Exile and the Narrative Imagination

Exile
and the
Narrative
Imagination

Michael Seidel

YALE UNIVERSITY PRESS
New Haven and London

Designed by Nancy Ovedovitz and set in Garamond No. 3 type by The Composing Room of Michigan, Inc. Printed in the United States of America by Cushing-Malloy, Inc., Ann Arbor, Michigan.

Library of Congress Cataloging-in-Publication Data
Seidel, Michael, 1943–
　　Exile and the narrative imagination.

　　Includes index.
　　1. English fiction—History and criticism.　2. Exiles in literature.　3. American fiction—20th century—History and criticism.　I. Title.
PR830.E93S45　　1986　　823'.009'353　　85-17787
ISBN 0-300-03498-9

The paper in this book meets the guidelines for permanence and durability of the Committee on Production Guidelines for Book Longevity of the Council on Library Resources.

10　　9　　8　　7　　6　　5　　4　　3　　2　　1

For Daniel and Matthew

Contents

Preface

An exile is someone who inhabits one place and remembers or projects the reality of another. [1] Henry James, returning to America after a more than twenty-year exile in Europe, sensed that his physical absence from home had made him extracognizant not only of the new but of what he remembered of the old. The first time around he had absorbed experience unthinkingly; now he *sees* consciously. He asks in *The American Scene* why he missed things earlier, and answers that his previous opaqueness was "all, doubtless, in the very interest, precisely, of this eventual belated romance, and so that adventures, even of a minor type, so preposterously postponed should be able to deck themselves at last with a kind of accumulation of freshness."[2] Belatedness broadens the product of the imagination by postponing its romance until consciousness knows what to do with it. In Jamesian terms, the temporal twists and turns of a phrase like "preposterously postponed" reflect etymologically the experience that exile registers imaginatively.

There is another moment in *The American Scene* when James centers and foreshortens the exilic experience. He returns to Ashburton Place in Boston to revisit two familiar old houses he had last seen just after the Civil War. These houses held cherished memories for him and he is moved to see them again. His nostalgia runs so deep that he returns a month later to repeat the visit. But during this short interval the houses were demolished. James is unnerved. He uses the occasion to comment on the longer exile that has marked his life: "That, however, seemed just to give me, as I have hinted, the whole figure of my connection with everything about, a connection that had been sharp, in spite of brevity, and then had broken short off. Thus it was the sense of rupture . . . that I was to carry with me."[3]

The task for the exile, especially the exiled artist, is to transform the figure of rupture back into a "figure of connection." I do not mean to suggest that aesthetic recompense is sufficient for history's countless refugees, expellees, émigrés, and dispossessed suffering what Nabokov describes in *Pale Fire* as "the cold hard core of loneliness which is not good for a displaced soul."[4] Exile can be a grim fate and its recourses equally grim. When, in *A Portrait of the Artist as a Young Man,* Joyce has Stephen Dedalus recommend exile—along with silence and cunning—as preparatory courses for a new Irish trivium, his words could apply as readily to a life of exilic terror as to a life of exilic art. But Joyce would surely wish to emphasize the latter over the former. And he is not alone. So many writers, whatever their personal or political traumas, have gained imaginative sustenance from exile—Ovid, Dante, Swift, Rousseau, Madame de Staël, Hugo, Lawrence, Mann, Brecht—that experiences native to the life of the exile seem almost activated in the life of the artist: separation as desire, perspective as witness, alienation as new being.

In *Speak, Memory,* Nabokov writes of the consequences of his exile after the Russian Revolution, and he claims, despite years of anguish and his unique sense of Russophilia, that the "break in my own destiny affords me in retrospect a syncopal kick that I would not have missed for worlds."[5] Like his young poet, Fyodor, in *The Gift,* Nabokov summons up by writing what he calls his "shorthand" for "Russia far." Fyodor learns that the imagination not only compensates for exilic loss but registers that loss as aesthetic gain.

> Ought one not to reject any longing for one's homeland, for any homeland besides that which is with me, within me, which is stuck like the silver sand of the sea to the skin of my soles, lives in my eyes, my blood, gives depth and distance to the background of life's every hope? Some day, interrupting my writing, I will look through the window and see a Russian autumn.[6]

The move at the end of this passage is crucial: the Russian autumn emerges during a pause in the imaginative activity that evokes it.

What is gestating inside the exile's writerly skull displays itself as a kind of hologram. When Fyodor thinks of actually getting back to Russia, he understands that he has, in effect, already done so. Russia is reachable in only one real way: "I know only that when I reach it, it will be with pen in hand."[7] For the exile, native territory is the product of heightened and sharpened memory, and imagination is, indeed, a special homecoming.

• • •

In the course of the chapters that follow I pay close attention to works written in English by a Pole, a Russian, an Irishman, an American, and two Englishmen. Insofar as language is a locating and dynamic figure in exilic narrative, I do not wish to introduce the distraction of writing in one language about books written in another.[8] This choice is essentially tactical, and the range and variety of the narratives I treat, from *Robinson Crusoe* to *A Sentimental Journey,* from *Lord Jim* to *The Ambassadors,* from *Ulysses* to *Pale Fire,* partially make up for my own reluctance to sustain a detailed argument on the basis of Continental fiction in translation or, for that matter, Latin American fiction in translation.

If I have placed some controlling limitations upon myself in terms of the books I am ready to treat, I also recognize that I do not pursue certain approaches to the subject of exile with the same fervor I pursue others. Had I decided to proceed along strictly thematic lines I would have perhaps focused on different kinds of material or focused differently on the kinds of material I do treat. For instance, I do not deal in any systematic way with the post-Romantic condition of exile as a metaphor for the alienated or marginalized modern consciousness whereby individuals are alienated not only from the place they inhabit but from the things they do or the things they are. In this sense, alienation, as part of artistic consciousness, can register without one ever leaving home, without a poet, say, ever leaving the streets of Blake's chartered London, or a wanderer ever leaving the terrain of Wordsworth's lake country, or an insomniac ever leaving the comforts of Proust's bed. It is the imagination that relocates or repairs the experience of being exiled, as it were, while still in place. Though I recognize the currency of such notions and occasionally invoke them, generally I do not dwell on exile as a form of modern alienation, whether as a metaphor for psychic "difference" or as a Marxist allegory of separation—separation from worth, from satisfaction, and even from material equity.[9] Similarly, I recognize but do not dwell on exile as a Freudian analogue charting the path from the totalizing perversities of infantile consciousness to the separating perversities of adult neurosis, from the womb to the anteroom of the "alienist" (only later softened to "analyst").

For different reasons, I have also resisted the impulse to write excessively on modern exilic politics and émigré conditions, choosing for example to focus upon the metaphor of politics in the Robinson Crusoe myth rather than upon Conrad's expatriate Polish sympathies or Joyce's hostility to Irish Fenians in America or on the Continent. If these more modern matters touch on issues of contemporary concern, they demand and deserve a kind of fire-in-the-belly commitment that I think it a sorry gesture on my part to cultivate for the mere pose of it. Though it is often difficult to separate the fervor of exilic politics from the literary structures of political imagining, I do not wish to isolate in an imaginative context issues that still possess an immediate, soulful, sometimes devastating reality to thousands of actual exiles and émigrés. There is a discipline of modern academic research called Exile Studies that is much better suited to deal with the fate of displaced populations and exilic communities in the modern world.

I hope instead to focus on literary representations of exile, especially representations in which exile or expatriation is foregrounded as a narrative action. I will not—as should become obvious as I proceed—flinch from elaborating the encompassing, if metaphorical, nature of the exilic experience in life or in art, but I will concentrate on exile as an enabling fiction, or at least a fiction enabling me to address the larger strategies of narrative representation. Part one of the book describes narrative ventures that define the boundaries of exilic action, and part two details the sense of lack or loss that stimulates exilic crossings. In practice, each chapter absorbs material already presented in the introduction and reflects material taken up in subsequent sections of the book. The first set of chapters concerns the exilic adventure as an allegory of narrative properties; the second set, an elaboration of that allegory in terms of narrative and cultural "otherness."

Robinson Crusoe inaugurates the notion of exile as an originary action. The processes of exilic replication and exilic supplementation that serve Crusoe during his island exile mirror the processes that serve the larger narrative enterprise in which Defoe is engaged. The chapter on Conrad, placed after *Crusoe,* essentially relocates the source of exilic experience from narrative place to narrative voice. Issues of fictional sovereignty, always at the heart of exilic narrative, arise in this chapter in conjunction with the strains and ironies implicit in the Western imperial adventure. James Joyce's role in this first set of chapters details the transformation of the exilic experience into a full and intricate aesthetic of cultural paranoia and rivalry: rival places, rival voices, rival artists. Exile for Joyce is a kind of capital narrative stock against which he can redeem an almost endless series of national, personal, aesthetic, and linguistic debts.

The chapters in the second part of the book have a Continental bias. I begin with Sterne's *A Sentimental Journey* because that short comic narrative is in so many ways a primer on expatriate imagining. Its commerce in border crossings of one sort or another displays many of the notions of difference and distance that make the exilic situation metaphorically and generatively central to narrative representation. Henry James, in *The Ambassadors,* elaborates on what Sterne depicts as the fetish of expatriation while making his novel's action expansive enough to contain the larger dimensions of an international strife-epos. The exilic condition in this extraordinary novel marks the clash, at times comic and at times epic, between emerging and eclipsing Western cultures. I conclude the second set of chapters with Nabokov's *Ada* and *Pale Fire* because these works (and Nabokov's fiction generally) represent the most sustained and resourceful exercise of the exilic imagination in modern fiction. My last chapter stands as a kind of *summa* for issues raised throughout the book.

I have turned for advice, while working on this book, to the same friends I have turned to before, and in thanking them again I feel somewhat like Claude Rains as the police inspector at the end of *Casablanca:* "Round up the usual suspects." Of course, Rains speaks with considerable affection, and he knows that those summoned cannot really be blamed for the deed that he, in fact, has just perpetrated.

Everyone who was good enough to read or talk with me about portions of this book has aided me in what I hope are recognizable though not blamable ways: Martin Meisel, Ed Mendelson, Edward Said, and Ted Tayler at Columbia; Alfred MacAdam at Barnard; David Bromwich, Maria DiBattista, Alvin Kernan, and David Quint at Princeton; Paul Fry at Yale; Beth Hedrick at the University of Texas; Paul Hunter at the University of Rochester; and James Nohrnberg at the University of Virginia. I have also had considerable help in the preparation of the manuscript from students at Columbia, Diana Henderson, Gary Hentzi, Alan Kifferstein, Aaron Schneider, Martin Van Delden, and Mary Dering.

This is the second project on which I have worked with my editor at Yale Press, Ellen Graham, and her skill and grace are as impressive as they have always been. It is a great pleasure for me to thank her yet again, and, in addition, to thank Michael Joyce and Cecile Watters for their inestimable help in preparing the manuscript.

Chapters or parts of chapters have appeared in *Yale Review, ELH, PMLA, Genre,* and *Criticism,* and I am grateful to these journals for the permission to include material herein revised for the purposes of this book.

INTRODUCTION

Postexilic Eminence

"Now I *know* we're not in Kansas"

The word *exile* derives from *ex* ("out of") and the Latin root *salire* ("to leap"), the same etymological root that produces the word *exult*. Joseph Conrad understood this intuitively when as a young man he made what he called his exilic "jump": "I verily believe mine was the only case of a boy of my nationality and antecedents taking a, so to speak, standing jump out of his racial surroundings and associations."[1] The experience split him in two, made him, as he put it, into "homo duplex," a sailor and writer whose extraterritorial perspective worked to soothe his exilic conscience.

Exile is a compelling subject and a propelling action; it names a figure and establishes a narrative ground. At the very beginning of D. H. Lawrence's *Women in Love,* Gudrun contemplates the nature of life's subjunctive mood, the "if" which serves as a narrative radical, and remarks: "If one jumps over the edge, one is bound to land somewhere." Lawrence, of course, is more concerned with the daring of the gesture and the mystery of the destination than with the exilic trauma of the leap or the moral weightlessness that attends it; but the space of the exilic leap, what Conrad calls in *Lord Jim* that "everlasting deep hole,"[2] is a powerful, perhaps even constitutive, metaphor for the genesis and disposition of narrative itself. This becomes emphatic later when Conrad deposits Jim in faraway Patusan and has Marlow record that neither "Stein nor I had a clear conception of what might be on the other side when we, metaphorically speaking, took

I

him up and hove him over the wall with scant ceremony."[3] Narrative is a kind of speaking metaphor, a crossover, and its scene is set by the projection of activity in a mimetic and illusionistic space, a "conception of what *might be* on the other side."

Exilic domain is new action, what Joyce calls in *Ulysses* "postexilic eminence."[4] Chroniclers from Moses to Homer, from Ovid to Joyce have memorialized the primacy of the exilic fable in narrative, and characters from Daedalus of Athens to Dedalus of Dublin have enacted it. Joyce cites as his epigraph for *A Portrait of the Artist as a Young Man,* the conclusion of the following passage from the *Metamorphoses* on the Ovidian Daedalus's Cretan exile.

> Daedalus, hating Crete and his long exile [*longumque perosus exilium*], and longing to see his native land, was shut in by the sea. . . . "yet the sky is open, and by that way will I go. Though Minos rules over all, he does not rule the air." So saying, he sets his mind at work upon unknown arts, and changes the laws of nature [*et ignotas animum dimittit in artes*].[5]

Ovid's exiled Daedalus turns for solace to illusion. To be an imaginer soaring beyond the borders of place and across the borders of certain states of consciousness is, as Nabokov later puts it, to be a "secret agent in an alien country."[6]

But the exilic mind, no matter where it projects, no matter how unknown its arts, emanates from familiar or local territory. Imaginative powers begin at the boundaries of accumulated experience. In *Either/Or,* Søren Kierkegaard offers a parable of the imagination that plots its orienting and exilic energies.

> If I imagined two kingdoms adjoining one another, with one of which I was fairly well acquainted, and altogether unfamiliar with the other, and I was not allowed to enter the unknown realm, however much I desired to do so, I should still be able to form some conception of its nature. I could go to the limits of the kingdom with which I was acquainted and follow its boundaries, and as I did so, I should in this way describe the boundaries of this unknown country, and thus without ever having set foot in it, obtain a general conception of it. And if this was a task that engrossed my energies, and if I was indefatigable in

my desire to be accurate, it would doubtless sometimes happen that, as I stood sadly at my country's boundary and looked longingly into the unknown country, which was so near me and yet so far away, some little revelation might be vouchsafed to me.[7]

What Kierkegaard describes as a mental borderland is controlled by the generative notion that the line marking the end of the familiar is the same as that marking the beginning of the unknown. The line that limits is also the line that dares. At this juncture, the creative mind is capable of a necessary recourse: projection images proximity, imagination reinforms, allegorizes, and enlivens material already assimilated; or, to put it another way, new accounts draw from funds already on deposit.[8] Joseph Conrad remembers gazing at the known and unknown spaces of the map for hours as a youth, and he claimed that his early efforts gave conveyable dimension to his imagination: "I have no doubt that star-gazing is a fine occupation, for it leads you within the borders of the unattainable. But map-gazing, to which I became addicted so early, brings the problems of the great spaces of the earth into stimulating and direct contact with sane curiosity and gives an honest precision to one's imaginative faculty."[9] The imagined outland is a version of the inland; the possible a version of the previous.[10]

To cross into the bounds of imagined worlds and do so honestly is to begin from that point Conrad calls "sane curiosity," or the point a movie director in Nabokov's *Ada* defines as infinity: "the farthest point from the camera which is still in fair focus."[11] Even the most remote and distant projections, the imaginative "nowheres" of science fiction, are versions of a "somewhere" already there.[12] Anthony Burgess is fond of citing the shortest science fiction fantasy on record, the utopian inversion from Plato's *Statesman:* "The sun rose in the west." What is involved here, of course, is not merely the extravagance of the proposition but the familiarity of its phrasing. The day merely orients as an occidental occurrence.

If the "other side" of the boundary traditionally represents a moment of differentiation, it also represents a cloning or twinning. W. H. Auden invokes boundary figures as terminal and initiatory twins.

> O Lords of Limit, training dark and light
> And setting a tabu 'twixt left and right:
> The influential quiet twins
> From whom all property begins . . .[13]

It is not surprising that literary theorists and interpreters tend to linger, like their patron Hermes, at imaginative borders in the hopes of catching metaphor in its natural act of replicating by carrying across. However free, unrestrained, unencumbered, extravagant, or outlandish things appear beyond bounds, the imagination, in Kierkegaard's phrase, vouchsafes its little revelations home. This is one of the reasons the exilic condition is so readily an image and an opportunity for narrative projection. Territory beyond borders is appropriated and familiarized. When, for example, Judy Garland as Dorothy in *The Wizard of Oz* looks down at her dog Toto and up at the beautiful Witch of the North standing over them and says, "Now I *know* we're not in Kansas," her famous words only partially construe the principle upon which her boundary crossing is devised. For it is the metamorphosis of an all-too-familiar Kansas (in Technicolor) that sustains the action of the outland. Oz is a place over the rainbow whose boundaries are exilic but whose allegorical energies translate local fears and homegrown desires.

Unreal Estate

If the imaginative boundary separates and supplements, differentiates and replicates, it is worth speculating for a moment on what happens to Kierkegaard's parable from *Either/Or* if the imaginer, instead of peering across the border from the known territory to the unknown, finds himself in an opposite position on the unknown side of the border trying to sustain the image of distant familiarity. Properties have, in effect, changed places. The imaginer remembers from where he used to project. And the experience resembles what Nabokov's crazy expatriated Russian, Hermann, notices in *Despair* about the sense of dissociation wherein one becomes "aware that imp Split had taken over" and one's imaginative life manifests "at a remove."[14]

Writers more at home, for whatever reasons, in the conjured spaces of their works than in their actual homelands—Dante, for example, or Joyce, or Nabokov, or, in a special sense, Proust—feel real or imagined constraints upon them that make an artistic virtue of exilic necessity. In *Speak, Memory,* Nabokov writes of inheriting from his mother special verbal powers of memorial reconstruction even before the Russian Revolution that exiled him: "Thus, in a way, I inherited an exquisite simulacrum—the beauty of intangible property, unreal estate—and this proved a splendid training for the endurance of later losses."[15] Walter Benjamin makes a similar argument for Proust, claiming that the effort in *Remembrance of Things Past* is to re-create a place from which time has barred the artist who would forget the urgencies of the present as many would forget the memories of the past. Proust, as Benjamin reads him, desires most of all to return to the image he creates while living in a present that merely exiles him further from what he desires. Imagining, in this sense, may be the only tangible property of the narrative estate. Proust sought, according to Benjamin, the recurring image, or the image restored, "the image which satisfied his curiosity—indeed, assuaged his homesickness. He lay on his bed racked with homesickness, homesick for the world distorted in the state of resemblance, a world in which the true surrealist face of existence breaks through."[16] Benjamin calls this exilic conjuring *das Bild,* and means by it a "fragile, precious reality" of another place in which the imagination is sovereign. What is created in the Proustian exilic supplement is not only a new space to exercise one's being but a medium through which to reimagine one's beginnings.

Exilic necessity derives from exilic anxiety, a lifelong scenario of estrangement, which can also be located in Proust in the opening scenes of the *Remembrance* when the child suffers upstairs in his bedroom the agony of separation from his mother downstairs at an evening dinner party, an agony he calls his banishment. It later turns out that the young narrator preferred the torture of separation to the solace of his mother's eventual visit because the imaginative anticipation was greater than its resolution. In a further Proustian twist, the narrator's realization that his mother's staying the night with him will not be infinitely repeatable makes the experience nostalgic even while it is happening. It is almost as if the imagination requires the impediments of time or distance to activate it.

Franz Kafka has a similar (and actual) childhood memory, in which he recalls his father banishing him from the bedroom one night to the outside balcony (*pavlatche*) because he was whimpering in his bed for a glass of water. These experiences suggest that exile, even in miniature, accounts for some of the intricate patterns projected in narrative from not belonging or not knowing. Kafka's father's action was, to the boy's mind, groundless, but the meditation on its groundlessness became a fixation and something like a recurring plot. Charles Bernheimer, in his recent study of Flaubert and Kafka, treats the pavlatche episode as originary: "That exile is the place of *Vorstellung,* the groundless place where inside and outside vacillate."[17] His discussion of the scene also locates its oedipal origins, a construct of imaginative beginnings that assumes the deepest anxieties of exilic experience, the witnessing of an inside action from the outside. The scene from which everyone is exiled is the most intimate place of origin, to which physical and psychological reaccess is forever barred except in the domain of the imagination. What Bernheimer describes is indeed archetypal; it even includes, with all the resonances of childhood petulance, a narrative scene such as Satan skulking around the perimeters of the creative seat in Milton's *Paradise Lost.*

That Satan eventually gets into Paradise is an authorial dispensation; he also occupies Hell and would Heaven, too, if Milton and God allowed it. This is to suggest the obvious: not only exilic imaginers seek to capture supplemental spaces but so too characters, readers, and interpreters. Imagined terrain is a strange or alien place by definition—*strange* in the sense of its cognates, *extraneous* (meaning "outside") and *extra* (meaning "supplemental"). The conventional compliment for a well-realized narrative projection—it is as if one has entered "another world"—applies equally to *Journal of the Plague Year* or to *Gulliver's Travels,* to *The Adventures of Alice* or the popular television soap opera simply called "Another World." Whether imaginative space is deemed London or Houyhnhnmland, Wonderland or Television City, characters either occupying it or experiencing it are there by the grace of exilic passports.

There is a fine instance of the nature of imaginative habitation in a passage that Kafka deleted from the text of *The Castle*. K.'s lover, Frieda, explains the conditions under which the stranger-in-exile is allowed to circulate in the region of the Schloss and the village. From her explanation we can extrapolate the general conditions under which fictional characters and readers inhabit space whose full imaginative presence is, with a stroke of the pen, authorized.

> As a stranger you have no right to anything here, perhaps here we are particularly strict or unjust toward strangers, I don't know, but there it is, you have no right to anything. A local person, for instance, when he needs assistants, takes such people on, and when he is grown up and wants to marry, he takes himself a wife. The authorities have a great deal of influence in these matters too, but in the main everyone is free to decide for himself. But you, as a stranger, have to make out with what you are given; if it pleases the authorities to do so, they give you assistants; if it pleases them to do so, they give you a wife. Even this, of course, is not merely arbitrary, but it is a matter solely for the authorities to decide, and this means that the reasons for the decision remain hidden. [18]

These observations are presented in the voice of a character who for mimetic purposes, or, it might be better to say, fictionally contractual purposes, represents herself as part of the narrative system that separates the local from the strange. But, in essence, her residence in the village is no more legitimate than K.'s unless we accept the authority that decides such things for us as readers. Frieda's "authorities" seem to know what they are doing and possess what keys there are to hidden meaning in the region, but she pluralizes what ought to remain singular. The only dispensing authority is *The Castle*'s author. To imagine otherwise is to let the whimsy of naive realism commute the exilic sentence of fictional being.

"In exitu Israel"

If exile is a symptomatic metaphor for the state of the narrative imagination, it is also a material resource for legend, literature, and history in the West. The exilic projection is originary, whether the Tartarian and Luciferian expulsions, the trek east from Eden, the sagas of Io and Europa, the flight of Daedalus, the exposure of Oedipus, the voyage of the Argonauts, the Exodus, Captivity, and Diaspora of the Jews, the wanderings of Odysseus, the displacement of Aeneas, the trials of the prodigal son, the medieval and gothic myths of the Wandering Jew, the journey of Dante the pilgrim, the outlawry of El Cid, the "fugitive" fable of the castaway Robinson Crusoe, the river odyssey of Huck Finn, even the intercontinental trauma of Tarzan and the intergalactic adventure of Superman. In the exilic plot the extraneous becomes foundational, the blighted and ill-fated from one sphere become instigators and originators in another. The powers of exilic imagining represent desired territory, lost or found, as narrative fate.

When Dante explained to his patron, Can Grande, how the layering processes of narrative allegory worked, he cited the first line of Psalm 113 (Psalm 114 in the Protestant Bible) on the parting of the Red Sea at Exodus: "in exitu Israel de Egypto."[19] Exile inaugurates, the long way around, the redemption of individual souls, cities, and nations. Often in the exilic fable the home place is destroyed, rendered illegitimate, contaminated, or taken over by conquerors or rival claimants. Without a native place (or possibly a government) recognized as secure, home territory itself is invalidated for those forced to remain behind in it. Thus those in exile are saving remnants; they imagine in new surroundings the conditions that existed before the trauma that necessitated their displacement. Aeneas measures the Mediterranean in his quest for a future Troy, but he pauses to express the tearfulness of things, *lachrymae rerum,* when he sees in Carthage the wall paintings of the events that led the original city to fall. Similarly, it is when the Jews, who in captivity would muster the enormous energies required to codify Talmudic law, sit by the flowing rivers of Babylon that they remember most fervently their own Jerusalem and the nearby waters of the Jordan.

Dante's own great poem took up the same cadences of exilic refashioning and exilic anguish. In *Paradiso xvii* of the *Commedia,* we hear the terms of Dante's future exile from Florence.

> The blame, as always, will follow the injured party, in outcry; but vengeance shall bear witness to the truth which dispenses it. You shall leave everything beloved most dearly; and this is the arrow which the bow of exile shoots first [*e questo è quello strale che l'arco de lo essilio pria saetta*]. You shall come to know how salt is the taste of another's bread, and how hard the path to descend and mount by another man's stairs. And that which shall most weigh your shoulders down will be the evil and senseless company with which you shall fall into this vale; which shall then become all ungrateful, all mad and malevolent against you, but, soon after, their brows, not yours, shall redden for it. Of their brutish folly their own conduct shall afford the proof, so that it will be for your fair fame to have made you a party by yourself.[20]

As scapegoat, Dante the pilgrim is a type of redeemer, a prophet without honor in his own land. He becomes a citizen of the cities of the afterworld, which reflect the Florence that he has departed and that has departed him. Dante's exile, and the vision of Florence created by it, bear the standard of the native citizen's righteousness. Especially if exile is the result of contingent political circumstances or self-imposed ideological ones, its victim claims to possess the values of his native place, as it were, in proxy—he is the truer version of the place from which he is barred. It is in this sense that Coriolanus banishes Rome in the Shakespearean play or that Conrad's exiled Razumov rants in *Under Western Eyes:* " 'Russia *can't* disown me. She cannot!' Razumov struck his breast with his fist. 'I am *it.*' "[21] The empowered community, on the other hand, casts the exile as an outlaw, a figure legally or quasi-legally deprived of credentials for a land in which he would, if he could, circulate with impunity.[22]

Ovid in exile along the cold, uncultured shores of the Euxine is an intriguing case in this regard. For reasons muddled by the conspiracy of silence around them, Augustus exiled the poet to Tomis, but the emperor and his successor, Tiberius, allowed the poet's works to be circulated in Rome. Ovid spent ten years trying to write his way home, whether by humble petition, by testimonial, or by apologia. Finally, he instructs the first poem in his collected *Tristia* to travel to Rome in his stead. He requests that the poem redeem him and, in effect, metaphorically embody him at home.

> My own wit has brought me exile. But do you go in my stead, do you, who are permitted to do so, gaze on Rome! Would that the gods might grant me now to be my book!—and think not, because you enter into the great city as one from foreign lands, that you can come as a stranger to the people. Though you should lack a title, your very style will bring recognition.[23]

In time, Ovid becomes his book (*possem nunc meus esse liber*) and his reputation makes him still one of the noblest Romans of all. In a subsequent poem from the *Tristia,* he thanks his muse (*grata, Musa, tibi*) for granting him Roman immortality in poetry while the authorities in Rome were prepared to let him die in exile.[24]

Another imaginative solution to the exile's anguish is to export just enough of the homeland to the outland to metonymically purify it. Something like this occurs not only in Dante's *Purgatorio* but in Shakespeare's *Tempest,* where the key Milanese usurpers are magically deposited on Prospero's island—"Hell is empty," says Ariel, "And all the devils are here!" (1.2.214–15). Prospero sorts out native virtues before he returns to native land. Defoe, in direct imitation of *The Tempest,* has Robinson Crusoe similarly screen a band of English mutineers for loyalty near the end of his island exile before he returns them (and himself) to England.[25]

Exile sets in motion the allegory of separation that circles around to a differently disposed, perhaps even differently located, home. The typical exile in literature, although by nature a wanderer, is also by habit a homebody. Home is locus, custom, memory, familiarity, ease, security, sanctuary. And centuries of tradition do not alter the power of home as an image. George Eliot writes of what home means in *Daniel Deronda* (a novel, in good part, about rootlessness).

A human life, I think, should be well rooted in some spot of a native land, where it may get the love of tender kinship for the face of the earth, for the labours men go forth to, for the sounds and accents that haunt it, for whatever will give that early home a familiar unmistakable difference amidst the future widening of knowledge: a spot where the definiteness of early memories . . . may spread not by sentimental effort and reflection, but as a sweet habit of the blood.[26]

The memory of home becomes paramount in narratives where home itself is but a memory. In a talk prepared for his seventieth birthday celebration in Los Angeles, the exiled Thomas Mann pointed out that the German word *Elend,* meaning "misery," once applied to a person living in an alien land, so that exile named its primary emotion.[27] In exile, the expression of the desire for home becomes a substitute for home, embodies the emotion attendant upon the image. It is in this sense that so many of the adventures of Odysseus try to dim the hero's homeward compulsion by making exilic space a substitute for the home island. Similarly, Odysseus finds himself at the beck of island lovers to replace the Ithacan Penelope, and he enjoys abroad the successes the suitors would wish for themselves with Penelope back on Ithaca. That the substitute is in some ways a replicate is not merely something that happens to Odysseus but something that he is bound to desire, that has been on his mind. Hence the spatial frame of the narration: Odysseus, temporarily domesticated at the furthest bounds of the Mediterranean on Calpyso's isle, dreams of domestication with Penelope at its Ithacan center. In so doing, he displays not only the full range of the exilic course, extension and return, but the full power of exilic imagining, extension *as* return.

Of course, in variant versions of the Odysseus legend, which make up an epic subculture undoubtedly known by Homer and later resurrected by Dante, Tennyson, and Kazantzakis, the hero's renewed desire for the voyage out, even after his return to Ithaca, is something that is also part of his nature. This instinctively makes Odysseus reject, in the Homeric version, the promise of immortality Calypso offers on *her* isle. It is not just that Calypso prevents the hero's return to Penelope, but that her domain is too much like the domestic *tedium vitae* that will reactivate the great homecomer's wanderlust. For Odysseus, supplemental desire is what ought to be given over with the promise of *nostos,* though it may never be given over entirely. Defoe played on just such an impulse in the continuation of the *Crusoe* saga. Satisfaction at home could not rival the desire activated in exile. It is common enough even in actual cases of exilic return that the mental energy expended on the image of home in absence proves incommensurate with the reality of home as presence.

The displaced condition or "state" of mind of the exile at times results in a decidedly ambiguous relation with both the place of remove and the place of resettlement. The younger generation of murmuring Jews of the Exodus, for example, who know little of their promised land before reaching it and who have begun to forget the miseries of their ancestors' Egyptian past, seem as agonized at the prospect of leaving a temporary home, an oasis like Elim in the Sinai, as Moses, who knows much more, is agonized at the prospect of staying. The theme of uncertainty in exile is more pronounced in the *Aeneid,* where Aeneas, praying to have done with his trials, attempts to found a new version of Troy on each of the Trojans' marginal landfalls in the Mediterranean.[28] He acts on the chance that the gods have destined the place where he happens to be as the place where he is supposed to be. On a smaller scale, Robinson Crusoe goes through a comparable experience on his island, first despairing at his desolate condition then thanking his providential stars that he can make something like a home in a place that has never been home to anyone else. He begins to forget the outside world when he is by the outside world forgot: "I look'd now upon the World as a Thing remote, which I had nothing to do with, no Expectation from, and indeed no desires about . . . so I thought it look'd as we may perhaps look upon it hereafter, *viz.* as a Place I had liv'd in, but was come out of it; and well might I say, as Father *Abraham* to *Dives, Between me and thee is a great Gulph fix'd.*"[29]

An even more complex relation exists in Dante's *Commedia* between the places of exile and the image of Florence that serves for home. The poet is in exile from his home city, while the pilgrim is, so to speak, merely on leave from it. He journeys as Dante the pilgrim before he knows what will happen to him as Dante the poet. The itinerary of that journey, however, pictures Florence as already distributed through the afterworlds. Dante has taken up part of the promise of immortality that Odysseus rejected on Calypso's isle, the part that makes the future seem like the present. Virgil offered a historical version of the same process in the sweep of the *Aeneid*'s descent, where the symbol of the new city, Rome, and of its citizens appears as a vision before either it or they exist in future form.

The underworld descent, for a host of reasons, is one of the most profound narrative models for the exilic experience in literature. From the early fragments of the Greek *nekuia,* the summoning of the shades, to the fully developed underworld where the light shines in Elysium before Erebus swallows it in the depths of Tartarus, the descent myth relays secrets from the world of the dead for the benefit of life's vital format. Joyce catches the gist of the matter when Bloom, in the "Hades," or descent chapter of *Ulysses,* thinks: "Read your own obituary notice they say you live longer. Gives you second wind. New lease on life."[30] The full Virgilian descent is the exile's dream, a new lease on future property. It offers the leader of a nation in diaspora an image of the future as prologue, and it grants him access to powers of utterance that are both memorial and prophetic. Descent is that ending which is also a telling, that exile which conjures up imaginable territory. The spatial and temporal magic of the descent is a powerful emblem of the narrative imagination at work: supplemental spaces conceived are supplemental spaces controlled.[31] Only those with special visionary powers, either powers possessed or powers granted, can negotiate these depths. As Poe writes: "It is all very well to talk about the *facilis descensus Averni;* but in all kinds of climbing, as Catalani said of singing, it is far more easy to get up than to come down."[32]

Exilic Alibis

Exile serves narrative as an initiating and supplementing action, and it also serves, as Dante pointed out, as a figure for allegory itself.

Because of the doubleness implicit in exilic positioning, the record of exile in narrative is an alien voicing, which is what the word *allegory* means (*al*, "other"; *goria*, "voicing"). James Nohrnberg provides a list of words related to allegory's first syllable, which, as he notes, sounds "like a catalogue of the basic concepts for any theory of allegory: *also, alternate, alteration, parallel, alien, else, ulterior, as, alibi.*"[33] The last is my favorite, deriving as Nohrnberg points out, from the Latin word for *elsewhere*. Joyce may have been thinking along these lines in the "Proteus" chapter of *Ulysses* (where everything turns into something else) when Dedalus remembers the trick of carrying punched tram tickets "to prove an alibi if they arrested you for murder somewhere. Justice. On the night of the seventeenth of February 1904 the prisoner was seen by two witnesses. Other fellow did it: other me. Hat, tie, overcoat, nose. *Lui, c'est moi.* You seem to have enjoyed yourself."[34] As Buck Mulligan, Stephen's other me, puts it in his parodic play title from *Ulysses*, confusing self-enjoyment with imaginative genesis and proliferation, *"Everyman His own Wife / or / A Honeymoon in the Hand.*"[35] Joyce seems to have understood that "otherness" generated from self is the Ur-allegory of literature. He has Stephen work out just such a notion in his theory of Shakespearean art in *Ulysses,* and Shem the Penman (in perpetual need of alibis and aliases as a forger) gives every last bit of himself to art in *Finnegans Wake,* some of it in forms none too savory.

A good deal has been written on the complexities of allegory as an imaginative and verbal activity, and whether those complexities involve the status of allegory in a post-Nietzschean world, the place of allegory in deconstructive poetics, or the relation of allegory to other literary figures and tropes (including irony, which is a kind of subversive allegory, a doubling that cancels), they all assume the central feature of allegory: its figures must represent something "other" to signify, even if that other is the process of signification itself.[36] This is perhaps why the exilic fable, one that seeks out otherness as its very subject, is so natural an allegory. The urge to read Odysseus's experiences, or Dante's, or Crusoe's, or Gulliver's, or K.'s into something other is irresistible. Consider Kafka's *The Castle.* K. is mysteriously called over to an alien land (or *not* called, as the case may be) to await his duties in the village and at the out-of-bounds Schloss. His job becomes a quest to make things signify, allegorically comparable to the narrative that tries to render it. What is intriguing and invariably frustrating about K.'s dilemma is that once he crosses into the environs whose survey he cannot satisfactorily comprehend, he seems fully committed to the notion that his allegorical lot is the same as his exilic one. He is in for the duration. The space of narration is all allegorical potential, and from such a space, if that is one's only space, there is no escape.[37]

In hinting at significance or meaning that might or might not reside in its figures, allegory tends to weaken naturalistic mimesis but widen mimetic range.[38] Something akin to this occurs when Odysseus shouts his name at the monster, the Cyclops, punning on the particular Greek syllables that render proximations of "I am Odysseus" and "I am Noman."[39] Odysseus announces his nominal presence and hints at his ontological absence. He both names and obliterates the identity that the narrative he is in works to prescribe, and he does so at the boundary in the adventure between the human and the monstrous, at the very point that narrative itself divides the constituent properties of allegory, its mimetic figures and its alien nature, its being and its figuring forth.

In a schematic sense, narrative worlds are filled with people and objects that represent the very allegorical principles upon which they were conceived: Mr. Hyde infuses radical otherness directly into Dr. Jekyll; Raskolnikov's name means split personality; secret sharers and doppelgängers allegorize mimesis as doubling. What holds for characters also holds for narrative places, and it is here that exile enters as allegory or alibi, a necessary *elsewhere*. Narrative forges two kinds of scenes, the first a counter or allegorical space where the "I am" of character projects a being that sustains an inscriptive sovereignty, and the second a mimetic space that limits the absolute otherness of the "I am" by supposing a recognizable world to which it is answerable.[40] To a greater or lesser degree both scenes are present in any narration, and the structure of their relation determines what I plan to discuss throughout this book as the implicit allegory of exilic imagining.

I will limit myself here to an example from Samuel Beckett's *Molloy* in which Molloy seeks to isolate himself in a forest near his region, allegorically to live in fictional space, mimetically to free himself from all familial and local obligations. His exile becomes his sovereignty: "For being in the forest, a place neither worse nor better than the others, and being free to stay there, was it not natural I should think highly of it, not because of what it was, but because I was there. For I was there."[41] But Molloy as character soon comes to understand that he cannot remain apart just as his "fiction" refuses to rest secure in its absolute otherness.

> But I could not, stay in the forest I mean, I was not free to. That is to say I could have, physically nothing could have been easier, but I was not purely physical, I lacked something, and I would have had the feeling, if I had stayed in the forest, of going against an imperative, at least I had that impression.[42]

Lack, in narrative terms, is defective allegory, a loss of that otherness that makes the narrative "read," or, in mimetic terms, the dread of that imperative that makes the narrative end. Molloy wonders whether he could have or should have remained alone in his forest "without remorse, without the painful impression of committing a fault, almost a sin." This sequence occurs at the point in the narrative when Molloy's story, insofar as it is one, does actually end; but more important it occurs at the point when Molloy's entire narrative is about to be penetrated by another exilic quest, the bourgeois Moran's, almost as if the imperative that disallows the insularity of the fictional domain is the difference that separates fictional sovereignty from the pretense that its world is complete.

Fictional mechanisms writ small in *Molloy* had earlier been writ large in the exilic narrative I will turn to in my first chapter, Defoe's *The Life and Surprizing Adventures of Robinson Crusoe*. And in all the following chapters I hope to refocus the issues I have raised in this introduction as they contribute to the contours of a larger argument on the foundational, allegorical, imaginative properties of the narrative estate.

PART ONE
EXILIC BOUNDARIES

CHAPTER ONE

Crusoe's Island Exile

Homemade

In *Ulysses,* Leopold Bloom, the Irish Odysseus, poses an exile's question to another exile whom Joyce called the English Ulysses: *"O, poor Robinson Crusoe! / How could you possibly do so?"*[1] Bloom's lilting refrain comes from a popular turn-of-the-century song that recalls a haunting moment in *Robinson Crusoe* when Defoe's castaway, alone at that time for six years, hears the disembodied voice of his previously trained wild parrot, Poll, ask, *"Robin, Robin, Robin Crusoe, poor Robin Crusoe, where are you Robin Crusoe?* Where are you? Where have you been?"[2]

Before Crusoe was startled by the parrot's words he had been on a reconnaissance mission, or *periplous,* sailing around part of his island in a small canoe, or *periagua.* He had almost been carried beyond the island by ocean currents, at which point he looked back on the place of his exile as a kind of paradisaic home.

> Now I look'd back upon my desolate solitary Island, as the most pleasant Place in the World, and all the happiness my Heart could wish for, was to be but there again. I stretch'd out my Hands to it with eager Wishes. O happy Desart, said I, I shall never see thee more. O miserable Creature, said I, whither am I going: Then I reproach'd my self with my unthankful Temper, and how I had repin'd at my solitary Condition; and now what would I give to be on Shore there again. Thus we never see the true State of our Condition, till it is illustrated to us by its Contraries; nor know how to value what we enjoy, but by the want of it. [p. 139]

Exile for Crusoe is now anywhere *but* his island, including the great sea whence he came. Fortunately, he negotiates the treacherous cur-

19

rents, beaches the canoe, and heads on foot toward his inland bower, or country house, for a miniature homecoming of sorts. His trek exhausts him, and he is half asleep when he hears the parrot's baffling questions. Poll, having flown in on its own accord from Crusoe's seaward settlement, chooses this occasion to repeat, by imprint, the sounds it has recorded during the early, more trying years of Crusoe's exile. So in the same sense that a loner's experience is rather like talking to other versions of himself, the questions the parrot asks of Crusoe are the same as those asked earlier by Crusoe. The questions themselves possess a double structure, hinting at two times and two places, at the Crusoe who hears them (where *are* you?) and the Crusoe who asked them (where have you *been?*).[3] The exile faces the dilemma that he is, indeed, of two places. Or, to put it another way, where he is displaced becomes his home place. Paradoxically, the answers to both the parrot's questions are in a generic sense the same: home. Home is where Crusoe now is, and home is where he had been. It is as Elizabeth Bishop puts it in her poem, "Crusoe in England": "Home-made, home-made! But aren't we all?"

Crusoe himself recognizes the mental and territorial transformation when he comments much earlier on the first night he ever spent away from his original settlement, the seaward hutch, after exploring the inland savannas: "I spent all that Evening there, and went not back to my Habitation, which by the Way was the first Night, as I might say, I had lain from Home" (p. 99). The locution "as I might say" makes the condition figurative but no less real for Crusoe in exile. Several months later, he undertakes an exploration of the island by foot and, after about thirty days, gets homesick.

> I cannot express what a Satisfaction it was to me, to come into my old Hutch, and lye down in my Hamock-Bed: This little wandring Journey, without settled Place of Abode, had been so unpleasant to me, that my own House, as I call'd it to my self, was a perfect Settlement to me, compar'd to that; and it rendred every Thing about me so comfortable, that I resolv'd I would never go a great Way from it again, while it should be my Lot to stay on the Island. [p. 111]

Of course, it is in Crusoe's wandering nature to abjure this particular promise or any like it upon the shortest possible notice, but of more immediate interest is the psychological appropriation of exilic space entailed by his coming "home." Crusoe refers to his island exile as "my Reign, or my Captivity, which you please" (p. 137). By whatever principle of abundant or redundant locution we do please, that place from which the exile is blocked becomes the model for the place in which he resettles his imagination. Crusoe's habit of mind has been "made" permanently binary, a process or, more accurately, a figuration represented in Crusoe's ledger "Accompt," where the tension between the anxieties of separation and the activities of resettlement are represented in graphic (or written) shape in double columns on the page.[4] He records on the side of separation: *"I am divided from Mankind, a Solitaire, one banish'd from humane Society"*; and on the side of resettlement (in every sense): *"But I am not starv'd and perishing on a barren Place, affording no Sustenance"* (p. 66). Crusoe's ledger conforms to his condition as exile: displacement and replacement are something of the same phenomenon.

The way Crusoe thinks in exile effects the way Defoe writes him up. Language mimics perception as the horror of isolation turns into the relief of deliverance: "as my Life was a Life of Sorrow, one way, so it was a Life of Mercy, another" (p. 132). Crusoe's way of articulating his condition reinforces the pattern that courses through the entire narrative, the double-entry accounting that transvalues experience. In his initial despair, Crusoe's hutch was but a hovel. Later, in full pride of place, his shelter becomes an estate; his estate, a kingdom; his kingdom, a paradise. When, and for whatever reasons, Crusoe's insecurities return, his paradise shrinks to his cave. If he feels fearful or hostile, his cave becomes his fortification. Crusoe's exile is an invitation to conversion, not simply a turning or movement from place to place but a transformation—imaginative and psychological—of one place or state of mind *into* another. This is, of course, also at the heart of the fictional record that makes up his exilic story.

"My brain bred islands"

It is precisely the exilic doubleness of Crusoe's situation or placement that accounts for the generative and allegorical texture of the narrative. When Defoe got around to commenting, seriously or otherwise, on his fictional strategies in *Crusoe,* he recognized that, however great his urge to substantiate a particular story, any sequence of narrative carries with it the pattern for interchangeability or duplication. Such a notion finds its way into the text of *Robinson Crusoe,* and Crusoe himself articulates it on his Brazilian plantation before he had any way of knowing about his subsequent island exile: "I used to say, I liv'd just like a Man cast away upon some desolate island, that had no body there but himself." Crusoe points out that those who utter such words may have heaven "oblige them to make the Exchange" (p. 35). Indeed, both heaven and Defoe so oblige.

Defoe writes at greater length of narrative interchangeability in his extended commentary on the story of the exiled Crusoe, *Serious Reflections during the Life and Surprizing Adventures of Robinson Crusoe* (1720). His voice is nominally that of Crusoe as a fictional being but actually that of himself as an authorial being: "In a word, there is not a circumstance in the imaginary story but has its just allusion to a real story, and chimes part for part and step for step with the inimitable Life of Robinson Crusoe."[5] Defoe cites as an example of what he means an illustration chosen not from the original narrative but from a later section of *Serious Reflections.*

> For example, in the latter part of this work called the Vision, I begin thus: "When I was in my island-kingdom I had abundance of strange notions of my seeing apparitions," &c. All these reflections are just history of a state of forced confinement, which in my real history is represented by a confined retreat in an island; and it is as reasonable to represent one kind of imprisonment by another, as it is to represent any thing that really exists by that which exists not. [3:xii]

Fable achieves a kind of reality by calling to mind replicative sets of experience.[6] "My brain bred islands," as Bishop puts it in "Crusoe in England." In *Serious Reflections,* Defoe makes a claim for what he calls the allegorical historical method of narration while defending himself (in the guise of Crusoe) from those who have charged him with lying.

> I Robinson Crusoe, being at this Time in perfect and sound mind and memory, thanks be to God therefor, do hereby declare their objection

is an invention scandalous in design, and false in fact; and do affirm that the story, though allegorical, is also historical; and that it is the beautiful representation of a life of unexampled misfortunes, and of a variety not to be met with in the world, sincerely adapted to and intended for the common good of mankind, and designed first, as it is now farther applied, to the most serious uses possible. [3:ix]

Defoe writes in Crusoe's name but leaves the possibility open that what is described as Crusoe's life happened to someone else: Crusoe's story is the fabrication of other "real" events. This much is, at least, half true. Crusoe's story is a fabrication. Defoe, still in Crusoe's voice, suggests that the process of reading is naturally allegorical—that the mind makes one thing stand for comparable things no matter what the real or invented status of the events narrated. In essence, Defoe is trying very hard to shift the grounds of the argument surrounding fictional invention from verifiability to application.[7] Now we have before us the possibility that the island adventure did not take place but that its writing makes it real for those reading it. The book is, after all, read and experienced. Its contents empty into one's brain. Crusoe had less wittingly already offered a similar argument during his actual island adventure when, after an ague-inspired vision, he saw before him a terrifying Avenging Angel: "No one, that shall ever read this Account, will expect that I should be able to describe the Horrors of my Soul at this terrible Vision, I mean, that even while it was a Dream, I even dreamed of those Horrors; nor is it any more possible to describe the impression that remain'd upon my Mind when I awak'd and found it was but a Dream" (p. 88). The phrase "that even while it was a Dream, I even dreamed of those Horrors" can mean only that the unreal action of dream *as dream* left a real impression. On just such terms would Defoe defend the validity of fictional event as "real." It is *made* real to the reader and therefore takes on tangible status in regard to the uses to which it might be put.

"There are a great many sorts of those people who make it their business to go about telling stories" (3:106), Defoe writes in *Serious Reflections*. Among them are those who, out of the forge of invention, "hammer out the very person, man or woman, and begin, 'I knew the man,' or 'I knew the woman'" (3:106). But the selling or writing a parable or an allusive allegoric history, is quite a different case, and is always distinguished from this other jesting with truth, that it is designed and effectually turned for instructive and upright ends, and has its moral justly applied. Such are the historical parables in the Holy Scripture, such "The Pilgrim's Progress," and such, in a word, the adventures of your fugitive friend, "Robinson Crusoe." [3:107]

Once relieved of justifying fiction merely by verifying the occurrence of its events, it becomes possible for Defoe to encourage his readers to think about the significance and design of events relayed as narrative sequence, so that, for example, a reader might expand allegorically upon the idea of solitude from that "which I have represented to the world, and of which you must have formed some ideas from the life of a man in an island" (3:3). As Defoe writes in another context: "Things seem to appear more lively to the Understanding, and to make a stronger Impression upon the Mind, when they are insinuated under the cover of some Symbol or Allegory, especially when the Moral is good, and the Application easy."[8] Allegory always represents one thing *in* another, and this representation, as we have seen, is very close to what the word *allegory* means: a speaking otherwise where difference itself becomes a form of duplication. Crusoe is more conscious than most fictional characters that an allegory of one kind or another has been going on around him. He even begins a journal that repeats the allegorical shape of the adventure he is in by mirroring its key word and recurrent theme, deliverance, in terms of his impulse to write it up. He writes, as he puts it, in order to "deliver my Thoughts from daily poring upon them, and afflicting my Mind" (p. 65).[9]

Defoe understands that writing serves to intensify action, imbue it with calculated strangeness, remoteness, liminality that engages as it expands one's interest. The adventures of Crusoe in the original volume are both *Strange* and *Surprizing*. In *Serious Reflections,* Defoe as Crusoe—or Crusoe as Defoe—compares himself to "the teacher, like a greater [Christ], having no honour in his own country." Such a teacher knows that "Facts that are formed to touch the mind, must be done a great way off, and by somebody never heard of" (3:xiii). Familiarity breeds contempt; strangeness or remoteness attracts attention. Crusoe hedges a bit as to whether the adventures he has experienced happened where he represented them, on an island near the mouth of the Orinoco, or somewhere much closer to home. Having raised the allegorical stakes, Defoe wonders whether his readers would lose interest "when you are supposing the scene, which is placed so far off, had its original so near home?" (3:xiii). The question comports with Defoe's notion that a unique metaphoric configuration makes a greater impression on the mind than a familiar literal one, but it also opens up the territory of the imagination as an exilic supplement.

Home, of course, is a key word in the text of *Crusoe* itself and around it is organized the potential for allegory. To strike home is to startle into realization: "The world, I say, is nothing to us, but as it is more or less to our relish. All reflection is carried home, and our dear self is, in one respect, the end of living" (3:4). The self-discovery that is the object of the interpreting mind is imaged constantly in the allegorical discovery that takes place in the sequence of narrative duplications. The allegorical self is a homebody. Crusoe's discovery of an old goat in his cave is perhaps an apposite example. He need not even know exactly what he means when he says it, but when he comes upon the goat he comes upon Crusoe allegorized: "I durst to believe there was nothing in this Cave that was more frightful than my self" (p. 177). Crusoe in exile is always discovering himself.

In a more general sense, ten months into his stay Crusoe hits upon the principle that rules the narrative: "Having now secur'd my Habitation, as I thought, fully to my Mind, I had a great Desire to make a more perfect Discovery of the Island, and to see what other Productions I might find, which I yet knew nothing of" (p. 98). This not only repeats the central pattern of action, the narrative and psychological temptation to enlarge the perimeters of experience, but it provides a resource for the analyzing, performing, and, in the final analysis, the imagining mind. It is as "Discovery" that the status of the island encourages the generous range of allegorical propensities that seem given over to it. The island is located in the fantasy of its own sovereign imagining, that "true" space, as Melville says of Quee-queg's island in *Moby Dick,* that "is not down in any map; true places never are." [10] Elizabeth Bishop's "Crusoe in England" makes the same point.

> . . . but my poor old island's still
> un-rediscovered, un-renamable.
> None of the books has ever got it right.

Robinson Crusoe is the only book that does get it right. It proliferates meaning from its island exile: linguistic, temporal, psychological, spiritual, political. Crusoe himself participates in and encourages the process, reading and misreading [11] the nature of his experience, sup-plementing his adventure by creating other versions of it that, in narrative terms, never happened: "I spent whole Hours, I may say whole Days, in representing to my self in the most lively Colours, how I must have acted, if I had got nothing out of the Ship. How I could not have so much as got any Food, except Fish and Turtles; and that as it was long before I found any of them, I must have perish'd first. That I should have liv'd, if I Had not perish'd, like a meer Savage" (p. 130). Robinson Crusoe's story is so allegorically bountiful that it supplements its own island supplement.

> "Why did you leave your father's house?"
> "To seek misfortune."

Defoe does not presume a single, privileged allegorical reading for Crusoe's adventures at the expense of the narrative's general power as a saga of adaptation and endurance, as a study of isolation and fear, and as a tale of the mobile fantasy and transforming imagination. But from the beginning of the action it seems clear that the pattern of separation and exile is at the heart of the narrative no matter how we would read it, and that the initiating event of all the action, Crusoe's disobedience to the wishes of his father that he stay at home, is complexly implicated in the run of the adventure abroad.

Crusoe steadfastly disobeys despite, perhaps even because of, his father's proposal to settle him: "In a word, that as he would do very kind things for me if I would stay and settle at Home as he directed, so he would not have so much hand in my Misfortunes, as to give me any Encouragement to go away" (p. 5). Every word here is rich, from the hint of originating authority, the "word," to the countercommand of adventure, "stay," to the multivalent "settle," to the allegorical "Home," to the archetypal "Misfortunes." The last plays on the paradigm of the prodigal son as Joyce plays on it in *Ulysses*—leaving the father's land or motherland "to seek misfortune" (*Ulysses*, p. 619)—and becomes the essence of exilic alienation.

In one sense, perhaps a political one, Crusoe's spirit during his years of exile represents the antithesis to patriarchal home rule;[12] in another, Crusoe's anguish at his original disobedience (he calls it his original sin) is genuine, though most severe when he feels least secure. Crusoe never does quite sort out the difference in motive between sin and impulse, and the question for the narrative action is whether resistance to his father's demands serves him better than had he succumbed to them. Crusoe is positioned so that his initial resistance to his home is the prelude to a crisis or series of crises that are themselves steps in a process of self-substantiation and return. The measure of Crusoe's hard-won settlement is the degree to which his impulses force him to avoid too easy a settlement too soon. This process, I will later argue, provides the political basis of the narrative's exilic structure. Crusoe's father's advice has to be tempered by the exclusionary nature of its focus. Some obvious courses of action cost more in anguish to follow than to resist, and there are times when the secure and complacent life he recommends is worse than the necessary errantry of a liberated soul. "I broke loose" (p. 7), Crusoe says of his initial sea voyage, and he is always doing so. His island exile is the final project of his "rambling Designs" (p. 40).

At one point in the *Farther Adventures of Robinson Crusoe,* a merchant in the Bay of Bengal tries to talk Crusoe into a sailing expedition. His argument reflects back on the initiating scene of the first volume: "For what should we stand still for? The whole world is in motion, rolling round and round; all the creatures of God, heavenly bodies and earthly, are busy and diligent; why should we be idle?" (2:214). The notion of rootedness is associated with the buzzword *idleness*. Defoe's narratives count on the principle of mobility, self-propulsion, and self-extension. Motion is fate. Near the beginning of Defoe's *Memoirs of a Cavalier,* the hero's mother dreams that she wanders out into the middle of a field in order to give birth to a son who, in half an hour's time, sprouts a pair of wings and flies away. The incipient cavalier is dreamed up as one of narrative's bird signs; his is an inborn tendency to fly the coop. As is the case for Crusoe's "wandring Inclination" (p. 4),[13] the cavalier has elsewhere built into his nature.

Defoe's fiction gains its power by playing the mobile self off the desiring self.[14] Moll Flanders, for example, whose mobility is class-inspired, and whose energies are sexually keen—a better word might be *smart*—seeks the security of the sobriquet *gentlewoman,* but finds herself removed to the very borders of the English-speaking world in America to attain it. Moll tests the status of gentility, which she seems to think means enterprising but which her first employer knew meant flesh peddling, with a set of prodigal relations in Virginia. Because of the exigencies of bourgeois fate, her new husband turns out to be her brother, and her mother-in-law her mother *in deed.* If on Crusoe's faraway island the values of hard-won sovereignty come up against the threat of cannibalism, in *Moll Flanders* newfangled gentility contests with a primordial taboo, incest. Moll's New World interlude is a paradigm of limits; it sets the contours of activity not merely in the simple sense of casting a character to the extremes but in the more complex sense of reaccommodating that character to his or her sense of center once the extremes are subsumed as part of experience. The mobile fantasy entails negotiation at the boundary between extreme circumstance and the formation of character. Usually, matters are turned to profit. As appalled as Moll was at what she called her undoing in Virginia, her brother/husband's estate eventually stakes her future. By the end of the narrative she literally "capitalizes" the incest taboo, which works for her the way Crusoe's Brazilian plantation worked for him as a land bank in exile.

The voyage out for Defoe is the sovereignty the self establishes over contingency. This is part of the reason that Crusoe first frames his "irresistible Reluctance . . . to going home" (p. 16) as a negative power: "I had several times loud Calls from my Reason and my more composed Judgment to go home, yet I had no Power to do it" (p. 14). He knows that settlement brings its own rewards, but he operates under a different imperative. Even when his reason tells him to stay put in Brazil and he is willing to admit, given his previous ill luck, that his voyaging scheme is "the most preposterous Thing that ever Man in such Circumstances could be guilty of" (p. 40), he feels compelled to undertake it. Later, when his rhetorical and religious guard is down on the island, he tells us what really drives him: "I seldom gave any Thing over without accomplishing it, when I once had it in my Head enough to begin it" (p. 168). He refers to his conviction that in time he would have figured a way to brew beer, but his sentiment applies to almost all his actions and it resides at the center of his sometimes mercurial character.

"Freedom lives hence, and banishment is here"

When Defoe speaks, as he does at length in *Serious Reflections,* of Crusoe's adventure acting the role of allegory to bring the remote nearer home, he means by home any and all familiar mental territory. But he also has an exilic fable in mind that makes Crusoe's island, as a home away from home, politically allusive. Crusoe's displacement overlaps a time in English history near, if not dear, to Defoe's heart. It does not tax the imagination, beyond the levy Defoe has already allowed it, to consider the interplay between the narrative's temporal configuration and the fold of years "at home" that coincide with Crusoe's time on his island. Defoe placed Crusoe in "banishment," as he calls it, from 1659 to 1686 (he returns to England a year later in 1687), a period of twenty-eight years that virtually parallels the years of the Stuart Restoration in England. [15] In a deliberate and calculated sense, Defoe makes of Crusoe's reign a government in exile.

For reasons that Defoe never forgot, the Stuart Restoration seemed apostolic to him. [16] Crusoe is cast ashore on the island a year before the return of Charles II, and he does not set foot on English soil until over a quarter century later just as arrangements for the Williamite succession are under way, a succession that would follow a Glorious Revolution Defoe considered foundational. As is characteristic of the exilic reflex in narrative, Defoe represents on Crusoe's island an ideological supplement separated from home but effectively replacing the regime in power. Crusoe, without any real political awareness of his own, sustains, like so many exiles, the values of his original land during a time when that land seemed incapable, at least in Defoe's view, of sustaining them properly itself. Defoe felt about the Stuarts at home in England what Kent felt about Lear's daughters: "Freedom lives hence, and banishment is here" (1.1.180). Subsequently, just prior to the time James II and his Stuart supporters are exiled, Defoe ushers his island sovereign home to forecast England's renewed legitimacy or its return to its senses.

Again, I am making an argument not for Crusoe's awareness of the temporal politics of his exilic fable but for Defoe's. He felt that the important gap in the continuity of English history was not the dramatic parliamentary revolution from 1641 through the Cromwellian Protectorate but those alien years from 1660 to 1688, coincidental also with the first twenty-eight years of his own life, during which his family was victimized, at least early in the Restoration, by the oppressive Clarendon codes. [17] *Robinson Crusoe* takes its place alongside traditional narratives where exilic duration is a kind of test until national history is, in a way, ready to legitimize itself. Individuals and peoples best represent themselves by metaphorically standing outside their land. [18]

The Stuarts, in Defoe's view, had two-timed the home island, enshrined a legitimacy founded on worn-out principles of Divine Right and Passive Obedience, and secured the safety of the realm in its later years by the swiftness and exigency of the executioner's ax. It is possible to say that the Restoration, in which most of Defoe's narratives are set, is the epoch that most haunted his imagination, and the notion of the period as a kind of *trou,* lapse, or hiatus is not one to which Defoe turns for the first time in *Robinson Crusoe*. He began his career with a pamphlet attack on the Stuarts, and his major early works capped, so to speak, the alien politics of the previous century. *The Consolidator* (1705) and *Jure Divino* (1706) are both relentless, detailed indictments of Stuart tyranny. Defoe specifically called *The Consolidator,* his first sustained fictional narrative, an "allegorick Relation," and the action sets a lunar philosopher on the moon to talk out and act out the precepts of the 1688 Glorious Revolution while explicitly attacking "lunar" (or lunatic) politics, the much less glorious practices of the Stuart kings, or any who would follow Stuart policies into the eighteenth century.

From the beginning of his career, Defoe had a countermyth in mind, one that depicted the true course of English history not as passive obedience in the face of *jure divino* but as a project or speculative adventure. It is in this sense that many readers have intuited that Crusoe stands for something central in the English experience, even if he does so without a sense of national mission.[19] His exile is a kind of blind trust, a metaphorical account that earns its interest not only as a new kind of sovereignty but as a new national enterprise. In his first full-length work in the 1690s, *Essay upon Projects,* Defoe offers up the Crusoe type and symbol in incipient form, the merchant adventurer with practical vision who, in the face of all manner of risk, is still "the most intelligent Man in the World, and consequently the most capable, when urg'd by Necessity, to Contrive New Ways to live."[20] He repeats the essence of this notion much later in his career, after *Robinson Crusoe,* when he refers to the English merchant as a kind of cycle of redemption in and of himself, an allegory of risk, endurance, and profit: "The English tradesman is a kind of phoenix, who rises out of his own ashes, and makes the ruin of his fortunes be a firm foundation to build his recovery."[21]

The inauguration of Crusoe's trials always involve risk devolving from capital venture. His island exile proper begins after several intervening commercial years that include imprisonment after capture by pirates and, upon his escape from North Africa, the establishment of a plantation in Brazil.[22] Crusoe claims that setting up the plantation puts him in the same settled stay-at-home condition his father recommended to him "and which if I resolved to go on with, I might as well ha' staid at Home, and never have fatigu'd my self in the World as I had done" (p. 35). It is not so much Crusoe's conviction speaking here that events such as his earlier capture by the Moors, his escape to the African coast, and his hacking a plantation out of the wilds of South America are the equivalent of taking a law degree—to which his father was willing to stake him—as it is his conviction that he is destined for a more risk-filled life than he happens to be living at the time.

Crusoe departs Brazil 1 September 1659 and he comes to ruin on 30 September 1659.[23] The prelude to his island adventure, as death stares him in the face aboard a foundering ship, previews the ultimate exilic fate, the crossing into another world: "In a word, we sat looking upon one another, and expecting Death every Moment, and every Man acting accordingly, as preparing for another World, for there was little or nothing more for us to do in this" (p. 43). Crusoe is thrust on his island, and his very survival is a rebirth into a new condition or "state," which seems to repeat the scene near the beginning of the narrative when the young Robinson swoons during his first shipwreck only to awake "with Horror of Mind and the Thoughts of what was yet before me" (p. 13). In this earlier scene the future plot of the whole plays out in its adverbial part; what is later "before" Crusoe after his second wreck is the battle for life that becomes his restoration.

> Nothing can describe the Confusion of Thought which I felt when I sunk into the Water; for tho' I swam very well, yet I could not deliver my self from the Waves so as to draw Breath, till that Wave having driven me, or rather carried me a vast Way on towards the Shore, and having spent it self, went back, and left me upon the Land almost dry, but half-dead with the Water I took in. [p. 44]

The sea comes at Crusoe, again as a landed form and then as an enemy: "for I saw the Sea come after me as high as a great Hill, and as furious as an Enemy which I had no Means or Strength to contend with" (p. 44). Crusoe's business, at least in the metaphoric language with which he relays his experience, is to serve as his own self-regulator or governor: "[to] Pilot my self toward the Shore" (p. 45). Later, when the wrecked ship appears for his salvaging and Crusoe loads a raft with booty, he steers toward a cove near the mouth of an island creek to moor his vessel and, in an almost symbolic gesture, marks his sovereignty by "sticking my two broken Oars into the Ground" (p. 52). When he considers future trips to the wrecked ship for salvaging, his self-sovereignty becomes participatory: "I call'd a Council, that is to say, in my Thoughts" (p. 54). From disaster comes a plan, or council, for the beginnings of a new order of things. Of course, if we credit the possibility of a temporal juxtaposition with English home rule, we also credit Crusoe's language of resettlement as conventional to a fault. We have seen its metaphoric equivalent with every crucial change of government in England, particularly with the host of encomia for the Stuart beachhead in 1660 that figure the return of Charles II as the restoration of calm after a storm at sea. Dryden, for example, compresses the king's exile and return in the following lines:

> To all the Sea-Gods *Charles* an Off'ring owes:
> A Bull to thee *Portunus* shall be slain,
> A Lamb to you the Tempests of the Main:
> For those loud stormes that did against him rore
> Have cast his shipwrack'd Vessel on the shore.
> ["Astraea Redux," lines 120–24]

Defoe need not have remembered the specific Dryden passage here—that is not the point I am making. What is significant is the antithetical nature of Crusoe's beachhead in 1659; his new estate signals what Defoe always believed, that the true Englishman was compromised when the Stuarts were in his "home" and he was, so to speak, "out of it." Restoration means resupply or restocking, literally laying away for the future. Crusoe is as well established, in this sense, as his temporal sovereign rival; in fact, one of the plus items on his ledger sheet of miseries and comforts is that from the ship he has "*gotten out so many necessary things as will either supply my Wants, or enable me to supply my self even as long as I live*" (p. 66). He repeats this comfort a few paragraphs later, commenting on the "store" in his cave: "it look'd like a general Magazine of all Necessary things, and I had every thing so ready at my Hand, that it was a great Pleasure to me to see all my Goods in such Order, and especially to find my Stock of all Necessaries so great" (pp. 68–69). Crusoe landed is Crusoe restored.

Oppositions

Timing is no accident in *Robinson Crusoe*. Both Defoe and his "fugitive hero" are sensitive to coincidence, Crusoe, for example, noticing that "there was a strange Concurrence of Days, in the various Providences which befel me; and which, if I had been superstitiously inclin'd to observe Days as Fatal or Fortunate, I might have had Reason to have look'd upon with a great deal of Curiosity" (p. 133). That Defoe sets the adventure when he does becomes yet another element of the narrative's readable potential. The politics of the island exile are live issues for Defoe: sovereignty, property, natural law, and toleration. Crusoe reinvents what the Stuarts abused, though in the instance of toleration it requires a few years worth of taxing conversation between Crusoe's self and soul on the subject of cannibalism to sort out the issues involved.[24]

Crusoe's adventures on the island are such that they conform to the standard exigencies of exilic experience. During the earlier years on the island, he is trapped between his desire for settlement and his readiness to depart an uninhabited, strange, and lonely place. He is vaguely aware that he must organize his territory on what he comes to call "my beloved Island" so that he can both transform it as a new home and keep paramount any opportunity to leave it. To place himself any distance from the seaward part of the island, from which he could be more easily rescued if circumstance permitted, would, as he puts it, "anticipate my Bondage" (p. 101). But until the time is ready in the larger scheme of things that Crusoe calls Providence, he is tethered. Crusoe may plan an escape by carving a huge canoe out of a felled tree, but to his dismay he realizes that he has no way of hauling the finished craft to the sea. Poor Crusoe tries to make too much of opportunity before opportunity is ready to make something of him.

The turning point of Crusoe's stay on the island, the point at which the slow process of opportunity begins to shape the necessity for departure, is also the point at which the idea of sovereignty begins to take on different dimensions. This process begins with the famous footprint episode, during the fifteenth year of Crusoe's isolation. Crusoe himself recognizes the moment as an incursion that is also a turning or transition point in his exile: "But now I come to a new Scene in my Life" (p. 153). Perhaps no scene in fiction better illustrates the subtle workings of surface and depth patternings that narrative has available to it.[25] Crusoe, wandering over now familiar territory, comes on a startling sight, the image of a single footprint in the sand. This stark impression provides his hard-won resettlement—his recessed allegorical history—its most dramatic surface test. At the appearance of the print, Crusoe's lingering despair at his separation from the world he once knew turns into an absolute and immanent fear of having his sovereignty violated, his settlement in exile penetrated. The paradox of the exilic condition is fully realized in a single narrative incident: the necessitous strength of character that allows Crusoe to re-create a version of home abroad also inhibits and distorts the exile's traditional *Drang nach Hause,* his will to return to his original place.

The footprint episode recalls Crusoe's earlier shock at the sudden greeting of his wild parrot, when the sound of another voice so rattled him that it took him "a good while before I could compose my self" (p. 143). But Crusoe is not so fortunate after sighting the print which, even years later, still "discompos'd me very much" (p. 157). He is at first thunderstruck "as if I had seen an Apparition" (p. 153), and his recidivistic response is to wander up and down the beach just as he had done when he set his own foot on the island nearly fifteen years before. He immediately adjusts his language to suit his material circumstances; homecoming now becomes a form of self-defense: "like a Man perfectly confus'd and out of my self, I came Home to my

Fortification, not feeling, as we say, the Ground I went on" (p. 154). Out of himself, he is like the apparition he thinks he has just seen, but his supposed apparition has a very tangible quality to it—it makes a real impression or, at least, a footprint—whereas Crusoe is so scared his feet barely touch the ground.

The confusion here of Crusoe's self with sign—later he hopes the footprint, like the imprint of the parrot's voice, would turn out to be his own—derives from the strength of his desire that his settlement, once so separable from all he had known, now be integral as all he has left.[26] The print in the sand is both an image of trespass on the exile's territory and a strong but necessary reminder that the exile's isolated condition is an unnatural one. Crusoe's fear initially renders him as wild as any being who might have made the print, that is, renders him too native an inhabitant—one with no civilized history other than his island life. He ran home

> terrify'd to the last Degree, looking behind me at every two or three Steps, mistaking every Bush and Tree, and fancying every Stump at a Distance to be a Man; nor is it possible to describe how many various Shapes affrighted Imagination represented Things to me in, how many wild Ideas were found every Moment in my Fancy, and what strange unaccountable Whimsies came into my Thoughts by the Way. [p. 154]

When Crusoe tries to soothe himself with the hope that the footprint might, after all, be his own, that hope is dashed in an appropriate externalization of internal apprehension: the print turns out to be too large. For the fearful Crusoe, the mysterious impression on the beach assumes in size a power opposite to the self-diminishment he experiences on seeing it.[27] The print is even more threatening in its singleness: one print suggests its complement, its "other." To put its significance differently, Crusoe learns from the surface appearance of the footprint a deeper exilic lesson he ought never to have forgotten and will remember for the rest of his stay on the island: one simply cannot go it alone forever. By its singleness, which is to say its incompleteness, the one print in the sand is both a complement to Crusoe's condition and a corrective to any permanent historical notion about the possibility or desirability of the exile's lone sovereignty. By the habit of abundant years, Crusoe had already begun to cultivate permanent thoughts that ought to have remained provisional: "when I began to regret the want of Conversation, I would ask my self whether thus conversing mutually with my own Thoughts, and, as I hope I may say, with even God himself by Ejaculations, was not better than the utmost Enjoyment of humane Society in the World" (pp: 135–36).

An earlier passage in which Crusoe, aware of the hyperbole, describes the nature of his supposed sovereignty suggests why the appearance of the print on the beach is so crucial a point in the narrative: "I was Lord of the whole Mannor; or if I pleas'd, I might call my self King, or Emperor[28] over the whole Country which I had Possession of. There were no Rivals. I had no Competitor, none to dispute Sovereignty or Command with me" (p. 128). "Rivals," "Competitor," and "Sovereignty" are key words here, and the sighting of the footprint signals the imposition of new circumstances for Crusoe, circumstances that are, willy-nilly, political. If Defoe chose to represent Crusoe's island reign as coincidentally "occupying" the Restoration hiatus in England, he also gave considerable thought to what sort of action affects the alteration of historical circumstance. In the exilic state, rivalry is opportunity; in the usurped state, rivalry is disaster. The two possibilities conform to the status of narrative as sovereign on the one hand, sufficient unto its made-up self, and representational on the other, reflecting the contingencies and necessities of the supposed real world it imitates. This is the same point I make in the introductory chapter about the double quality of Molloy's "region," both insulated and penetrated, in the Samuel Beckett novel that serves as a modern comic analogue to the Crusoe dilemma. Fiction is threatened or, as Edward Said would put it, molested by its own compulsion to penetrate its exilic allegory with the figure of oppositional reality.

The footprint in Defoe's narrative is incontestably a sign of opposition to Crusoe—surely he reads it that way—and, given the care

Defoe takes in marking its appearance in the fifteenth year of Crusoe's reign, the historically temporal parallel at "home" is intriguing. Crusoe sees the footprint in 1674, assuming he lands on the island in 1659, as he originally says, and not in 1658, as he later seems to think.[29] Nearly every observer of the course of Stuart history pointed to a different set of circumstances after the first fifteen years of Charles II's reign. Those actively involved in the politics of the period such as Andrew Marvell, Anthony Ashley Cooper, Algernon Sidney, and John Locke, and those that were to write of it in the next generation, Laurence Echard, John Oldmixon, and Daniel Defoe, marked 1674 as a transition from the earlier monarchical consolidation of power to the emergence, within the context of plots and conspiracies, of a newly named opposition party and a new crisis in national sovereignty. In his *Growth of Popery and Arbitrary Power* (1678), Marvell wrote that after 1674 the king's new party, the Tories, tried to stir the old royalist antirevolutionary fervor against the new Whigs: "They begun therefore after fifteen years to remember that there were such a sort of men in England as the old Cavalier party; and reckoned, that by how much the more generous, they were more credulous than others, and so more fit to be again abused."[30]

For the Stuarts, the emergence of a powerful opposition after 1674 plotted the beginning of a long road to the end; for Crusoe, the end to his unviolated hegemony during 1674 plotted the beginning of a long road to a new beginning. The potential represented by the footprint is what is required to get Crusoe back to his first home, his "real" home, the one on the map. In the oft-cited "Chequer Work of Providence" passage, Crusoe admits the absurdity of having feared as violation what he ought better to have welcomed as possible salvation.

> For I whose only Affliction was, that I seem'd banished from human Society, that I was alone, circumscrib'd by the boundless Ocean, cut off from Mankind, and condemn'd to what I call'd silent Life; that I was as one who Heaven thought not worthy to be number'd among the Living, or to appear among the rest of his Creatures; that to have seen one of my own Species, would have seem'd to me a Raising me from

Death to Life, and the greatest blessing that Heaven it self, next to the supreme Blessing of Salvation, could bestow: *I say,* that I should now tremble at the very Apprehensions of seeing a Man, and was ready to sink into the Ground at but the Shadow or silent Appearance of a Man's having set his Foot in the Island. [p. 156]

Crusoe may be ready to recognize the irony of his initial reaction, but he is not yet prepared to alter his behavior. He has the exilic terms reversed, if his desire is historical reprise: "In my Reflections upon the State of my Case, since I came on Shore on this Island, I was comparing the happy Posture of My Affairs, in the first Years of my Habitation here, compar'd to the Life of Anxiety, Fear and Care, which I had liv'd ever since I had seen the Print of a Foot in the Sand" (p. 196). Someone made that print and Crusoe is unready to deem that someone savior or friend. In fact, for years he reacts to his opposition, real or presumed, as would the worst of tyrants securing the safety of his tyranny: "these Anxieties, these constant Dangers I liv'd in, and the Concern that was now upon me, put an End to all Invention, and to all the Contrivances that I had laid for my Future Accommodations and Conveniences" (p. 176). In the political pattern of the action, Defoe ironically endows his governor in exile with the most oppressive features of the Stuart regime whose reign he temporally counters. In the strictly narrative pattern, Crusoe's exaggerated fears for his own security obsessively protect a "created" realm by putting an end to its invention, by ceasing to create it: "I had the Care of my Safety more now upon my Hands, than that of my Food. I car'd not to drive a Nail, or chop a Stick of Wood now, for fear the Noise I should make should be heard; much less would I fire a Gun, for the same Reason" (p. 176).

"At this hour lie at my mercy all mine enemies"

It takes Crusoe several years of paranoid defensiveness to get used to the notion that what seems to be his opposition might actually be the means by which he can alter his condition as exile. The sighting of the print refocuses the exilic dilemma—that which had been appropriated as a substitute has become for Crusoe a necessity. Something has gone wrong in ways that even Crusoe comes to recognize, and in the latter years of his stay he begins the process of reconversion and recivilization. He makes positive again what his father, in overstressing security at home, had so many years before envisaged as strictly negative: "I could not satisfy my self in my Station, but was continually poring upon the Means, and Possibility of my Escape from this Place" (p. 195). The neutral, indeed, almost scathing "Place" tells much of the story. Like Odysseus's renewed urge for home while tethered on Calypso's island, or like Prospero's homeward turn after burying his staff on his magical isle, Crusoe reexperiences the exile's original desire: any place but home for him now is undifferentiated. Once Crusoe's counterturn is set in motion things move, if not as quickly as he would choose, at least decisively. He readies himself for actual homecoming by planning a preliminary beachhead on the cannibal mainland.

> All my Calm of Mind in my Resignation to Providence, and waiting the Issue of the Dispositions of Heaven, seem'd to be suspended; and I had, as it were, no Power to turn my Thoughts to any thing, but to the Project of a Voyage to the Main, which came upon me with such Force, and such an Impetuosity of Desire, that it was not to be resisted. [p. 198]

Crusoe gives up his scheme to go to the cannibal Main only when one very useful cannibal comes to him. Friday's companionship during the last few years of Crusoe's exile provides an actual other who becomes a second self in initiating the strength of will toward repatriation. Friday sees his own land from a vantage point on the high side of Crusoe's island: "*O joy!* Says he, *O glad! There see my Country, there my Nation!*" (p. 223). These stirring words are voiced just after Crusoe anticipates the spatial collapse of the distance between the place of exile and his own home island nation by referring to himself and Friday as "comforted restor'd Penitents; we had here the Word of God to read, and no farther off from his Spirit to instruct, than if we had been in *England*" (p. 221). The solace of one land for Friday and the mention of another by Crusoe prime the narrative for what is about to happen.

After Friday's arrival, and without precisely knowing why, Crusoe assumes his deliverance is again providentially opportune, telling of "the great Hopes I had of being effectually, and speedily deliver'd; for I Had an invincible Impression upon my Thoughts, that my Deliverance was at hand, and that I should not be another Year in this Place" (p. 229). The impression that the times are ready for him to return seems as telling in its way as the impression of the footprint years before. Crusoe loses his fear of having his island penetrated when he loses the desire to remain isolated.

In the interim between Crusoe's thoughts about redirecting his efforts toward home and his opportunity to make the break, he begins to revise his notions of what sovereignty ought to mean to him in historical rather than fictional terms. He turns to the law of civilized nations,[31] and he does so by readjusting his view of those cannibals whose intermittent presence on the island had so reduced him to quivering paranoia and unaccountable bloodlust.[32] Divine Right, Crusoe decides, ought to be in the hands of a Divinity, not in the hands of a self-appointed vice-regent. God has not called on him, Crusoe says, "to take upon me to be a Judge of their Actions, much less an Executioner of his Justice; that whenever he thought fit, he would take the Cause into his own Hands, and by national Vengeance punish them as a People, for national Crimes; but that in the mean time, it was none of my Business" (p. 232).[33] Any one individual, namely Crusoe in this instance, cannot afford to be a scourge on an entire nation, and at the end of his stay, his energies are better employed against those few who have falsely usurped a power that they have no right to hold, that is, against the English mutineers who run riot in conspiracy and betrayal.

At the original sighting of the mutineers and their unfortunate captives, matters come to a head.[34] Crusoe approaches the captives with the mutineers out of earshot and chooses to ally himself with those who face either an exile like his own or, worse, death. That is, he allies himself with historical legitimacy, with the rightful captain of the English vessel. As soon as matters indeed "right" themselves, the English usurpers and mutineers are cast out from that which they have misappropriated. Later we learn that their fate, too, becomes exilic: "they would much rather venture to stay there, than to be carry'd to *England* to be hang'd; so I left it on that Issue" (p. 276). The politics of Crusoe's narrative are played out in miniature by the scoundrels suffering what they would have wished upon the forces of legitimacy.

While still in dire straits, the English captain contemplates the bizarre figure of Crusoe as ally coming toward him, a bedraggled version of the mythical stranger-savior figure of legendary tales.[35] Crusoe says to the captain: "But can you put a Stranger in the way how to help you, for you seem to me be in some great Distress? I saw you when you landed, and when you seem'd to make Applications to the Brutes that came with you, I saw one of them lift up his Sword to kill you" (p. 254). The captain looks at this apparition and elevates Crusoe beyond or, as Crusoe's father would see it, higher than his merits: *"Am I talking to God, or Man! Is it a real Man, or an Angel!"* (p. 254). Crusoe's self-identification is significant here after twenty-eight years on the island and nearly thirty-seven years away from home: "I am a Man, an *Englishman,* and dispos'd to assist you" (pp. 254–55). The island sovereign now names himself citizen of his native country, bringing his alien status and resettling impulse into alignment. Again, like Prospero, Crusoe is a magic (or imagined) island recluse willing to become a national subject once certain conditions are met, certain contracts arranged, certain powers displayed. Friday, as commentators have noticed, is Crusoe's Ariel.

> Let them be hunted soundly. At this hour
> Lie at my mercy all mine enemies.
> Shortly shall all my labors end, and thou
> Shalt have the airs at freedom. For a little,
> Follow, and do me service.
>
> [*Tempest,* 4.1.262–66]

Crusoe's actions at the end reveal a homeward turn of mind and a set of principles based on necessity. His advice about firing on, and possibly killing, the mutineers justifies violence for legal, not tyrannical, ends: *"Necessity* legitimates my Advice" (p. 256).[36] And Crusoe's forces advance in the name of rightful authority: "At the Noise of the Fire, I immediately advanc'd with my whole Army, which was now 8 Men, *viz.* my self *Generalissimo,* Friday, my Lieutenant-General, the Captain and his two Men, and the three Prisoners of War, who we had trusted with Arms" (p. 267). Perhaps this force is not so impressive as the advance guard of William III riding into England, but it is surely more effective than the hopeless army in which Defoe may have fought that suffered ignominious earlier defeat at Sedgemoor against the forces of James II in 1685.

Crusoe arrives back in England on 11 June 1687.[37] He comes home truly substantiated, both in status—as returned wanderer, a man of archetypal value—and in funds from his Brazilian plantation, which Defoe totals later at "above a thousand Pounds a Year, as sure as an Estate of Lands in *England*" (p. 285). Defoe's analogy exceeds even the wishes of Crusoe's father: his exile progresses metaphorically as adventurer from the merchant class to the settled gentry. Crusoe's accumulated property allows him to return, in a sense, properly islanded. Perhaps in a broader sense, Crusoe's substantial return to his native place allows Defoe to realize the full potential of an action in which the exile, abroad and restored, is always sovereign.

CHAPTER TWO

Conrad after Crusoe: *Lord Jim* and *Heart of Darkness*

Isolation and Narrative Power

Conrad is much less interested than Defoe in salvaging the exilic experience for reconstitutional—indeed, for commercial—sovereignty than he is in writing up or "into" the moral confusion embedded in the life of the renegade, a figure whose fate signals the lot of those who violate communal principles in which Conrad is somewhat embarrassed to believe in the first place. The dilemma in Conrad's fiction, at least before the severe irony of his skepticism obliterates even the sentimental romance of communal obligation, is that the narrative capacity to describe the effects of isolation is effaced by the mysterious, silent powers of the *isolato*. Marlow writes of the renegade exile, Tuan Jim on Patusan, that, as a figure on narrative ground, he has become even more powerful than the words that give him life.

> I can't with mere words convey to you the impression of his total and utter isolation. I know, of course, he was in every sense alone of his kind there, but the unsuspected qualities of his nature had brought him in such close touch with his surroundings that this isolation seemed only the effect of his power. His loneliness added to his stature. [1]

It is with a characteristic feint toward the notion of authenticity that Conrad plays one of the realist's trumps in suggesting that his exiled hero's experience is so primal that a mere sequence of inked impressions on a page cannot fully convey his stature. It "is as if loneliness were a hard and absolute condition of existence; the envelope of flesh and blood on which our eyes are fixed melts before the outstretched hand, and there remains only the capricious, unconsolable, and elusive spirit that no eye can follow, no hand can grasp" (p. 180). Jim gains in narrative fascination from the moment he begins to claim sovereignty over the only material he has left at his disposal, his exilic power, having given up all other rights to that communal territory which his actions and his fate have denied him. Like Kurtz in *Heart of Darkness,* the isolated Jim has kicked himself loose from the earth and kicked the earth loose in the process.[2]

Marlow insists that Jim's legend in Patusan is imbued with the mystery of the silent land that harbors it; it is not subject to the loud clarion call of the goddess Fama: "Its voice was not the trumpeting of the disreputable goddess we all know—not blatant—not brazen. It took its tone from the stillness and gloom of the land without a past, where his word was the one truth of every passing day. It shared something of the nature of that silence through which it accompanied you into unexplored depths, heard continuously by your side, penetrating, far-reaching—tinged with wonder and mystery on the lips of whispering men" (p. 272). To wedge one's way into a place that emits mostly silence is, paradoxically, the way Conrad's renegades exist in worlds made for their narrative action.[3] What Conrad says of Jim holds as well for Decoud on the Great Isabel or for Kurtz at the heart of darkness—at least before Marlow's urge to hear Kurtz talk himself up. Marlow describes the Kurtzian interior.

> How can you imagine what particular region of the first ages a man's untrammelled feet may take him into by the way of solitude—utter solitude without a policeman—by the way of silence—utter silence, where no warning voice of a kind neighbour can be heard whispering of public opinion? These little things make all the great difference. When they are gone you must fall back upon your own innate strength, upon your own capacity for faithfulness. [p. 116]

Isolation is the state of silent remove, which is also the material terrain for the illusion that sustains the mimetic performance. But the depiction of isolation, somewhat like the narrative depiction of any event, requires the validation of voice to inaugurate and corroborate the existence of its silent circumstances.[4] Marlow had already speculated in *Lord Jim* on the aesthetics of the outland: "But do you notice how, three hundred miles beyond the end of telegraph cables and mail-boat lines, the haggard utilitarian lies of our civilization wither and die, to be replaced by pure exercises of imagination, that have the futility, often the charm and sometimes the deep hidden truthfulness of works of art?" (p. 282).

The outcast's experience is powerful only insofar as its written or spoken record reveals it, at which point the experience becomes, as it does for Crusoe, for Kurtz, for Jim, a kind of sovereign narrative addendum. Marlow comments on the final crossing to Patusan, where the leap beyond bounds is a leap into the space that compels exilic imagining, playing on words, *extravagant* and *strange,* that at their very etymological core mean supplemental: "That's how he ascended the Patusan river. Nothing could have been more prosaic and more unsafe, more extravagantly casual, more lonely. Strange, this fatality that would cast the complexion of a flight upon all his acts, of impulsive unreflecting desertion—of a jump into the unknown" (p. 229). Jim works on Patusan, or lets Conrad work him, to remake his history; he is himself an image of supplemental human history, at once, as Stein puts it, "the youngest human being now in existence" (p. 219) and, as Marlow puts it, the oldest: "He dominated the forest, the secular gloom, the old mankind. He was a figure set up on a pedestal, to represent in his persistent youth the power, and perhaps the virtues, of races that never grow old, that have emerged from the gloom. I don't know why he should always have appeared to me symbolic" (p. 265).

Jim, in effect, is reimagined in Patusan as he would reimagine himself: "He left his earthly failings behind him and that sort of reputation he had, and there was a totally new set of conditions for his imaginative faculty to work upon" (p. 218). Patusan is "one of the lost, forgotten, unknown places of the earth" whose very existence is handed over *to* narrative as "the truth disclosed in a moment of illusion" (p. 323).

To signal the difference in *Lord Jim* between the communal story of the earlier *Patna* disaster and the exilic supplement of Patusan, Marlow reformulates his own narrative, beginning anew with an inaugurating lure: "I don't suppose any of you had ever heard of Patusan?" (p. 218). Once Jim gets into such a space "it would be for the outside world as though he never existed" (p. 232), even though one piece of the maritime world's flotsam, a derelict habitué of the sea-lanes, the misnamed Gentleman Brown, conspires in the end to penetrate Jim's boundaries, violate his sovereignty, and ruin his illusion. When Marlow, for his part, leaves Jim in Patusan, he senses that the place would retain only a supplemental status, "it would slip out of existence, to live only in my memory till I myself passed into oblivion" (p. 323). Or, by implication, it would live when he reimagines it. As Marlow's ship takes the final bend in the river, the land "dropped out of my sight bodily, with its colour, its design, and its meaning, like a picture created by fancy on a canvas, upon which, after long contemplation, you turn your back for the last time. It remains in the memory motionless, unfaded, with its life arrested, in an unchanging light" (p. 330).

Marlow admits the almost generic insularity of Jim's experience in Patusan by enclosing its status when he separates it from the main body of the story in a letter, written after Jim's death, to one of his previous listeners: "The story of the last events you shall find in the few pages enclosed here. You must admit that it is romantic beyond the wildest dreams of his boyhood, and yet there is to my mind a sort of profound and terrifying logic in it, as if it were our imagination alone that could set loose upon us the might of an overwhelming destiny" (p. 342). The nature of that destiny, framed here in terms of the power or "might" of its imaginative projection, makes of Jim's isolation one of the more mysterious and generative voicings available to narrative, a message from the world of the dead. When Stein's brigantine master, a kind of half-caste Captain Malaprop, prepared to deposit Jim on the shores of Patusan, he made some interesting observations to Marlow: "the gentleman was already 'in the similitude of a corpse.' 'What? What do you say?' I asked. He assumed a startlingly ferocious demeanour, and imitated to perfection the act of stabbing from behind. 'Already like the body of one deported' " (p. 240). In this case, the deportation to Patusan and departure to a world beyond turn out to mean something of the same thing.

Whatever base actions by other base renegades end up getting Jim shot and killed, it is precisely the reinscription of territory within which to act that renders Jim his undying opportunity. When Marlow says of Jim that indeed "no man could have appeared less 'in the similitude of a corpse' " (p. 241), he means that Jim has already been revived from the dead. The opportunity provided by his departure to and isolation in Patusan supplements an earlier loss. Conrad's language makes this clear. When Jim received the sentence of the court for his actions aboard the *Patna*, Marlow noted: "These proceedings had all the cold vengefulness of a death sentence, had all the cruelty of a sentence of exile" (p. 158). In Patusan, the figurative implications of the *Patna* sentence are literally enacted; but the very opportunity returns to Jim his credentials or, at least, issues him a new set to repair the loss that originally stripped him of the right to circulate on familiar seas and in familiar ports. Loss for Conrad is the trauma of inadequacy in the human concourse, and reparation for that loss takes place in an isolated zone where conscience is purged by a renewed sense of moral sovereignty.

"Community of Inglorious Toil"

Conrad remains intrigued with the narrative power of isolation as the silent test of the human spirit even in his later political fiction. In *Nostromo*, Martin Decoud undergoes his solitary dark night of the soul on the Great Isabel island in the Bay. In *Under Western Eyes*, before we learn of the agony of Razumov as social pariah, we learn of a legendary Russian émigré known as the heroic fugitive or great exile, whose journal narrative of fearful escape and long vigil in the Siberian forest becomes a European best-seller. Conrad's narrator heaps ironic scorn on the hypocritical uses to which the great exile later puts his adventures—their cachet enlists recruits for a mystical and phony revolutionary program based on the spirituality of the Russian female—but the mere image of the man makes a considerable impression, and this impression is intimately connected to the power of his experience and *its* expression. Conrad's Swiss narrator says that "this big pinkish poll evoked for me the vision of a wild head with matted locks peering through parted bushes, glimpses of naked, tawny limbs slinking behind the masses of sodden foliage under a cloud of flies and mosquitoes. It was an involuntary tribute to the vigour of his writing" (pp. 128–29). Like Jim, the great man in isolation is a walking allegory; he represents both his own moment in time and then, as in the very act of narrative re-creation, all moments done over again. In the wilds of Siberia, the great fugitive was an antithetical creature, reminiscent of Crusoe's recidivistic moments on his island or Kurtz's at the heart of darkness: "For it was as though there had been two human beings indissolubly joined in that enterprise. The civilized man, the enthusiast of advanced humanitarian ideals thirsting for the triumph of spiritual love and political liberty; and the stealthy, primeval savage, pitilessly cunning in the preservation of his freedom from day to day, like a tracked wild beast" (p. 122).

Though the trials of isolation in Conrad's fiction are powerfully evocative and reconstitutive, they invariably stem from misdealings of some sort or another within the communal arena. The misdealers in whom Conrad is especially interested tend to act from what Albert Guerard calls "exalted egoism."[5] Most of the countless beings alive and at work on the sea-lanes or in the great cities of the world either do not think terribly much about what they do or are lucky enough not to face the circumstances that might challenge the values they accept for no other reason than the unexamined fixity, as Marlow puts it, of their standards. What intrigues Conrad in his novels and tales is the dilemma that sets in for imaginatively charged individuals when the image of the world is no longer commensurate with the fixed image of their selves, when they are self-dispossessed, no longer their own property in a world of common ideologies and common material pursuits. The question asked by the despairing Razumov after his act of wretched bad faith in *Under Western Eyes* is one that serves many of Conrad's hero-victims: "Was it possible that he no longer belonged to himself?" (p. 301). Suicide or exile is the solution in the grimmest of these cases. Something like this happens in *Lord Jim* to the presiding official at Jim's *Patna* hearing, Captain Brierly, whose mysterious suicide hints at the dissolution of the fiction of perfect soundness by which he thought he lived in the world of the sea. Brierly's mate says: " ' neither you nor I, sir, had ever thought so much of ourselves' " (p. 65).

Crisis for Conrad's characters occurs in that worldly gap between a self-aggrandizing ideology and the riot of communal activity. In *Lord Jim,* it is the young sailor's misfortune to fall directly into this gap or, to make matters worse, jump directly into it. Jim is, in a way, predisposed to do so. His mental preparation for what ended up not happening on the infamous *Patna* encouraged his imagination to perform in a scene other than that provided by the events. Here is Jim before the moment of his crisis on the *Patna:* "His confounded imagination had evoked for him all the horrors of panic, the trampling rush, the pitiful screams, boats swamped—all the appalling incidents of a disaster at sea he had ever heard of" (p. 88). In effect, his imagination creates a supplement of chaos for which the actual occurrence—an ominous bump in the night and a typical ocean squall—has neither space nor time. Jim summons a nightmare more naturally the provenance of castaways, isolatoes, or paranoids: "Those striving with unreasonable forces know it well,—the shipwrecked castaways in boats, wanderers lost in a desert, men battling against the unthinking might of nature, or the stupid brutality of crowds" (p. 88). The panic over which no single individual would have control is so strong an imagined circumstance that it drives out the passive opportunity to do nothing at all, which, for those who maintained their communal posts, was the simplest and most acceptable response to what faced them at sea.

Just as Jim was unprepared in his vision of heroic self-capacity to consider the result of his panic—the image of its reality was so strong—he was also unprepared for the "element of burlesque in his ordeal" (p. 105). Humiliation in the face of wrong imaginings makes him "a seaman in exile from the sea" (p. 4), and plays no small part in activating his later desire for a faraway rather than a local opportunity to write burlesque out of his self-romance.[6] The failings that put the soul in exile for Conrad become complicated and compelling subjects for narration, but they tend not to get worked out as subjects in the same theaters of action in which they occur. Short of suicide, or at least, in Jim's case, before a kind of suicide, remove is the Conradian ground of repair. Jim will set himself at some kind of rest by a series of actions more severe than the "burlesque" one that set him awry. He will make an extravaganza-in-exile out of contrition, which is the full flowering of the ironic Conradian plot.

One of the problems in *Lord Jim* for Conrad's young hero involves the nature of the language used to represent him in a world for which he becomes increasingly unfit. Conrad centers the issue on the symbolic word *sovereignty,* a word of historical import for the exilic and imperial fiction. Jim circulates along the commercial circuit like a false sovereign, a counterfeit coin: "He looked genuine as a new sovereign, but there was some infernal alloy in his metal" (p. 45). Jim's own dreams of deeds have a "gorgeous virility" (p. 20) about them, but the first thing Marlow says of him when he sets eyes on his face is that he "had no business to look so sound" (p. 40). His dreams are like his image—he simply replicates the appearance more than the substance of fine metal, "nothing more rare than brass" (p. 46).

The word *sound* is one of those Conradian verbal bells that keeps tolling in different pitches through the action. *Sound* is a property of being, moral value, moral health, and a property of voicing, musing, telling. The equivocal action in the novel is that unsoundness is a false issuance, whether verbalized or traded. Marlow never gives over worrying about "the subtle unsoundness of the man" (p. 89), and, indeed, his tersest insult to Jim touches on a version of the same metaphoric implication when, remarking on one of Jim's abandoned jobs, Marlow says, "'You haven't as much sense as a rat; they don't clear out from a good ship'" (p. 195). Marlow, of course, senses immediately, perhaps even concurrently, the image of the *Patna*, a ship that seemed no more than a sinking tin, floating into port forlorn but still *sound*. And when he follows with an irreverent, "'This business ain't going to sink,' says I," Jim literally reenacts his original failing: "He gave a big jump" (p. 195).

The notion of sovereignty and unsoundness, legitimacy and debased utterance, gains a special significance when it is repeated in the context of Marlow's increasing doubt concerning the nature of standards for human activity that takes place within the communal sphere, "the doubt of the sovereign power enthroned in a fixed standard of conduct" (p. 50).[7] Moral conduct for Conrad is, as he writes in the *Nigger of the "Narcissus,"* based on a few boldly chosen sentimental lies, especially the idea of community, the "strong, effective and respectable bond of a sentimental lie" (p. 155). In his *Personal Record*, Conrad is good enough to provide the essence of these simple sentimental lies: "Those who read me know my conviction that the world, the temporal world, rests on a few very simple ideas; so simple that they must be as old as the hills. It rests notably, among others, on the idea of Fidelity" (p. xix). Of course Conrad also knows full well that these necessary lies are neither universally practiced nor even universally understood. But they ought to be, even if the *ought* remains a part of an "unofficial sentimentalism (which, like the poor, is exceedingly difficult to get rid of)."[8]

What causes Marlow to doubt sovereign communal power in *Lord Jim* is not so much Jim's having violated such standards, though he surely does, but Jim's seeming imperviousness to their fixity, an imperviousness decidedly not displayed by such stolid and, finally, uninteresting types as the Malay helmsman who refuses to leave his post on the *Patna* or, later, the French lieutenant who boards the ship as it drifts into port. These men are sailors and employees—what they lack in imagination they make up in steadfastness, a virtue that for the sake of narrative interest is honored more in the breach than in the observance.

Marlow works to change the focus of his perspective on Jim from the sovereign standards of his occupation to the sovereign possibilities of his imaginings. In the world of occupations, Jim's imagination is unfit. It is less withering for him to have performed badly as a sailor in the *Patna* episode than not to have had a situation in which his performance might have conformed to a notion of his desires: "He had no leisure to regret what he had lost, he was so wholly and naturally concerned for what he had failed to obtain" (p. 83). Even after the fact he is bothered less by what he did than by what people conclude about his capacities. This is what Marlow claims is at the "heart"—always a charged word in Conrad's fiction—of his "impossible world of romantic achievements" (p. 83). Later, Jim still gets the focus of his action wrong; he relives the incident once again, imagining its potential proportions if the ship had actually foundered. Jim considers that he might have been strong enough to float on a piece of the wreck, proudly pounding his chest: " 'There's nothing the matter with *my* heart' " (p. 131). He fails to make the crucial distinction between the heart as an organ of romantic endurance and the heart as a measure of moral obligation.

Jim, of course, does not really belong to the world of occupations, to what Marlow calls the "community of inglorious toil" (p. 50). As Albert Guerard puts it, a "man is what he does, which in Jim's case is very little that is not equivocal."[9] Marlow's first efforts at placing Jim once again in the world of maritime commerce are disastrous. The expiation process after the *Patna* demands "something in the nature of an opportunity" (p. 202), but it must be understood that this demand is also what Jim wanted before the *Patna*. What transpires as action in narrative is almost always a repeat in some other key of what was sounded before, just as the jumble of letters that constitute the place Patusan contain within them the ship *Patna*.[10] The issue in *Lord Jim* is complicated by Marlow's wanting an opportunity too, but his opportunity is in Jim as a figuration of seaman adventurer, as narrative's opportunity to once again set the contours of a "telling" phenomenon, an experience that is at once representational and illusional. Marlow tries to evoke the very themes that do not enter Jim's head as cogent: "Don't you see what I mean by the solidarity of the craft? I was aggrieved against him, as though he had cheated me—me!—of a splendid opportunity to keep up the illusion of my beginnings, as though he had robbed our common life of the last spark of its glamour" (p. 131). But what he really invokes in Jim is the generative source for narrative performance, just as he invokes in Kurtz of *Heart of Darkness* the generative source for narrative voice. There is in Jim's story an undeniable narrative vein: "Indeed this affair, I may notice in passing, had an extraordinary power of defying the shortness of memories and the length of time: it seemed to live, with a sort of uncanny vitality, in the minds of men, on the tips of their tongues" (p. 137). Mere words seem enough to take Jim's measure before he gets to Patusan.

Curious Argonauts

When Jim finally arrives at his opportunity in Patusan he turns away from the communal, material, sovereign venture, marked by particular images of "order and progress" abjured: "The point, however, is that of all mankind Jim had no dealings but with himself, and the question is whether at the last he had not confessed to a faith mightier than the laws of order and progress" (p. 339). With the depiction of Jim's work on Patusan—"the certitude of rehabilitation" (p. 248) in a place where the "things that made him master had made him a captive, too" (p. 247)—Conrad elaborates the paradigm of sovereign isolation available to the novel from the time of the exilic island saga *Robinson Crusoe.* But it is precisely the abandoning of what sovereignty had come to mean in a fable such as Crusoe's that provides Conrad with a different idea of isolation as enterprise. [11] I will return to Jim in a moment, especially to Jim in commercial straits before the Patusan adventure, but first I would like to set the exilic imperial tale in a more general and wider historical context, taking it back, in fact, to its beginnings.

Both Defoe and Conrad touch obliquely on the original myth of colonial venture in the West, the search for the city of gold, El Dorado. Defoe's Crusoe, by his own calculations, figures his island to be in the proximity of the Orinoco river basin, the cannibal country that presumably granted access to the mythic city. When Defoe places Crusoe near the Orinoco, he updates the myth of New World adventure inaugurated by Sir Walter Raleigh and others. Defoe does so partly because it *is* a myth and partly because he would prefer a different, more viable version of that myth as New World history. Defoe has colonization (of cannibal lands) and trade with European nations in mind much more than the fabulous, legendary discovery of hidden cities.[12] Conrad's most stunning imperial venture is set in a different river basin, the Congo, but he ironically includes in the supporting cast of *Heart of Darkness* a group of unsavory modern-day adventurers and greed merchants with the intentionally misplaced Orinoco name of the Eldorado Exploring Expedition. If Defoe's Orinoco castaway is a substitute version of the imperial adventure, Conrad's Eldorado exploiters are a debased version of the imperial crusade: "reckless without hardihood, greedy without audacity, and cruel without courage" (p. 87). By absorbing the most prominent symbol of the venture quest, El Dorado, into *Heart of Darkness,* and by placing a bit of the Orinoco myth in the Congo adventure, Conrad, like Defoe, ties the colonial dream of the Renaissance to its more recent expressions. But whereas Defoe universalizes the exploitational idea for what he assumes is the better, Conrad universalizes it for the worse. He speaks of the myth with scorn in his essay "Geography and Some Explorers."

> I suppose it is not very charitable of me, but I must say that to this day I feel a malicious pleasure at the many disappointments of those pertinacious searchers for El Dorado who climbed mountains, pushed through forests, swam rivers, floundered in bogs, without giving a single thought to the science of geography. Not for them the serene joys of scientific research, but infinite toil, in hunger, thirst, sickness, battle; with broken heads, unseemly squabbles, and empty pockets in the end. I cannot help thinking it served them right. It is an ugly tale. [pp. 3–4]

The host of self-sovereigned exiles and egotistical globe-trotters who appear in Conrad's venture narratives are, in one way or another, parodies of the same ugly tale. This is as true, say, for Kurtz as it is for the bepatched harlequin figure, the rag-tag man possessed of the remnants of *techné* in his marked-up copy of "An Inquiry into some Points of Seamanship" (p. 99), who leaps out of the jungle like a goat-skinned Crusoe to greet Marlow in *Heart of Darkness*.[13] But the most deliberate and telling critique, almost a travesty, of the materialist assumptions that govern the imperial venture occurs in *Lord Jim*. Just before Marlow makes the crucial decision to act on Jim's behalf, he and Jim confront "a curious pair of Argonauts" (p. 169), a West Australian gadabout con man of the seas, Chester, and his ancient partner, a Captain Robinson, with his umbrella and his "white beard with amber streaks hung lumpily down to his waist" (p. 163). Conrad, Chester, and Marlow marvel at the crusty sea dog, a legend in his time: " 'Old Robinson. Yes; *the* Robinson. Don't *you* know?' " (p. 162).

Captain Robinson's reputation haunted the oceans: opium smuggler, seal executioner, infamous castaway. The mere name is narratively talismanic, and Conrad turns his tale back upon Robinson the First when he dashes that of Robinson the Second with more than a soupçon of cannibalism, a recurring subject in Crusoe's adventure, especially during the latter years of his island reign when he arms himself to the teeth against the encroachments of those cannibals from the Orinoco Main who would chew him. *Lord Jim*'s Robinson is therefore not only "Holy-Terror Robinson" but "Cannibal Robinson": " 'Cannibal?—well, they used to give him the name years and years ago. You remember the story?' " (p. 162). Shipwrecked long before on Stewart Island with seven mates, he was discovered by the crew of His Majesty's *Wolverine* " 'kneeling on the kelp, naked as the day he was born, and chanting some psalm-tune or other' " (p. 162). " 'Alone? Of course' " (p. 163). His mates had gone the way of some flesh.[14] Of this relict and present partner, Chester says: " 'Three weeks afterward he was as well as ever' " (p. 163).

Whereas Defoe's Robinson Crusoe feared cannibalism above all things—not the doing of it, but having it done to him—Conrad's Captain Robinson commits what Tony Tanner sees as the ultimate symbolic, even anthropological violation, mistaking the all-too-humanly raw for the all-too-temptingly cooked. In an essay indebted to the structural anthropology of Lévi-Strauss, Tanner argues that Conrad's fascination with cannibalism is at its core a "readable" phenomenon. Tanner's essay attempts, more seriously than my description of it is likely to imply, to place imperial discourse in the context of dining, in distinction to that elementally hostile human scene when one's dinner companion is also one's meal. It is interesting, in this sense, that Conrad's "actual" native cannibals in his fiction, the crew of the river boat in *Heart of Darkness,* are among the most discreet of all his characters operating under cannibal temptation. The cannibal crew members, despite their hunger, show admirable restraint because, as Conrad implies, they honor the letter of their obligations over the spirit of their appetites. Restraint among the cannibals is urged as a social value, whereas lack of restraint among Conrad's Western El Dorado adventurers is presented as a palpable excess. [15]

The Cannibal Robinson episode in *Lord Jim* appears in the narrative at a crucial moment, the moment that Marlow has to decide whether to abandon Jim to the debased parody of the imperial materialist ethic, an action that would deaden his imagination permanently, or to forge a different opportunity, based first on work that Marlow approves and then on a conscious experiment (with Stein's help) of moral, not commercial, rehabilitation in isolation. What Chester and Captain Robinson offer Jim is a position as lord and protector over an island heap of bat guano—"Fortune on that fair isle!" (p. 169). This can only evoke for Marlow a perverse version of the Crusoe castaway myth: "I had a rapid vision of Jim perched on a shadowless rock, up to his knees in guano, with the screams of sea-birds in his ears, the incandescent ball of the sun above his head; the empty sky and the empty ocean all a-quiver, simmering together in the heat as far as the eye could reach" (p. 167). Marlow is appalled. Jim would sit on his island perch in bat excrement as the maniacal Kurtz grubs the Congo for ivory. Guano rather than gold serves as the debased symbol of the adventure of the West, as it would again when Conrad turns to the political version of the same farce acted in the aptly named Costa

Guana of *Nostromo*. Removal from the active world of the sea may be in store for Jim, but sovereignty over bat droppings under the aegis of Chester and old Cannibal Robinson—" 'That's the man for me' " (p. 163)—will not be his actual or narrated fate.

At this point, more accurately *because* of this point, Marlow takes pen in hand and decides formally to write Jim out of the range of these disreputable old salts. He corresponds with friends on Jim's behalf just at the moment Chester and Robinson threaten to jump on the blank page and inscribe their befouled, aggrandizing schemes all over Jim: "All at once, on the blank page, under the very point of the pen, the two figures of Chester and his antique partner, very distinct and complete, would dodge into view with stride and gestures, as if reproduced in the field of some optical toy. I would watch them for awhile. No! They were too phantasmal and extravagant to enter into anyone's fate" (p. 174). Marlow enters the action, writes into it in a sense, to keep these two out. The narrative extravagance of Jim's future romance will counter the debased extravagance of this material venture of the seas. Of course, it is testimony to the structural clever-ness of Conrad's irony in the novel that Jim's rehabilitation is sand-wiched between an opportunity that Marlow took the liberty of re-jecting for him—the bat guano caper—and the one Marlow arranges for him in which he is finally done in by the actions of a Gentleman Brown, so derelict an adventurer that the sea world disallows him the title Captain and insists on the ironic genteel sobriquet. Brown as outcast, pirate, and thief is the final retributive reflex of the imperial materialist ego.

Venture as Voice

What Jim needs is another chance, not to remake himself for the commercial world of the sea that had canceled him, but to remove to a place where his self-romance can regain its sovereignty and Marlow can give it voice. This is not an unambiguous proposition, as the deeply confused and confusing remark of Stein's to Marlow about dreams and destructive elements attests, but it is a generative one—it does allow for an exilic "jump," which is the root meaning of the word *exile*. Marlow and Stein offer Patusan. Jim is cast out and cast over to what Marlow calls the "other side," an image that describes not only Jim's "lot" but, as discussed in my introductory chapter, the general relation of narrative projection to the supposedly real circumstances it imitates: "Neither Stein nor I had a clear conception of what might be on the other side when we, metaphorically speaking, took him up and hove him over the wall with scant ceremony" (p. 229).

The transition from venturing to narrative voicing is an even more pronounced feature of Conrad's *Heart of Darkness* than it is of *Lord Jim*, though there is an apparent imperial din in all Conradian tales of the sea, seaboard, and river basin: silver, gold, ivory, bat guano. Of *Heart of Darkness*, Conrad readily admitted, and many of his friends and contemporaries recognized, [16] that the tale was a vicious fictional assault upon the imperial idea of exploitation in an area of the world that played host to "the vilest scramble for loot that ever disfigured the history of human conscience and geographical exploration" ("Geography and Some Explorers," p. 17). Conrad's rendition of the imperial venture in the tale extends back to the Romans on the Thames and implies all those other European "advents" over the centuries in other river basins of the world: the Amazon, the Orinoco, the Mississippi, the Ganges, the Yangtze, the Niger, the Nile, and the Congo. Conrad assumes the awe if not the full irony of the men of the wagging tongues in the "Aeolus" chapter of *Ulysses* on the same subject of the Roman triremes and maritime exploitation.

Imagine the feelings of a commander of a fine—what d'ye call 'em?—trireme in the Mediterranean, ordered suddenly to the north; run overland across the Gauls in a hurry; put in charge of one of these craft the legionnaires—a wonderful lot of handy men they must have been, too—used to build, apparently by the hundred, in a month or two, if we may believe what we read. Imagine him here—the very end of the world, a sea the colour of lead, a sky the colour of smoke, a kind of ship about as rigid as a concertina—and going up this river with stores, or

orders, or what you like. Sand-banks, marshes, forests, savages,—
precious little to eat fit for a civilized man, nothing but Thames water
to drink. No Falernian wine here, no going ashore. [p. 49]

Much of Conrad's awe, some of it clearly sardonic, derives from his
personal and narrative interest in what he envisions as an imperial
romance, "knights errant of the sea," sailing out from the Thames
basin: "What greatness had not floated on the ebb of that river into
the mystery of an unknown earth! . . . The dreams of men, the seed
of commonwealths, the germs of empires" (p. 47). When Conrad
describes what he had in mind for *Heart of Darkness* in a letter of 31
December 1898 to William Blackwood, his syntax does not quite sort
out the difference between his grudging admiration of the imperial
venture and his detestation of it: "The criminality and pure selfishness when tackling the civilising work on Africa is a justifiable
idea." The sentence seems to equivocate on whether the justice resides
in the idea or in its fictional treatment. In fact, whatever the idea
ultimately lacks in justice it sustains in energy, something that Marlow articulates in *Heart of Darkness* about imperial conquest. Again,
he sounds like someone out of *Ulysses,* perhaps this time Leopold
Bloom: "An idea at the back of it; not a sentimental pretence but an
idea" (p. 51). Conrad is far from overwhelmed at the legitimacy of the
idea, but he recognizes its force.

There is, of course, a place for the imperialist idea in Conrad's own
life—it was not mere curiosity that drove him on his Congo expedition aboard the appropriately named imperialistic Belgian ship, the
SS *Roi de Belges,* and kept him keenly interested, even after a disheart-
ening experience, in turning a possible profit from the venture. But
finally, the attacks in the narrative against the conditions that inspired ventures such as the Congo enterprise and the conditions that
control it are so obvious that Marlow hardly even needs Kurtz to make
him realize that his boyhood dream of African adventure has been
turned into the nightmarish ravaging of a continent's bowels. If there
were anything of intrinsic appeal to Conrad or to Marlow in the
imperial romance of *Heart of Darkness,* the dying Kurtz would not

work their imaginations quite the way he does. Kurtz is much more (or much less) than what he epitomizes in the imperial theme—the company's best agent who had "collected, bartered, swindled, or stolen more ivory than all the other agents together" (p. 113).

What may have begun as a geographical seduction tale belonging to the myth of Western colonization—the lure of a dark, mysterious place on the map—ends as an uncanny plunge into the realm of an ivory factor "gone *fantee*," as Ian Watt puts it.[17] Marlow says of Kurtz: "I looked at him as you peer down at a man who is lying at the bottom of a precipice where the sun never shines" (p. 149). This figure registers an almost exquisite irony in that the boast attributable to virtually every overseas empire since the Renaissance is the rule of a domain upon which the sun never sets. Kurtz, upon whom the sun never shines, seems to open up an inspired new dimension of imperial bearing. His life is an abuse of possession, a desire that has metamorphosed into violent and lustful longings, *having* and *needing* as impure sovereignty: "'My Intended, my ivory, my station, my river, my ——' everything belonged to him" (p. 116). A debilitated Kurtz teaches us from the heart of darkness that the true imperialist is also the truly demented: "He desired to have kings meet him at railway-stations on his return from some ghastly Nowhere, where he intended to accomplish great things. 'You show them you have in you something that is really profitable, and then there will be no limits to the recognition of your ability'" (p. 148). The important word "intended" is buried into Kurtz's material hubris, the very word that seems so interchangeable at the end of the tale with the aspirated voicing, "the horror."

Kurtz is what he voices; his is the horror of a certain kind of intent. Marlow's compulsion to speak to Kurtz is a compulsion to penetrate "an impenetrable darkness" (p. 149), to confront an alien nature that may be the nether side of all humanity at a point virtually at hell's gate near the center of the earth.[18] Marlow comments on the literal and metaphoric end of the African adventure as the "farthest point of navigation and the culminating point of my experience" (p. 51). He describes, in essence, both a narrative series of points along an ex-

tended line—the Kurtz story—and the act of its voicing—the totality of his experience in confronting (and listening to) Kurtz as the
narrative other, the outcast who is pure voice. Kurtz is the power of
the voice that is barely mediated utterance, the groan of a Tiresian or
Nietzschean muse.

On his way in and down to what he calls the blank spot on the map,
Marlow participates in a bizarre, hellish incident. During the frenzy
of the native attack near the last river station, the boat's helmsman is
run through with a spear. A puddle of blood drenches Marlow's socks
and shoes. He is morbidly uncomfortable and takes one shoe off and
flings it overboard: "I flung one shoe overboard, and became aware
that was exactly what I had been looking forward to—a talk with
Kurtz. I made the strange discovery that I had never imagined him as
doing, you know, but as discoursing. I didn't say to myself, 'Now I
will never see him,' or 'Now I will never shake him by the hand,' but,
'Now I will never hear him'" (p. 113). One of Marlow's listeners
delivers civilization's punctuation mark at this juncture, "'Absurd'"
(p. 114), and when a match is struck—that is, when Marlow's voice
is no longer out of the dark—he, too, resumes his ironic presence:
"'My dear boys, what can you expect from a man who out of sheer
nervousness had just flung overboard a pair of new shoes!'" (p. 114).

In discussing this scene, strange as its logic seems, Conrad's most
commonsensical interpreter, Ian Watt, insists there is a perfectly
reasonable explanation for it. Marlow links his discomfort to Kurtz's
name because the demise of the helmsman makes him think that
Kurtz, too, might be dead as a result of the fray. Blood at his feet
signals the possible death of the man for whom he has made his
journey. But not only is Marlow thinking of Kurtz but the loss of the
story that *is* Kurtz. His shoe is a frustrated offering or tribute to "the
devil-god of that river" (p. 114) in unwitting hopes of gaining access
to something "other." A bloodied civilized remnant is exchanged for
voice: a shoe, an epiphany, a name. Having gotten so far, the final
thought of no story, no voice, no utterance is unbearable. For Marlow, the possibility augurs a kind of disconnectedness: "I couldn't

have felt more of lonely desolation somehow, had I been robbed of a belief or had missed my destiny in life" (p. 114).

Marlow hurling his shoe at the river recalls, in its way, the scene of frustration and fear when Robinson Crusoe discovers the single print in the sand, a scene in which the shoe, so to speak, was decidedly *not* on the other foot. As mentioned in my *Crusoe* chapter, after an initial period of mental tumult, in which, among other things, he thinks the print was made by the devil, Crusoe, at least in his narrative reconstruction of the episode, reworks the impression into a symbol of complementarity or connectivity. One print, like humanity itself, requires the "other." Crusoe is on the inside desiring to get out; Marlow is on the outside desiring to get in. What is wanted in both instances, finally, is the voice of the other.

In *Heart of Darkness,* we do not hear much of Kurtz's fabled voice, but we read enough into it. In the excerpts Marlow provides from Kurtz's report, the supracivilized sentimentalist finds his antithesis in the brutal dementia that drives him. [19] Kurtz is the "author" of the report whose conflicting entries confuse the rhetoric of civilization and the violence of primal savagery, that is, they inscribe the man, a progressive imperialist punctuated by a horrific moment of Hobbist retrogressive desire. "'By the simple exercise of our will we can exert a power for good practically unbounded,'" writes Kurtz, who then appends the dementia of a sovereign isolato gone wild as postscript— "'Exterminate all the brutes'" (p. 118).

What little we actually hear of Kurtz touches not only, as Marlow says, upon "an exotic Immensity ruled by an august Benevolence" (p. 118) but upon the confusion of accumulation and articulation that gives him his measure.

> Kurtz discoursed. A voice! a voice! It rang deep to the very last. It survived his strength to hide in the magnificent folds of eloquence the barren darkness of his heart. Oh, he struggled! he struggled! The wastes of his weary brain were haunted by shadowy images now— images of wealth and fame revolving obsequiously round his unextinguishable gift of noble and lofty expression. [p. 147]

In his isolation, Kurtz is another side of the Tuan Jim legend: the antithetical being whose fate is unregenerate, but whose power resides in the discovery and challenge at the center of the narrative space—its heart, its animus, its obsessive, if imprecise, generic voice.

> Do you see him? Do you see the story? Do you see anything? It seems to me I am trying to tell you a dream—making a vain attempt, because no relation of a dream can convey the dream-sensation, that commingling of absurdity, surprise, and bewilderment in a tremor of struggling revolt, that notion of being captured by the incredible which is of the very essence of dreams. [p. 82]

Marlow hears in Kurtz the voice whose story is more sound than sense in the way Conrad hints in his *Personal Record* that the "power of sound has always been greater than the power of sense" (p. xi). Or, as he says in *Lord Jim*: "There is a weird power in a spoken word" (p. 174). At his loudest Kurtz is all roar, at his softest an aspirated "horror," that Marlow in a later sequence of palliating bourgeois discourse in fact renders interchangeable with the name of Kurtz's "Intended," suggesting, as much else tends to suggest in the narrative, the antithetical properties of primal scenes and words. Of course, Marlow's substitution of the name (and object) the "Intended" for "the horror" embodied in Kurtz links the notion of imperial violation with the image of its bourgeois dream. Narrative has a way of properly allegorizing experience only when it speaks its true intent.

Telling Secrets

Marlow at the heart of darkness, a place as forbidding and isolated as any in the world, to which he has beckoned his own muse, should not be overly surprised at the discovery of Kurtz's ambiguous and ambivalent powers of voice in the name of reclamation and extermination. After all, the rationality of "straightforward facts" (p. 61) is what he abjured when he entered the African gloom. And in telling the tale Marlow is almost Kurtz's medium; indeed his listeners sense that he, because of the darkness of the narrative scene, is "no more to us than a voice" (p. 83). This is the exact phrase Marlow employs for Kurtz: "He was very little more than a voice" (p. 115). So we can assume that in the repeated rhythms of the narrative, Marlow and Kurtz, whether by intent or result, produce something of the same effect, even if each is engaged in an enterprise as different as fiction (narration) ought to be from ivory grubbing and unspeakable rites. But, as we have learned from the most renowned of imperial narrative descent myths, the *descensus Averni*, it is through the gates of ivory that the dream or nightmare voices itself to the world of light. Of Kurtz Marlow says:

> The point was in his being a gifted creature, and that of all his gifts the one that stood out preeminently, that carried with it a sense of real presence, was his ability to talk, his words—the gift of expression, the bewildering, the illuminating, the most exalted and the most contemptible, the pulsating stream of light, or the deceitful flow from the heart of an impenetrable darkness. [pp. 113–14]

Marlow, too, is a compulsive talker, disdainful of listeners, eager to penetrate to those secrets that pervade narrative experience, to those supplemental realms where only imagination gains access and about which only the evoking powers of language can utter the words that become images of the narrative scene. Thus Marlow says of the din of the inhuman, prehistoric sounds along the banks of the dark river: "An appeal to me in this fiendish row—is there? Very well; I hear; I admit, but I have a voice, too, and for good or evil mine is the speech that cannot be silenced" (p. 97). Narrative will plummet the depths for its resonant if not exactly articulated secrets. To enter these depths is also to read into a world where utterance is suggestive and deflective, where meaning, insofar as one would wish to call it that, is something less provided than extracted. Conrad's word for the process by which narrative, without exactly revealing discrete particles of applicable meaning, informs on experience is a version of his favorite word, *secret*. He repeats the word in several of his titles and in many of his major statements on the evocative powers of art, including the most famous one from the preface to the *Nigger of the "Narcissus"* where the words of a tale have the power to reveal the rescued fragment's color and substance, to "disclose its inspiring secret" (p. x). In *Heart of Darkness,* the secret in "the silence of the land went home to one's very heart—its mystery, its greatness, the amazing reality of its concealed life" (p. 80).

Marlow's role as narrative medium, as revealer of secrets, is not the same in *Heart of Darkness* as in *Lord Jim.* Whatever the land's silence in the Congo region or in Patusan, Kurtz speaks up and Jim clams up. Marlow works them differently. He is Jim's voice-over; he is even a medium for the actionable, that is, he arranges for the very incidents he narrates, though he does not determine their results. Jim's verbal capacities are negligible. At best they are spasmodic; at worst, inactive. Part of Marlow's frustration is that Jim offers no contiguous, sequential, subordinated voice for him to parrot. Just after jumping the *Patna,* Jim remembers: "There are no words for the sort of things I wanted to say. If I had opened my lips just then I would have simply howled like an animal" (p. 124). Jim doubts after the *Patna* "whether he would ever again speak out as long as he lived. . . . speech was of no use to him any longer" (p. 33), a decided paradox in that the thing of least use to Jim is what Marlow must employ to piece him together both for the action represented in the narrative and for the narrative itself.

Whether by voicing the sounds and silences of darkness or by connecting the verbally disparate, narration has the power, as Conrad says in his oft-cited preface to the *Nigger of the "Narcissus,"* "to make you hear, to make you feel—it is, before all, to make you *see*" (p. x). *See* has its precise and its inspirational meaning—a thing one does with eyes and a thing one comprehends with whatever resources are available—just as another often used Conradian word *sense* means antithetically that which is intuited as that which is tangibly apprehended. When Conrad speaks about authorship and writing in his *Personal Record,* he picks up some of his key terms, especially voice, where the idea is not to project the author into the actional setting but to project the things he voices as presence.

> He stands there, the only reality in an invented world, among imaginary things, happenings, and people. Writing about them, he is only writing about himself. But the disclosure is not complete. He remains, to a certain extent, a figure behind the veil; a suspected rather than a seen presence—a movement and a voice behind the draperies of fiction. [p. xiii]

Conrad describes language, the medium of narrative representation, as possessing the same general features as narrative action: it both evokes and portrays, serving the same primal and mimetic urges. This is why Conrad's writing can at once be so charged with imprecision in the face of raw experience (violence, shame, sex) and so precisely ironic and chiseled in the face of more overtly portrayable, civilized phenomena like hypocrisy. In fact, it is typical of Conrad's style, and typical of some of the differences between his sense of social and political representation and his sense of adventure, that he writes directly into the teeth of hypocrisy but only along the ridges of moral trauma: language which can brilliantly gauge the surfaces of behavior can only sound its depths.[20] Marlow is a mediator in this sense since he possesses the powers of close articulation and lacerating irony, yet somehow yearns for those voices emanating from the holes and depths at the narrative boundary. He serves to make what sense is possible out of sound, and at his best he leaves the power of his tales intact, while at his most submissive (or at his most subtle) he palliates, as he does in the famous equivocation to Kurtz's Intended.

Conrad, of course, knows what he is doing with Marlow. He wrote *Lord Jim* at the same time as he did *Heart of Darkness* and has Marlow say of Jim's tale that this "was one of those cases which no solemn deception can palliate" (p. 97). When he faces Jim's Jewel, Marlow tells her, because the situation demands it, the painful truth of why the world does not want her lover back—" 'Because he is not good enough' " (p. 318)—just as he kept the truth, because the situation demanded it, from Kurtz's Intended. Or to put it another way, the irony of Marlow's encounter with Kurtz's affianced reveals both the truth and its palliation. The Intended is more than ready to believe Marlow's lie; Jewel is less than ready to believe Marlow's truth: " 'You lie!' " (p. 318), she says, when Marlow speaks to her of Jim.

Marlow is not only an intermediary as voice, but an intermediary as mariner. He partakes of the impulse to wander—an inscriptive impulse to write on the blank spaces of the map—but he always returns to the company of men, to the rational, communal order. He needs listeners to be Marlow even if those listeners are not always *with* Marlow. Conrad says of him in *Heart of Darkness:* "He was a seaman, but he was a wanderer, too, while most seamen lead, if one may so express it, a sedentary life. Their minds are of the stay-at-home order, and their home is always with them—the ship; and so is their country—the sea" (p. 48). Marlow points out with sarcasm the difficulty of making the boundary zone a comfortable subject for comfortable, moored listeners: " 'Here you all are, each moored with two good addresses, like a hulk with two anchors, a butcher round one corner, a policeman round another, excellent appetites, and temperature normal' " (p. 114). On the one hand he berates his listeners to the degree that he cannot mesmerize them; on the other hand he jests with his listeners to the degree that he feels comfortable in their presence.

It is in the telling, more than in any of his own actions, that Marlow makes what identification he can with his isolated subjects, his renegade exiles. In a passage that Conrad excised from *Lord Jim* describing the attendees at the *Patna* desertion hearing, Marlow makes what effort he can to get on Jim's fictional side, that is, to move toward his figurative and spatial separateness at the boundary: "I don't know what was the matter with me that morning but . . . they all seemed to me strange, foreign, *as if* belonging to some order of beings I had no connection with. It was only when my eyes turned towards Jim that I had a sense of not being alone of my kind, as if we two had wandered in there from some distant regions, from a different world. I turned to him for fellowship."[21]

But Marlow, because he is the record of types as various as Kurtz and Jim without in any final sense joining them, neither remains in realms marked out for fictional isolation nor succumbs to realms beyond articulation. For instance, just after his speechless reaction in *Lord Jim* to the murder of Jewel's mother, to what he calls an "irremediable horror," he seeks the order or reorder of language. The scene at first

> had the power to drive me out of my conception of existence, out of that shelter each of us makes for himself to creep under in moments of danger, as a tortoise withdraws within its shell. For a moment I had a view of a world that seemed to wear a vast and dismal aspect of disorder, while, in truth, thanks to our unwearied efforts, it is as sunny an arrangement of small conveniences as the mind of man can conceive. But still—it was only a moment: I went back into my shell directly. One *must*—don't you know?—though I seemed to have lost all my words in the chaos of dark thoughts I had contemplated for a second or two beyond the pale. These came back, too, very soon, for words also belong to the sheltering conception of light and order which is our refuge. [p. 313]

Marlow is a Western wordmonger who returns from the inside, from the concealed zones of human experience. His reordering effort here is similar to that moment when E. M. Forster's Fielding in *A Passage to India* crosses back into the precision and perspective of the Mediterranean after the sounded but senseless horror of the Ou-Boum in India's Marabar Caves. Marlow's compulsion is always different, more modest, more formal, than his subjects. As narrator, he admits to the most palliative of motives: curiosity. He says in *Lord Jim*, "curiosity is the most obvious of sentiments" (p. 42), and he also speaks of his natural connection to Jim as a man of the sea: "My fault of course. One has no business really to get interested. It's a weakness of mine" (p. 94). Marlow cannot help doing what narration always does for exiled renegades, take them home from the wild and remote to the ordered estate in which they can be read and powerfully remembered.

If Conrad's narratives end at the moment when the exilic story, like the memoirs of the "great exile" in *Under Western Eyes*, palliates adventure by working it through the medium of print into a kind of epilogue, the Joycean venture traced in my next chapter makes the exilic myth less a postlude than a prelude to varieties of artistic action and reaction. It is testimony to Joyce's comic and allusive genius that he can derive so much out of the tale of exile without ever releasing his characters far beyond the pale of Dublin and environs. For Joyce, exile is less an adventure than an aesthetic advent, a process that can be, that must be, enacted as a way of conjuring or forging subject matter intricately linked with aesthetic estrangement, usurpation, rivalry, and revenge.

CHAPTER THREE

Monte Cristo's Revenge
Joyce's *A Portrait of the Artist* and *Ulysses*

"Out of the land of Egypt into the house of bondage"

Stephen Dedalus has his moments of exultation in *A Portrait of the Artist,* but he is at his most controlled and calculated when he inaugurates his long-range defensive program for aesthetic revenge: "silence, exile, and cunning."[1] His program bears an inverse relation to the qualities exhibited by Irish stay-at-homes—palaver, paralysis, and sentimentality—in the first book that James Joyce completed in *his* European exile, *Dubliners.*

Exile is the least odd of the three strategies; even if its end remains unclear, it can, at least, be located as a tactic. Joyce became an exile;[2] he titled his one play *Exiles;* and he absorbed the most renowned of exilic themes, the Odyssean wanderings, into the texture of both his Irish epics. In the comic spectacle of *Finnegans Wake,* the artist Shem is a perpetual inscriber and a perpetual resettler (a "sooner") whose subject is his own sustenance in exile: "He even ran away with hunself and became a farsoonerite, saying he would far sooner muddle through the hash of lentils in Europe than meddle with Irrland's split little pea."[3] Shem the Penman makes exile into a form of autobiography, "self exiled in upon his ego" (p. 184).

Silence and cunning, as befit them, are less easily revealed as Joycean impulses. It is difficult to guess exactly what Stephen means by them unless we align the terms with attributes of narrative design—surely the Odyssean one and, more pointedly, the Daedalian one. Like Odysseus on Calypso's island at the western extreme of the

Mediterranean, Daedalus near its eastern extreme on Minos's Crete already suffers exile as part of his fate; he need not enjoin its necessity. Silence and cunning, therefore, are means to effect an exilic alternative, a Greek *nostos*. For the young Stephen Dedalus, of course, England's King Edward takes a less active interest in his affairs than the Cretan King Minos takes in those of Daedalus; nor is the Irish Catholic church so alluring a bride as Odysseus's island-binding goddess Calypso. Joyce's Dedalus must effect his problem before he can render its solution.

If in *Portrait* Joyce talks up the aesthetic program before the exilic adventure, in his play, *Exiles,* Joyce advances the cisatlantic connection beyond the point of exilic return. "Why the title *Exiles?*" he asks in a note to his play, and he answers his own question: "A nation exacts a penance from those who dared to leave her payable on their return."[4] Joyce goes on to note that only in the otherworldly wisdom of the biblical prodigal son story is the voluntary exile honored at home—"certainly not in Ireland." In *Ulysses,* Stephen Dedalus hints in the telegram he sends Buck Mulligan—a phrase cribbed from Meredith's *Ordeal of Richard Feverel:*"—*The sentimentalist is he who would enjoy without incurring the immense debtorship for a thing done*"[5]— that the only debt worth repaying is the one worth incurring. But it is crucial to recognize that for Joyce the notion of Irish debt has little to do with the dare of nationalist politics or the glory of Ireland's national cultural revival, at least in the usual way these issues were conceived, and much more to do with the redemptive exilic structures that underwrite the particular Joycean narrative enterprise. In *Exiles,* the returned writer, Richard, marks as worthless Robert's article in honor of his repatriation in Ireland because it contains a phrase about "those who left her in her hour of need" (p. 100).[6] All Ireland's hours are her hours of need, and loyalty to lost causes is decidedly not the penance that Joyce would pay, though such might have been the penance the native Irish would most want to exact from him. Dedalus made this point in *Portrait:* "—My ancestors threw off their language and took another, Stephen said. They allowed a handful of foreigners to subject them. Do you fancy I am going to pay in my own life and person debts they made? What for?" (p. 203).

In distinction to Richard Rowan's exile in the play, Joyce's own exile "dared" remain permanent. But did Joyce feel he still owed anything? And, if so, to whom? The penance Joyce reveals himself most willing to pay Ireland is the only return on his overseas investment that he deems worth anything, a return that contributes to Ireland a stock of literary increase as abundant as the booty Odysseus brought back to redeem a destitute Ithaca. He calls this in *Finnegans Wake* the burden carried by "Our homerole poet to Ostelinda" (p. 445), where home rule becomes a Homeric project and the Mediterranean adventure merges into a Norse saga. In *Stephen Hero,* Joyce's still diphthonged young Daedalus comments on the enlightened impulse of modern secular art that distances itself from presumptive States, Redeemers, and Churches: "It examines the entire community in action and reconstructs the spectacle of redemption."[7] Redemption is a making good after going out on account, and if Joyce, as Ireland's unreturned prodigal, ends up practicing any of what his first Daedalus preached, he pays up, in a fashion, by the full communal spectacle he represents in and with his exilic narratives.

One of the more expansive glosses on exilic redemption occurs in "Aeolus" in *Ulysses* (the only passage for which we have an extant recorded reading by Joyce) when Professor MacHugh recalls John F. Taylor's speech in response to Mr. Justice Fitzgibbon on the question of reviving the Irish tongue. Clearly, this was an issue that rallied nationalist fervor and constituted in most palpable terms the redemptive impulse of a culture that deemed itself in exilic bondage while another nation controlled its fate. "We were weak, therefore worthless" says Professor MacHugh about to recite Taylor's oratorical comparison of the Irish to the Israelites. Had Moses bowed before Egypt,

he would never have brought the chosen people out of their house of bondage, nor followed the pillar of the cloud by day. He would never have spoken with the Eternal amid lightnings on Sinai's mountaintop nor ever have come down with

the light of inspiration shining in his countenance and bearing in his arms the
tables of the law, graven in the language of the outlaw. [p. 143]

When in *Portrait of the Artist,* Cranly was trying to persuade Dedalus to consider the range of options open to him at home, he argued
that he need not look upon himself as "an outlaw" in Ireland (p. 245).
But by *Ulysses* that was precisely what appeared essential in terms of
the exilic pattern Joyce extracted from the narrative histories with
which he worked, the "epic of two races (Israelite—Irish)," and the
Ulysses myth transposed, as Joyce put it, *"sub specie temporis nostri."*[8]
Though Joyce had little sympathy for the issue that forms the Israelite
homology for Taylor and MacHugh, the revival of the Gaelic
tongue,[9] he found absorbing the notion that the meaning of a land's
destiny could derive from the range and full force of inscription,
conceived in language that opened the national adventure for a variety
of narrative adaptations: allusive, parodic, prophetic, homiletic, and,
by the time of *Finnegans Wake,* syllabic.

Stephen Dedalus's first public voicing in *Ulysses,* his "Pisgah Sight
of Palestine," based on what has gone on so far during his day, comes
as a rival vision to Taylor's oratory: "—I have a vision too" (p. 144).
Later, when the professor suggests the Latin title *"Deus nobis haec otia*
fecit" (p. 149), Stephen insists on the Old Testament parody of a
different prospect, the view from the exilic spaces of the promised
land. The elongated Latin pun "periplum" (or island circuit)[10] in
Stephen's subtitle "Parable of the Plums," perhaps gets some of the
classical element back, enabling Stephen to confront all Mediterranean precursors, to satisfy or fulfill the range of the material available
to him. His effort, feebly funny, represents, as many have pointed
out, the first time that he has positioned himself for an enterprise that
incorporates most of the elements that contribute to Joyce's larger and
later narrative efforts: the detailed stuff of his home city; the lore of
exilic imagining; the parody of urban nostos. Naturally enough, the
first word of Stephen's international parable is "Dubliners." The
duplication of the home space as the wandering space assumed by the
parable indicates the enlarged and enlarging role of exilic parody for

Joyce when the "rock" of narration no longer affords complete haven for the rooted consciousness of voice and when, as Stephen's parable implies, Dublin itself becomes at once alien and visionary ground.

There is, of course, another Dubliner in *Ulysses* whose story hovers around the homologic spaces of Palestine, Mr. Leopold Bloom of Eccles Street. Bloom is the son of a man who, in typical formulaic fashion, initiates an actual exilic experience, "who left the house of his father and left the God of his father" (p. 76), whereas Bloom himself must perform a double, or narratively allegoric, service for Joyce's exilic-redemptive scheme to work in *Ulysses*. In "Aeolus," a throwaway remark by Bloom contains within it the principle of exilic realignment. Bloom misconstrues the biblical Exodus—just as he misconstrues, with similar duplicity, the home rule sun rising in the northwest of Ireland—when he remembers the Pesach service and "that long business about that brought us out of the land of Egypt and into the house of bondage" (p. 122).[11] The exilic Bloom is generated by the very mythology the narrative establishes for him, "Leopold Bloom of no fixed abode" (p. 470) whose exodus from one land of bondage to another is part of his defense in the phantasmagoria of "Circe," "my client's native place, the land of the Pharaoh" (p. 463). The turning of the cliché makes Bloom's Ireland into the space of exile, a poor delivery in an unpromising, hostile land—or a stiff one if we consider the version of Irish delivery actually provided in "Oxen of the Sun"—until and unless Joyce converts the exilic place of wandering into the home place of rest and return in that promised land of "Ithaca."

Garrett Deasy in "Nestor" already condemned the Jews to eternal wandering over the face of the earth, and even Stephen contributes to the exilic myth in regard to Bloom. His thoughts, no doubt, have been touched by Mulligan's reference to Bloom's lusting Galilean eyes, but Stephen (or the text of "Circe" within Stephen's scope at the moment) cannot help making the comparison between Bloom and a local citizen whom everyone calls Dublin's humpbacked Jew. Stephen sees Bloom at the brothel and thinks, "A time, times and half a time" (p. 506), which amounts to his own review of the three times so far in which he knows that he and Bloom have crossed paths: once in the library, once in "Oxen of the Sun," and now (ongoing) in "Circe." With no break but a blank line, we read the Circean stage direction: "*Reuben J. Antichrist, wandering jew.*"[12]

After "Circe," Bloom and Stephen begin to talk in "Eumaeus," though largely at cross-purposes. The conversation touches upon those recurrent exilic questions: to whom does Ireland belong? and what sort of currency might earn its repossession? Stephen's is an impertinent version of the artist as exile with his Irish belongings on show (impertinent because as yet unrealized).

> You have every bit as much right to live by your pen in pursuit of your philosophy as the peasant has. What? You both belong to Ireland, the brain and the brawn. Each is equally important.
> —You suspect, Stephen retorted with a sort of a half laugh, that I may be important because I belong to the *faubourg Saint Patrice* called Ireland for short.
> —I would go a step farther, Mr Bloom insinuated.
> —But I suspect, Stephen interrupted, that Ireland must be important because it belongs to me.
> —What belongs? queried Mr Bloom, bending, fancying he was perhaps under some misapprehension. [p. 645]

Bloom, the outcast and the homebody, supposes Stephen speaks of the political cisatlantic connection—the exilic wild goose—but Stephen intends the principle of exilic resource, even though his efforts to that point have inscribed very little of the Ireland that belongs to him and returned very little of artistic worth to the nation that provides him exilic inspiration. To see how Joyce works with the cross-Atlantic and pan-European adventure, I would like to turn back to *Portrait of the Artist* before resuming with *Ulysses*. Dedalus works through a romantic exilic resource before Joyce discovers a classical Odyssean one.

"Madam, I never eat muscatel grapes"

The first resourceful plot, indeed the first plot of any kind after the adventures of baby tuckoo and the moocow, that absorbs the young

Stephen Dedalus's attention in *Portrait of the Artist* is not the Odyssean adventure that inspired Joyce at the age of twelve but the famous Dumas tale of the exiled Edmond Dantes who reappeared in Europe as the Count of Monte Cristo. Stephen acknowledges only a small part of the story, its renunciatory bravado. He says little of the tale's generative archetypes of great fortune, forbearance, and power. As a fable of exile and return, the whole of the Monte Cristo legend romances the Odyssean epic in bourgeois Europe and, retrospectively, glosses the theory of Shakespearean revenge proposed by an older Dedalus in the library chapter of *Ulysses*. Dumas's tale charts the havoc wreaked by the returned hero on local betrayers. Edmond Dantes is the ghost from *limbo patrum,* the dark avenger who makes retribution into a work of art, who weaves bits and pieces of retributive justice slowly, silently, elaborately into the fabric of a design until, as with the god-inspired interdiction against further Odyssean violence or with the equanimity of Bloom in bed, the Count abjures the very act of revenge as a final flourish preceding exilic rest.

It is this full story—and even the young Stephen presumably knows it, though he focuses on only one of its renunciatory scenes—that touches on the larger Joycean enterprise, the exilic fable that redeems as it disposes, that enlists, the way Bloom later proposes for Stephen, the "equal and opposite power of abandonment and recuperation" (*Ulysses,* p. 673). As future compositor and assimilator of fragments concerning all those heroes from the "atlantic and Phenitia Proper" (*Finnegans Wake,* p. 85), Joyce could well revel in the whole of the Monte Cristo legend. Consider its rudiments: a betrayed, abandoned, and returned mariner; an exile sewn into his own shroud and nearly drowned like a swollen bundle in the sea; a European *incog* someone calls an "Oriental, a Levantine, Maltese, Indian, Chinese; your family name is Monte Cristo; Sinbad the Sailor is your baptismal appellation";[13] the amasser of a personal fortune from the treasure hoard of an Italian prisoner greater than the one Leopold Bloom imagines inheriting from a Spanish prisoner's donation of "a distant treasure of valuables or specie or bullion lodged with a solvent banking corporation 100 years previously at 5% compound interest of the collective worth of £5,000,000 stg" (*Ulysses,* p. 718); the owner of an

eponymous Mediterranean rock-strewn island like the Ionian Ithaca—"this isle is a mass of rocks, and does not contain an acre of land
capable of cultivation" (1:269); and a Darkinbad Brightdayler whose
complexion migrates across the face of Europe, a complexion "so long
kept from the sun, had now that pale colour which produces when the
features are encircled with black hair the aristocratic beauty of the
man of the North" (1:188).

When the famous Count enters the Joyce canon through the open
portals of *Portrait,* the adolescent Dedalus sees him only as a superior
avenger, a Byronic hero, an insubstantial lover, a renouncer of cor-
poreal sustenance so that he might gain spiritual control. He exhib-
its, in short, the grand but weightless romantic temper described by
Daedalus in *Stephen Hero:* "blown to wild adventures, lacking the
gravity of solid bodies" (p. 78). Stephen's conjuring of Monte Cristo
is among his first imaginative projections beyond local borders. As a
lad between terms at Clongowes and Belvedere, he spends his long
summer days walking with his granduncle in and around the villages
just south of Dublin and his evenings reading Dumas's massive romance in translation, musing on Edmond Dantes, Mercedes, and
some freshly picked muscatel grapes.

> His evenings were his own; and he pored over a ragged translation of
> *The Count of Monte Cristo.* The figure of that dark avenger stood forth in
> his mind for whatever he had heard or divined in childhood of the
> strange and terrible. At night he built up on the parlour table an image
> of the wonderful island cave out of transfers and paper flowers and
> coloured tissue paper and strips of the silver and golden paper in which
> chocolate is wrapped. When he had broken up this scenery, weary of its
> tinsel, there would come to his mind the bright picture of Marseilles,
> of sunny trellisses and of Mercedes. Outside Blackrock, on the road
> that led to the mountains, stood a small whitewashed house in the
> garden of which grew many rosebushes: and in this house, he told
> himself another Mercedes lived. Both on the outward and on the
> homeward journey he measured distance by this landmark: and in his
> imagination he lived through a long train of adventures, marvelous as
> those in the book itself, towards the close of which there appeared an

image of himself, grown older and sadder, standing in a moonlit garden with Mercedes who had so many years before slighted his love, and with a sadly proud gesture of refusal, saying:

—Madam, I never eat muscatel grapes. [pp. 62–63]

The young boy's supplemental recall of the Dumas narrative is what some, in modern day parlance, call a strong reading, that is, an intentionally mangled one, though the "strong" reading in this case produces an intentionally "weak" grasp of the matrix of the original. Stephen's alternation between the libidinal urges of pubescent desire and the proud freedom of refusal seems to privilege what his more mature self deems as aesthetically unacceptable kinetic emotions: "Desire urges us to possess, to go to something; loathing urges us to abandon, to go from something. These are kinetic emotions" (p. 205). But we have seen nothing yet, nor are we yet ready, for Stephen the aesthetician. His boyhood meanderings on the *Monte Cristo* plot blithely cross into the kinetic domain of self-mythologizing and self-aggrandizement. He first reproduces the magical place of abundant treasure, Monte Cristo's island cave, the most powerful evocation of which comes Kubla Khan–like in the original as the result of a hashish trip; next he places the young Edmond Dantes on the sun-lined streets of Marseilles near his equally young and immensely alluring Mediterranean beauty, Mercedes; finally, Stephen evokes the older, shrewder, and resourceful Monte Cristo (Dantes) in the garden of the vaguely threatened Countess de Morcerf (Mercedes) in Paris.

After the lure of treasure and power, the clearest attraction of the passage for the young Stephen is indeed libidinal. But such an attraction also involves its clearest distortion. He has arrested Mercedes in her own youth or in his unsubstantial understanding of her—she is the "unsubstantial image which his soul so constantly beheld" (p. 65). Though Stephen ages the Count, he has trouble doing the same for Mercedes, and in a later allusion to this same scene we learn he hasn't moved Mercedes to Paris at all; the refusal scene literally takes place where she first appeared as a girl in the Irish Blackrock version of Marseilles: "He saw again the small white house and the garden of rosebushes on the road that led to the mountains and he remembered the sadly proud gesture of refusal which he was to make there, standing with her in the moonlit garden after years of estrangement and adventure" (p. 99). The muscatel grape scene is incorrectly set back at the place and at the time when Mercedes was most delectable. Hers is a sexual offering that Monte Cristo might accept or reject. Renunciation for a boy of Stephen's age is an appropriate control for romance given the amount he might know but the little he could expect from the pleasures of sexual initiation. Mercedes intrigues the young boy as sexual opportunity both available and rejectable, sex, that is, without grapes.

Before focusing on what the actual nature of Monte Cristo's renunciation might mean for the older Stephen, let me reset the scene in its proper perspective. The place and time have nothing to do with a moonlit garden in Marseilles and less to do with a sexual offering than might appear, though the memory of such opportunity certainly contributes to the force of the encounter. Mercedes at the time is a countess in her late thirties and the only person in Paris who has sensed Monte Cristo's real identity. She fears his presence even though she has little sense of the circumstances surrounding his earlier betrayal or the present circumstances surrounding his mysterious reappearance. It is not her own security she fears for, but rather the well-being of her only child, Albert, now a young man. What she senses in Monte Cristo's bearing is the implied threat of exilic or generational revenge for her own action years before in marrying a mere eighteen months after Dantes's imprisonment, an action to which Monte Cristo had applied the troubled Hamlet's remark, breaking into English to do so, "Frailty, thy name is woman" (1:235).

Mercedes has just coaxed Albert into maneuvering Monte Cristo toward her garden walk in the direction of the greenhouse: " 'The count will never accept an invitation to dine with us,' " she says as she implores Albert to " 'insist upon his taking something.' " Albert demurs but she repeats, as only a mother can, " 'Oblige me, Albert' " (2:150). Monte Cristo refuses the son as a kind of prelude for his refusal of the mother. During the stroll to the greenhouse, Mercedes tempts the count with grapes she picks from the vine. "'Pray excuse me, madame,' replied Monte Cristo, 'but I never eat Muscatel grapes'" (2:152). She then offers a peach: no, again. In calculated frustration, Mercedes says "'there is a beautiful Arabian custom which makes eternal friends of those who have together eaten bread and salt beneath the same roof.' 'I know it, madam,' replied the count; 'but we are in France, and not in Arabia. And in France eternal friendships are as rare as the custom of sharing bread and salt'" (2:152).[14]

Mercedes understands the nature of Monte Cristo's refusal only too well. She reoffers the grapes as a plea for familial safe conduct: "'Take some.'" Dantes refuses, now as an emphatic exercise of his own license to exact whatever revenge he sees fit: "'Madam, I never eat Muscatel grapes'" (2:154). Monte Cristo then concocts a story, an obviously false one, that points his moral and adorns his own tale. He tells of a young girl long in the past who was to wait for him on the isle of Malta but instead married during his absence. In response to Mercedes's question as to whether he had forgiven the girl, Edmond says he had pardoned her, implying, as Mercedes is quick to note, that there might be others whose fate was not—and would not be— so charitably disposed. With a mother's desperation she walks Monte Cristo back in the direction of young Albert and grasps the Count's hands, enfolding them over her son's: "'We are friends, are we not?'" (2:155).

As Mercedes leaves the garden, Albert assumes Monte Cristo and his mother have disagreed, and that assumption, at least for the time being, is accurate. Whatever young Stephen sees or misunderstands about the scene in the context of his own desires, it sets a fictional moment in which human bonds are broken, communal ones suspended, and the avenging will given the space to enact its retribution. The refusal to eat, to satisfy or partake under a hostess's roof, allows for the putative romantic reflexes of freedom and vengeance, the release from bonds that precedes the exercise of willed imperatives.

"Soulfree and fancyfree"

The suppleness with which Joyce works with the structure of allusion in narrative is such that Stephen's evocation of Monte Cristo's renunciation is of crucial importance to *Portrait* and, later, in a more general, or, as I shall argue, generic sense, to *Ulysses*. But not in the way Stephen initially conceives it. In fact, the Monte Cristo exemplum evaporates at the very moment Stephen hears a story similar to it. As self-romancer, Dedalus experiences a spiritual jolt worse than a whack from Father Dolan's pandy bat when the Jesuit priest at the retreat turns the fable of renunciation inside out. In the hell-fire romance, the priest evokes the plight of the nay-saying rebel angel Lucifer. Refusal becomes a literal disaster—a Miltonic star has his heroic lights put out: *"non serviam: I will not serve*. That instant was his ruin" (p. 117). Though later in *Portrait* and again in *Ulysses* Dedalus appropriates this exact phrase to abjure the bonds of family, religion, and country, when he first listens to the priest's mimicry of the Satanic utterance it petrifies him. In *Ulysses,* Mulligan still thinks Stephen has been frightened by the Jesuits from any Daedalian or Attic vocation: "—They drove his wits astray, he said, by visions of hell. He will never capture the Attic note" (p. 249).

At the time of the hell-fire sermons, Stephen, to some extent, was already primed for what the Jesuits would do to him. Sex and freedom turned in his mind with a reverse spin from his earlier reveries on Mercedes and Monte Cristo. The postpubescent sexual glut of his evenings in Nighttown had tarnished the cool economy of the Count's refusal. Stephen was a woeful future artificer trapped in Dublin's labyrinth, made queasy by the congealed ingredients of his city and its alphabetical symbols.

> The letters of the name of Dublin lay heavily upon his mind, pushing one another surlily hither and thither with slow boorish insistence. His soul was fattening and congealing into a gross grease, plunging ever deeper in its dull fear into a sombre threatening dusk, while the body that was his stood, listless and dishonoured, gazing out of darkened

eyes, helpless, perturbed and human for a bovine god to stare upon.
[p. 111]

After the retreat, Stephen travels the only path that remains open
to him; he moves toward, rather than from, the communal and
communicant fold. He becomes a functionary of religious sodalities;
he partakes of the church's sacraments; he eats of the bread and drinks
of the wine; and he even considers the priestly role of administering
the offering rather than the Cristofian role of abjuring it. But this is
an interim consideration. Dedalus's romantic nature resurfaces, and
he balks at the ceremonies of a vocation he will soon reject: "To merge
his life in the common tide of other lives was harder for him than any
fasting or prayer, and it was his constant failure to do this to his own
satisfaction which caused in his soul at last a sensation of spiritual
dryness together with a growth of doubts and scruples" (pp. 151–
52). [15]

The commonness of the action and its attendant obligations turns
Stephen away from the priesthood, and his renunciation approaches
the substance as well as the rhythm of Monte Cristo's refusal of the
muscatel grapes. The text of *Portrait* picks up the beat: "He had
refused. Why?" (p. 165). He aims, among other things, to separate
himself, to dodge "the challenge of the sentries who had stood as
guardians of his boyhood and had sought to keep him among them
that he might be subject to them and serve their ends" (p. 165). His
refusal to serve extends later to denying his mother's request that he
take Easter duty in the church. To partake of the eucharist under a
roof that may impose unwanted obligations upon him makes Stephen
fear a litmus change in his own nature: "the chemical action which
would be set up in my soul by a false homage to a symbol behind
which are massed twenty centuries of authority and veneration" (p.
243). Dedalus wants his soul free, as he soon exults, to forge other
symbols within its smithy.

The real significance of romantic renunciation, the first hint of
which had arrived even before the hell-fire sermons with Stephen's

heretical refusal to confess away the sins of a poet like Byron, is its presumed status as the mark of aesthetic integrity. Renunciation may impose the exilic brand of a Byronic Cain, but it also provides an initiatory impetus to action, a prelude to a fabulous career, a self-initiated career that invites freedom in the form of communal abjuration. This is what Dedalus proclaims in *Portrait* and this is what he begins anew the day of *Ulysses,* a good deal of which is spent, with ample drinking but little eating, ridding himself of encumbrances: the Irish Friend (Mulligan), the Irish Job, the Irish Samaritan (Bloom), even the Irish Wife (Molly) who has almost but not quite been offered to him. Stephen himself makes his case in *Ulysses* when theorizing on the beleaguered Shakespeare's manufactured life and vital art: "—There can be no reconciliation, Stephen said, if there has not been a sundering" (p. 195).

The figure who can afford such a renunciatory course must of needs rely on sustaining powers of genius. It is as Albert de Morcerf says of the exile, Monte Cristo, in the romance: " 'I really do look upon him as one of Byron's heroes, whom misery has marked with a fatal brand . . . who, disinherited of their patrimony, have achieved fortune by the force of their adventurous genius, which has placed them above the laws of society' " (1:428). Fatality is a singling out, a specialness, a dignity, recognized in Monte Cristo and obviously romanticized by Dumas whose hero says to Mercedes: " 'What I most loved after you, Mercedes, was myself, my dignity, and that strength which rendered me superior to other men; that strength was my life' " (2:344).

Such superiority knows no bounds, even national ones. Its exilic range is part of its power. As Monte Cristo says to the villainous prosecutor, Villefort, "You believe me to be a Frenchman, for I speak French with the same facility and purity as yourself. Well, Ali, my Nubian, believes me to be an Arab; Bertuccio, my steward, takes me for a Roman; Haydee, my slave, thinks me a Greek" (1:500). His very range inflates his ego: " 'I am a cosmopolite. No country can say it saw my birth; God alone knows what country will see me die. I adopt all customs, speak all languages. . . . You may therefore comprehend that being of no country, asking no protection from any government, acknowledging no man as my brother, not one of the scruples that arrest the powerful, or the obstacles which paralyse the weak, paralyses or arrests me [*pas un seul des scruples qui arrêtent les puissants ou des obstacles qui paralysent les faibles ne me paralyse ou ne m'arrête*]. I have only two adversaries,—I will not say two conquerors, for with perseverance I subdue even them,—they are time and space' " (1:500). It is most likely pure coincidence, but Monte Cristo's vocabulary, *paralyse* and *arrest,* and his vision of supplemental challenge, *time* and *space* (*distance* in the French) seem to have taken independent root in Joyce's own meanderings on aesthetics, whether in relation to the homegrown Irish of *Dubliners* or to the narrative time-space conundrums of *Finnegans Wake.* The real romance that takes place in *Portrait,* the one that will receive its classical form in *Ulysses* and *Finnegans Wake,* is the refabulation of a tale like Dumas's or like Homer's of exile and vengeance into a tale of artistic, cosmopolitan preparedness, a tale substantiated or filled out in Joyce's works that inscribe Ireland as they cast beyond her.

Stephen had inklings in *Portrait* of the direction in which renunciation might point him when, during his first epiphany of an artistic vocation, he saw clouds drifting westward from a Europe that "lay out there beyond the Irish Sea, Europe of strange tongues and valleyed and woodbegirt and citadelled and of entrenched and marshalled races. He heard a confused music within him as of memories and names which he was almost conscious of but could not capture even for an instant" (p. 167). In the same scene, Dedalus looks at his own city and instead of the glut of a congealed alphabet imagines all extraterritorial histories and mythologies plunging into Dublin through him. Dublin is pan-European: "A moment before the ghost of the ancient kingdom of the Danes had looked forth through the vesture of the hazewrapped city. Now, at the name of the fabulous artificer, he seemed to hear the noise of dim waves and to see a winged form flying above the waves and slowly climbing the air" (pp. 168–69). The scope extends from Scandinavia to Crete, from the northernmost to the southernmost reaches of Europe, from Odin to

Daedalus. Stephen has not yet set pen to paper, but he has moved beyond his native land to the exilic resources of Joyce's later Semitic-Hibernian *Odyssey* and his epic Irish *Wake*.[16]

Dedalus imagines the mysterious Europe and then he sees his vision, the lovely girl on the strand, "his ownest girlie," as Gerty MacDowell might put it. His muse is so stimulated that he seeks a landfall to sleep away his inspiration, still (and perhaps always) libidinous. As he dozes he enters a dream world, a supplement: "His soul was swooning into some new world, fantastic, dim, uncertain as under sea, traversed by cloudy shapes and beings" (p. 172). The opportunity is not unlike that promised by the hashish-peddling Count of Monte Cristo in his island sea cave, though I cite it as a Byronic parallel, not a direct allusion.

> "Are you a man of imagination,—a poet? taste this, and the boundaries of possibility disappear; the fields of infinite space open to you; you advance free in heart, free in mind, into the boundless realms of unfettered revelry. Are you ambitious, and do you seek to reach the high places of the earth? taste this, and in an hour you will be a king,—not a king of a petty kingdom hidden in some corner of Europe, like France, Spain, or England, but king of the world, king of the universe, king of creation." [1:284]

To forge a career as king of *his* world or, at least, of its language (*basilicogrammate*), Dedalus prepares himself, as Cranly puts it in *Portrait,* for "the mode of life or of art whereby your spirit could express itself in unfettered freedom" (p. 246). He seeks that exile that neither Odysseus nor Monte Cristo sought, but that found both and made both. Cranly continues: "—Alone, quite alone. You have no fear of that. And you know what that word means? Not only to be separate from all others but to have not even one friend" (p. 247). In *Stephen Hero,* Daedalus had told his brother: "Isolation is the first principle of artistic economy" (p. 33), and now in *Portrait,* Stephen's journal entry for 21 March reads "Free. Soulfree and fancyfree. Let the dead bury the dead. Ay. And let the dead marry the dead" (p. 248). Stephen's exultation upon the totality of release buries the conventionalized libido; his stay-at-home Mercedes, whoever she be, can, like Monte Cristo's, marry none but the barely living dead. Stephen's tactics then acknowledge the exilic program: "I will try to express myself in some mode of life or art as freely as I can and as wholly as I can, using for my defence the only arms I allow myself to use—silence, exile, and cunning" (p. 247).

Joyce's sweet Icarian bird of youth in *Portrait of the Artist* assumes that his aesthetic parabola will fly him by the nets of nationality, language, and religion, though it is one of Joyce's subtle turnarounds as a more mature, substantiating artist to make the innocuous little preposition *by* mean "with" as well as "past." Exile is an impetus, a positioning, and a perspective. As is the case for the general allegory of narrative supplementation I have presented throughout as part of the process of narrative genesis, one gets outside a space to look in and see wholly; on the other hand, the space created from outside is, willy-nilly, a projection, subject to laws generated and inspired by the imagining mind. Stephen's goal is an art whose powers are supreme, whose revenge is complete (satisfied), and whose stance is distant. But his words are initiatory and, as yet, unsubstantiated— they project the fabulous and heroic vision of romance and they sound similar to those of the dark avenger, Monte Cristo, who soars like the Daedalian artist: " 'I am free as a bird, and have wings like one. . . . I have my mode of dispensing justice, silent and sure, without respite or appeal, which condemns or pardons, and which no one sees' " (1:283). [17]

Rivals

The Monte Cristo legend, at least in its romance phase, dispenses special powers of retribution upon local wounders in direct proportion to the extent of real or perceived local wounds. Stephen Dedalus's exilic preparation stipulates the nature of the wounds he endures so that he might salve them abroad. In *Portrait,* he imagines that the forces of the entire nation conspire against him; in *Ulysses,* the rivalry seems to be centered in Mulligan, the parodic Irish genius who first appears in "Telemachus" mocking the vocation of the priest, a rival vocation that Dedalus had already rejected. Rivalry is the raw nerve of the Joycean enterprise and the spur to exilic recourse. Again, Joyce's notes for *Exiles* are helpful; indeed, the very first note for the play contains the germ of rivalry as both the rudimentary Joycean plot and the rudimentary Joycean character. Almost everything in Joyce can devolve from the initial gloss on Richard and Robert: rivals, twins, types, opposites.

> Richard-an automystic
> Robert-an automobile
>
> [p. 113]

The Joycean rival is the double gone in another direction. Automysticism implies the immobile, rooted consciousness, the omphalos centered universe, with more than a broad hint of the overromanticized version of the word Joyce meant when he described the first effect of the *Odyssey* on him—"I want to be candid: at twelve I liked the mysticism in Ulysses."[18] He means its self-absorbing magic, its wonder. Joyce confirms the implication of the first bit of his opening note for *Exiles* early in *Ulysses* when Stephen, parodying the automystic, thinks: "Will you be as gods? Gaze in your omphalos" (p. 38). Automobility, on the other hand, implies historical, dramatic, or narrative movement, what Stephen parrots in *Ulysses* as the Aristotelian "actuality of the possible as possible" (p. 25).[19] In a later note for *Exiles* we learn that automobility is primarily an exilic necessity: "Exiles—also because at the end either Robert or Richard must go into exile. Perhaps the new Ireland cannot contain both. Robert will go" (p. 123).[20] As an impetus to action or further action this is not altogether different from the opening chapter of *Ulysses* where the first emphatic comment Dedalus makes about anything refers to the Englishman Haines: "If he stays on here I am off" (p. 4). It soon becomes clear that Stephen's challenge is not so much intended for Haines as for Mulligan, which is precisely where Dedalus places it, silently, by the end of the chapter. "I will not sleep here tonight. Home also I cannot go." Thus the last word of "Telemachus" : "Usurper" (p. 23).

Rivalry sets exilic revenge in motion; usurpers desire the home-front, assault the body, banish the mind. As Dedalus says of the effect of Shakespearean rivalry: "The note of banishment, banishment from the heart, banishment from home, sounds uninterruptedly from *The Two Gentlemen of Verona* onward till Prospero breaks his staff, buries it certain fathoms in the earth and drowns his book" (p. 212). Just as Dedalus hits the peroration of his Shakespearean discourse in "Scylla and Charybdis," in walks Mulligan. Stephen's thoughts are ennobling to himself and damning to his rival: "Hast thou found me, O mine enemy?" (p. 197).

But there is more to rivalry in Joyce's works than its relation to betrayal. Rivals seem to contain each other from Shem and Shaun of *Finnegans Wake,* described by Adaline Glasheen, with her usual apt economy, as "identical twins, identical opposites"[21] to the rivalry that dominates the Irish politics of *Ulysses: "John O'Leary against Lear O'Johnny, Lord Edward Fitzgerald against Lord Gerald Fitzedward, The O'Donoghue of The Glens against The Glens of The O'Donoghue"* (p. 599). The figure of the rival as twin is so important to the structure of represented action in *Ulysses* that even the arch rival from the *Odyssey,* Antinoos, is divided in two for the day's action in Dublin. In a kind of allegorical literalization, the rival is doubled: Antinoos is both Mulligan and Boylan. Joyce, of course, has his reasons. For one thing, the suitor plot in *Ulysses* has little to do with Stephen whose mother is beastly dead; for another, Joyce desires that the offenses to his young artist be slighter, though not perceived so, than the offenses to his wandering Jew, Bloom. Stephen is in such a bad way from offenses he imagines that anything much more than the slights Mulligan commits would utterly paralyze him. Mulligan is ideal as a minor irritant, even if Stephen will make him a veritable Judas: "And that one was Judas" (p. 615).[22] Boylan, on the other hand, jauntily leaps into the hero's bed; his rivalry is unabashed.

Having made the tactical commitment to divide the rival role of Antinoos between Mulligan and Boylan, Joyce does all in his verbal power to bring the two together. It is as if all betrayal plots play alike on native turf. Early in *Ulysses,* when Mulligan stands at the forty-foot hole ready to dive into the water that Dedalus fears, he converts his action to a sense of sexual appropriation more fitting for Boylan's Antinoos: "Make room in the bed" (p. 22). Even the name "Buck" as a specific and general reference for sexual intruder unites Stephen's and Bloom's rivals. Mulligan's name is simple enough, but Boylan arrives at the same status by colloquialism. Bloom says of his wife's adviser (and admirer) in "Cyclops," after trying to avoid the topic entirely: "He's an excellent man to organise. Excellent." The chapter's narrator says: "That's the bucko that'll organise her, take my tip" (p. 319). Joyce tips his own hand in this respect with one of Stephen's references to a third party, Kevin (Buck) Egan, who serves as both betrayed wild goose Irish exile and betrayed husband, an Odysseus whom fate never returns home: "Loveless, landless, wifeless. She is quite nicey comfy without her outcast man, madame, in *rue Gît-le-Coeur,* canary and two buck lodgers" (p. 43). This exiled buck gets betrayed by versions of Stephen's Buck and Molly's bucko.

For Dedalus during the day, especially in the chapter of rivalry's named traps, "Scylla and Charybdis," the stark literalization of opposition turns into the very impetus for a transchannel exile: "My will: his will that fronts me. Seas between" (p. 217). The challenge is a great one for Dedalus because, in a notion Joyce had developed from the Icarian as well as Daedalian potential of *Portrait,* water is that crossing fraught with difficulties for the artistic fledgling. As Brother Michael had said of Stephen's aesthetics: "Many go down into the depths and never come up. Only the trained diver can go down into those depths and explore them and come to the surface again" (p. 187). The same talents, in the narrative contexts of supreme rivalry, belong to brine-saturated Odysseus and the ocean-emergent Edmond Dantes.

The first episode of *Ulysses* plays brilliantly upon these motifs, with their Byronic or *uebermensch* features divided between the artist and his ocean-submergent rival. Just before Mulligan readies himself to take the morning plunge into the sea from the rock at the forty-foot hole, the neutral narrative provides a mediating tableau for what will become, before the book is over, the outline of the new *Ulysses,* the bourgeois-maritime epic: "Two men stood at the verge of the cliff, watching: businessman, boatman" (p. 21). As the men speak of a drowning nine days before and watch a boat searching for the victim, Stephen thinks about the prospect and ventriloquizes himself into an image of the corpse: "The man that was drowned. A sail veering about the blank bay waiting for a swollen bundle to bob up, roll over to the sun a puffy face, saltwhite. Here I am" (p. 21). What Dedalus desires, though the prospect is daunting, is a voice that announces his presence after enduring what he imagines is the worst that fate has to offer, death by drowning, a matter that is still on his mind when he reads Milton's *Lycidas* with his students in the next chapter. But at the end of the first chapter only the rival's head bobs on the water, "a seal's, far out on the water, round" (p. 23). The chapter concludes with Stephen's fear of what rivalry entails, the usurpation of body and domain, the rival head that masters the waters.

Later in the day, Dedalus sees the rival as impetus; the artist needs his rival as a first principle of differentiation—if no rival exists, the artist will invent one. That is, after all, what Dedalus says about Shakespeare who makes a plot out of the plots that make him up: "His unremitting intellect is the hornmad Iago ceaselessly willing that the moor in him shall suffer" (p. 212). In this sense, the rival is also a supplement, a *lui,* as Stephen says, who is also a *moi,* or, as Joyce puts it in *Finnegans Wake,* the opposite who belongs to the self, "his polar andthisishis" (p. 177). Mulligan in *Ulysses* exists not only to threaten Stephen on the level of action, nor does Boylan exist merely to displace Bloom in bed; but in the larger Odyssean reconfiguration of *Ulysses,* Mulligan exists to encourage Stephen's comic horizons just as Boylan exists to energize Bloom's libido. As potential Irish chronicler, Stephen is potential Irish clown; he is enmeshed in Mulligan—he can't escape him whichever way he turns on whatever Irish ground. He in fact wears his shoes: "My two feet in his boots are at the end of his legs" (p. 37). Mulligan's boots at the end of Stephen's feet produce for Dedalus the strange phenomenon and the even stranger diction of a paradoxical self-hatred: "foot I dislove" (p. 49). Later, Dedalus feels the automobilic pressure: "His boots are spoiling the shape of my feet" (p. 210). It is one of the nicer jokes of *Ulysses* that when Bloom warns Stephen against Mulligan—earlier Mulligan had warned Stephen against Bloom—he picks an appropriate cliché to do so: "—No, Mr Bloom repeated again, I wouldn't personally repose much trust in that boon companion of yours who contributes the humorous element, Dr Mulligan, as a guide, philosopher and friend if I were in your shoes" (p. 620). The issue for Stephen is not that Bloom might wear his shoes, but that he, Stephen, wears Mulligan's. A little of the humorous element is not a negligible contribution to the tale of exile, silence, and cunning.

"Thomethinks to eath"

To be in a romantic plot is to be outrivaled, even when the rival is one's self. The classically exilic plot for Joyce emphasizes a different phase of rivalry—its subsumption into a larger comic, integrating action. Mercy is the archetypal religious response to the rival; abjuration the response practiced, finally, in the *Odyssey* and in *Monte Cristo;* equanimity the response felt by Bloom in *Ulysses;* and parodic indulgence the response displayed by Joyce in all his Irish epics. This is to say that the balance of power shifts in Joycean revenge where the rival turns serviceable in filling out the generic range of the action. One reads as much into the first two words of *Ulysses,* "Stately plump," where Mulligan, though Stephen is only intermittently aware of it, performs for the rival Irish artist in the same way he performs for Joyce—he increases the scope of the day by impregnating it with wit: *"Mr Malachi Mulligan. Fertiliser and Incubator. Lambay Island"* (p. 402).

Wit is one of the counterprinciples to the renunciations of romance, and contributes to the full notion of exile and nostos that makes up the classical narrative action, the embodying of all jocoserious potential in the material resources of the land and the culture. One of the ways Joyce localizes the range of the traditional exilic rivalry-revenge plot on Irish shores is by compacting, layering, and some might argue, stuffing its elements into the artist's soul, his ego, his smithy. And then he makes that artistic ego the metonymic property of the Western tradition. In the course of translating the aesthetic romance of *Portrait of the Artist* into the dimensions of *Ulysses* and *Finnegans Wake,* Joyce redeems the exilic idea by materially fulfilling it.[23] As he puts it of Shem in the *Wake,* he does "all the diddies in one dedal" (p. 179).

At the end of "Proteus" in *Ulysses,* Stephen turns and sees a schooner in the harbor, which we later learn bears the paradisal names of *notres dames,* "Rosevean." For Stephen the aura is mysterious: "He turned his face over a shoulder, rere regardant. Moving through the air high spars of a threemaster, her sails brailed up on the crosstrees, homing, upstream, silently moving, a silent ship" (p. 51). But we also later learn that aboard this material brick-carrying vessel from Bridgewater is the homebound sailor of *Ulysses,* the prevaricating sea dog Murphy, a parodic maritime voice whom Bloom identifies as "friend Sinbad and his horrifying adventures" (p. 636). The absorbing transition from boatman's to businessman's epic in *Ulysses* allows for the introduction of a gadabout low-life yarner like Murphy into Bloom's city. Parody sails home with adventure, makes it all-too-native.[24] One even wonders, though the allusion is far from definitive, whether Joyce remembered the very first sentence of *The Count of Monte Cristo,* which describes a cargo-laden schooner slipping into the harbor at Marseilles: "On the 24th of February, 1815, the watch-tower of Notre-Dame de la Garde signalled the three master, the Pharaon, from Smyrna, Trieste, and Naples" (1:1). The sentence is neutral, though aboard Dumas's three-master is Edmond Dantes who later, after his misadventures, returns a second time and signs himself in under the generic and jesting sailing name Sinbad the Sailor.

For Joyce, the accumulative, encyclopedic, generically diverse epic is the biggest and best natured of classical forms. *Stephen Hero's* Daedalus had said of the classical temper that its form in a way evolves out of "the materialism that must attend it" (p. 79)—the classical patiently fills out as it fills up: "By 'classical' I mean the slow elaborative patience of the art of satisfaction. The heroic, the fabulous, I call romantic" (p. 97). Stephen offers a distinction between classical and romantic based on the etymological meaning of satisfaction, that which is complete, entire, satiated, secure. His preliminary aesthetic distinction provides a special gloss on the *Monte Cristo* muscatel grape scene, with which Stephen begins his literary perspective in *Portrait*. There the Count's refusal to eat, in a kind of anthropology of generic action, reinforces the distinction between the weightless energy of romance and the recuperative powers of the fully constituted classical comic epic.

Earlier practitioners of comically replete narratives understood sustenance as a generic measure. Cervantes, for example, parodied chivalric romance by having Quixote, the Knight of the Rueful Countenance, refuse to eat "on the job" because Amadis of Gaul, to whom he swore chivalric fealty, always honored the quest over the feast. Classically epic heroes, on the other hand, tend to eat to surfeit. Homer's polytropic (all-round or fulfilled) Odysseus rarely refuses a morsel; Rabelais's giants eat and drink as embodiments of epic copia; Joyce's self-romancer and Irish "wildgoup," Shem, turned epic parodist in *Finnegans Wake,* mixes "merrier fumes" for a "new Irish stew" (p. 190)—he actually turns the gustatory tables on proud renouncers such as Quixote, who refuses the fare of La Mancha, and Monte Cristo, who abjures the figurative Arabian bread and the palpable bourgeois grape, when he asks his niggling, rivaled, twin brother, Shaun, metamorphosed into an anthropologist, "foh thomethinks to eath" (p. 149). In *Ulysses,* the first words we hear of the Dublin Citizen Mr. Leopold Bloom detail his habitual eating "with relish the inner organs of beasts and fowls" (p. 55). It is testimony to Bloom's satisfying impulses that by the end of the day in *Ulysses* he talks the recalcitrant Stephen into consuming a bit of liquid food under his roof at nostos, the Epps's mass-product cocoa, a homier and more marketable version of the eucharistic offering that Stephen so militantly renounced despite his mother's wishes that he partake in *Portrait*.

The classically defining words—*satisfaction, satisfied*—repeat like the tolling of a bell in *Ulysses,* especially at nostos. Referring to the Gold Cup race, the one taken by a rank outsider, Throwaway, the catechizer asks about Bloom's balancing of risk and gain, and though

Bloom seems to know little of the confusion surrounding his supposed tip on the winner that causes so much difficulty during the parodic chapters of wandering, he does sense that his actions have in some way or another sustained a narrative resolution.

> His mood?
> He had not risked, he did not expect, he had not been disappointed, he was satisfied.
> What satisfied him?
> To have sustained no positive loss. To have brought a positive gain to others. Light to the gentiles. [p. 676]

It is precisely at this point that Bloom makes the gesture of hospitality toward a gentile—"What supererogatory marks of special hospitality did the host show his guest"—in offering Stephen the cocoa. Bloom had been insistent all evening, from "Eumaeus" on, in getting Stephen to do what Mercedes could not get Monte Cristo to do: eat or, at least, drink. Food annoys Stephen, and, as unwashed bard and Icarian romancer, he finds nonalcoholic liquid, especially water, incompatible "with the erratic originality of genius" (p. 673). Most of Bloom's efforts had met with a negative response. When he offered a bun in the cabmen's shelter, "Try a bit," Stephen said: "—Couldn't." Bloom came back: "—Still, it's solid food, his good genius urged, I'm a stickler for solid food, his one and only reason being not gormandising in the least but regular meals as the *sine qua non* for any kind of proper work, mental or manual" (pp. 634–35). Bloom's good genius cannot leave the subject of the erratic genius's empty stomach alone, and his offerings forecast the fully satisfied strategy that will sustain the next Joycean work, *Finnegans Wake:* "but something substantial he certainly ought to eat even were it only an eggflip made on unadulterated maternal nutriment or, failing that, the homely Humpty Dumpty boiled" (p. 656).[25]

It is possible to argue that in the fulfilled and bulging figures of *Finnegans Wake,* including Humpty Dumpty, Joyce discovers not only a way to bring back to Ireland every exile and rank outsider from the ends of the earth but a way to satisfy every word, to make each alphabetical gesture a partaking guest of a potential host; indeed he makes satisfaction formally redundant by a kind of farce feeding, which causes forms to burst, to overflow, which is what *farce* means and what *Finnegans Wake* does with its words, letters, disseminations, and seminations, its "farced epistol to the hibruws" (p. 228). But it is also possible to see in the much more austere aesthetic theory of Dedalus in *Portrait* the beginnings of the urge for the structures of satisfaction that were to mark Joyce's later narrative efforts. Stephen's early program involved certain conceptions that Joyce never entirely deserted. What was missing from Stephen's speculations on artistic process and form was, of course, the energy and satisfactions of Joycean parody that so dominate in *Ulysses* and *Finnegans Wake*. In the rounded or modern classical narrative, the parodic voice is the material upon which the enterprise feeds.

Ulysses gains its bulk, according to Joyce's schema, by growing a body of various styles. Its growth sustains further growth as the parodic chapters ingest the day's events and add breadth and scope to the day's action. The ultimate gesture of parody in Joyce and for Joyce is the appropriation and subsumption of rival voices and exilic plots into the material and metaphoric medium of verbal resolution. There is an exchange in "Eumaeus" that suggests how the act of parodic writing both takes over and gives back as far as the structure of *Ulysses* is concerned. The very returned mariner, Murphy, whom Bloom calls a veritable Sinbad, talks about his travels but avoids a specific answer to Bloom about the Rock of Gibraltar, one of the few narratively tangible points of connection between the *Odyssey* and *Ulysses*. Among other wandering rocks and shamrocks, the book and the various styles of the day shift for themselves. Murphy says—in this chapter whose narrative voice is a parody of democratic periphrasis—"I'm tired of all them rocks in the sea, he said, and boats and ships. Salt junk all the time" (p. 630). Salt junk, of course, is Murphy's contribution to the Odyssean substrata of *Ulysses*'s day. The style then imitates itself: "Tired, seemingly, he ceased. His questioner, perceiving that he was not likely to get a great deal of change out of such a wily old customer, fell to woolgathering on the enormous dimensions of the water about the globe." Woolgathering is a perfect diversion in "Eumaeus," a chapter, like its parodic style, awaiting nostos and the greatest woolgatherer of them all, the weaver Penelope as the Gibraltar nymph, Molly Bloom. Stylistically, the relation of woolgathering to weaving is the same narratively as wandering to homecoming, be it understood that nostos for Joyce operates in the book's action on two levels, mimetic (after the fashion of plot) and aesthetic (after the fashion of process). Parody is that which extends adventure before nostos, and participates in the telling of the whole story, from the thousands of implicit allusions to the *Odyssey* to the intricate and conscious manipulation of language in all its guises to convey the accumulating details of *Ulysses*'s day and to round up material for satisfying the book's form.

"Another victory like that and we are done for"

What would *Ulysses* be without the exponential powers of literary, stylistic, and linguistic parody? More somber, perhaps? more chaste? But in a real sense much emptier. Though Dedalus in *Portrait* neither articulates nor even realizes the full narrative, comic, and parodic course Joyce would travel in an amended version of his bare-bones aesthetic theory, even Stephen's original notions included the key word—*satisfy*—that would become the basis of Joyce's later efforts: "beauty is beheld by the imagination which is appeased by the most satisfying relations of the sensible" (p. 208). Artistic production is the rendering of or striving for the beautiful, which turns out to have a plot similar to that initiatory move from romantic renunciation to classical satisfaction. Stephen expounds upon the Aquinian terms that he sets out for defining beauty—wholeness, harmony, and radiance—by suggesting what he calls "phases of apprehension" (pp. 211–12) whereby wholeness is knowable by a process of separation from the mass of other things; harmony is knowable by understanding the parts of the whole; and radiance is knowable as imaginative genesis, the birth of the supplement: "when the esthetic image is first conceived in his imagination" (p. 213).

The parodic manifestation of Stephen's theory finds Bloom in *Ulysses* examining the forms of statues at the museum for their classical, callipygian "holes." Shem is up to the same in *Finnegans Wake* when the fully classical plot implies a special commerce over the exilic void: "he winged away on a wildgoup's chase across the kathartic ocean and made synthetic ink and sensitive paper for his own end out of his wit's waste" (p. 185).

Dedalus, however, is very serious, even solemn, about aesthetic processes. That which he calls heroic or fabulous in *Stephen Hero* is in *Portrait* the preliminary whole known only by renouncing all else around it. To pretend the kind of integrity that Monte Cristo displays to Mercedes is tantamount to the aesthetic wholeness Stephen articulates as theory is to indulge, rather than work through, the powers of romance. Such pretense is by definition "insecure, unsatisfied, impatient" (p. 78). As for the pretenders, and this holds for young Stephen's Monte Cristo, "the mind that has conceived them ends by disowning them" (p. 78).

At its most innocuous, romance is all sentiment; at its most vicious, all rage. In *Ulysses* the romantic temper always manifests in parodic form—the bombastic mock heroism of "Cyclops" or the overt sentimentalism of "Nausicaa" (in many ways, companion chapters). And it is interesting that Gerty MacDowell's reveries in "Nausicaa" derive from what resembles the Monte Cristo template. Like the very young Stephen in *Portrait*, Gerty produces a version of the returned lover, grist for the libidinal female will just as Mercedes served for the young Stephen's libido. Gerty's hero—"She could see at once by his dark eyes and his pale intellectual face that he was a foreigner" (p. 357)—turns out to be the mysterious Mr. Bloom whose face was "the saddest she had ever seen" (p. 356) with "the story of a haunting sorrow . . . written" (p. 357) on it. Younger than her years, Gerty is ready for the unsatisfying union that displays adolescent sexual energies only in proximity to an object not in contact with it. Hers is a kind of emotional hoarding. Gerty wishes that her nobleman with the foreign name will "love her, his ownest girlie, for herself alone" (p. 358), and Joyce makes romance's mockery of emotion the sentimental equivalent of its possessive, vengeful ideology: all romancers are for themselves alone, and all Irish ones are *Sinn Fein*. When Stephen is about to smash the chandelier in "Circe" he provides a nice Irish "Shite" and in answer to Bloom's sympathetic "what?": *"Ah non, par exemple! The intellectual imagination! With me all or not at all. Non serviam!"* (p. 582). The extreme of renunciation here bears less, at least for readers of *Ulysses,* on young Dedalus's vision of Monte Cristo refusing the grapes or on the hell-fire sermon of *Portrait* than on the Citizen in "Cyclops" who says to Bloom"—*Sinn Fein! . . . Sinn fein amhain!* The friends we love are by our side and the foes we hate before us" (p. 306).[26]

Bloom, the all-round man of *Ulysses,* surely takes a very different view of violent self-assertion. The classically accommodating text judges him a pacifist: "he was reluctant to shed human blood even when the end justified the means" (p. 674).[27] Much of the action of the Ithacan nostos involves Bloom's resistance to hostility, a resistance in opposition to the revengefulness of the exilic romance. Bloom at home is Bloom in his proper battle station, that is, in bed, given an opportunity by the catechistic narrator to smile at betrayal as he considers the impression Boylan has made on his sheets before him. The smile (executed or not) is a satisfied response, commensurate with the formal properties of Joyce's classical reworking at nostos of the superior romance.

If he had smiled why would he have smiled?

To reflect that each one who enters imagines himself to be the first to enter whereas he is always the last term of a preceding series even if the first term of a succeeding one, each imagining himself to be first, last, only and alone whereas he is neither first nor last nor only nor alone in a series originating in and repeated to infinity. [p. 731]

Joyce's most decided revision of the heroic *Odyssey* in *Ulysses* is Bloom's final equanimity after betrayal. This is something he earns, and the impact of Boylan on the sheets is not the first impression the betrayer has made on Bloom during the day. When Nosey Flynn asks of the Blazes-run concert tour, "Who's getting it up?" (p. 172), the question is as insulting to Bloom as the mocking postcard (U.P.: up) to Breen, and it triggers the tumescent last line of the MacTrigger limerick when wives had the time of their lives as it *"grew bigger and bigger."* Bloom does indeed worry that he, the satisfied hero, comes up empty at Boylan's action: "He gets the plums, and I the plumstones" (p. 377). But, on the other hand, if we follow the recent arguments on the way the narrative line of *Ulysses* is played out in the dispositions of its words, phrases, and sentences (much as in *Finnegans Wake*), Bloom's remark about "Boland's breadvan delivering with trays our daily but she prefers yesterday's loaves turnovers crisp crowns hot" (p. 57) hints at the resolution of the day's story before its primary event. In a kind of narrative off-rhyme, yesterday's loaves or loves are preferable to Boland's or Boylan's daily delivery.

The entire matter of Bloom's retribution in *Ulysses* is complicated, of course, by the possibility that in sexual matters, as in aesthetic ones, the betrayal that necessitates revenge is partly a willed phenomenon. In "Eumaeus" Bloom says, in reference to the Parnell infidelity fiasco, that adultery is "a case for the two parties themselves unless it ensued that the legitimate husband happened to be a party to it" (p. 655). Bloom may require his own betrayal for his own reasons, vaguely aphrodisiacal, in the same way that in the play *Exiles* Richard says to Robert: "in the very core of my ignoble heart I longed to be betrayed by you and by her—in the dark, in the night—secretly, meanly, craftily. By you, my best friend, and by her. I longed for that passionately and ignobly, to be dishonoured for ever in love and in lust, to be . . ." (p. 70).[28] Richard goes on to suggest that he sets up the scene of betrayal from pride and longing and "from a motive deeper still." Richard seems to receive what he requires to sustain him, a deep wound, and Bertha seems to offer what he needs to sustain his vanity, a deep need: "You, Dick. O, my strange wild lover, come back to me again!" (p. 112).

The perverse ideology of betrayal as stimulus is played out systematically in *Exiles* as a credo. Richard explains to his son, masking a kind of sexual socialism, that to have something securely in one's possession is to have something that is vulnerable. It is only when one gives a thing away that one truly has it because it can no longer be taken. Richard says to his son, Archie: "While you have a thing it can be taken from you." Archie: "By robbers? No?" Richard: "But when you give it, you have given it. No robber can take it from you. . . . It is yours then for ever when you have given it. It will be yours always. That is to give" (pp. 46–47).

Frank Budgen, who was well aware of Joyce's own occasional propensities in this regard, with Nora Joyce as the potential gift, discussed the matter with Joyce in reference to Bloom; indeed, Joyce confirmed Bloom as a *mari complaisant*.[29] There are more than a few hints of this in *Ulysses,* one of which occurs near the time of the Molly-Boylan assignation and another of which occurs when Bloom's watch has stopped at the supposed time of Boylan's arrival at his home. In "Sirens," Bloom is most stimulated by the call of love, most captive by sexual intellect, while Boylan is literally in gear by sexual drive (the counterpoint of the chapter includes the clip-clop of Boylan's cab toward Eccles Street). And at the masturbatory moment in "Nausicaa," Bloom's release is accompanied by his imagination of Boylan's entry: "O, he did. Into her. She did. Done" (p. 370). Bloom guesses that Gerty's pleasures were also secondhand: "She must have been thinking of someone else all the time" (p. 371).

Naturally, the narrative's own taunting and parodic memory seizes upon the idea that Bloom manipulated his own betrayal. Among the charges and countercharges of "Circe" we get, as we often do in the parodies of *Ulysses,* outlandish articulations of possible Bloomian sentiments: "In five public conveniences he wrote pencilled messages offering his nuptial partner to all strongmembered males" (p. 537). Molly Bloom has some specially prejudiced and specially interested remarks-on similar topics. She describes Bloom as "trying to make a whore of me" (p. 740); at another point she seems to think that Bloom desires to expand the scope of his own sexual adventures with Josie Breen by expanding hers with Boylan: "hed never have the courage with a married woman thats why he wants me and Boylan though as for her Denis as she calls him . . ." (p. 773). Molly seems to sense that the Boylan rendezvous is not strictly her own affair. Even in reference to Stephen, Molly ponders the possibility of what, given the mood of "Eumaeus," may have passed through Dedalus's mind and increased his leeriness about an overnight stay at the Blooms. Of the photo that Bloom tells Molly he showed Dedalus she says: "I wonder he didnt make him a present of it altogether and me too" (p. 774). Finally, she confronts directly the idea of betrayal by design, though a kind of prideful ire contributes to her tone here: "Ill let him know if thats what he wanted that his wife is fucked yes and damn well fucked too up to my neck nearly" (p. 780).

It is not surprising in this context, as well as in a more humane one, that for Bloom retribution in the Odyssean or Cristofian fashion is out of the question: "Assassination, never, as two wrongs did not make one right. Duel by combat, no. Divorce, not now" (p. 733). Violent revenge is akin to what Stephen describes as Pyrrhic martial strategy: "*Another victory like that and we are done for*" (p. 24). Joyce's classicism may allow for artistic retribution—Stephen's "See this. Remember" (p. 192)—but never for the piling up of bodies as in the *Odyssey* or the last act of *Hamlet*. In fact, Shakespeare himself in "Circe" ventriloquizes the stuttering rage of Othello in revenging himself on his stay-at-home Penelope, Desdemona. The fabulous hero is overromantic in his temper: "How my Oldfellow chokit his Thursdaymomun. Iagogogo!" (p. 567).

Strangely enough, a seasoned and death-glutted Monte Cristo, of whom the young romantic Stephen makes no mention, comes to display similar profound misgivings about the project that had so long engaged him, but he does so only after most of the damage is already done. The exilic-return plot of *Monte Cristo* gains its final form when the Count renounces not the restriction upon revenge, as he had in the muscatel grape scene, but its actual exercise on Albert, Mercedes's son. He does so after the horror of his realization that his hounding of his other enemy, Villefort, results in the death of the prosecutor's innocent child, just the sort of obliteration Mercedes had feared for her son: "Until then he had been sustained by rage, by his strength of mind, by despair, by the supreme agony which led the Titans to scale the heavens, and Ajax to defy the gods" (2:516). The grief-stricken Villefort turns to the remorseful Monte Cristo: " 'You here, monsieur?' he exclaimed; 'do you then never appear but to act as an escort to Death?' " Monte Cristo senses that his vengeance engine is out of control and he along with it; the last thing the Count abjures is the impulse that in the romance "initiated" him. He must renounce the former principle of retributive freedom in order to satisfy his conscience.

Bloom handles his problem with a more subdued grace. He returns to bed envious of an experience he did not enjoy and jealous of Boylan who supplanted him, but transforms envy and jealousy into the more patient phases of classical progress: abnegation and equanimity. Bloom will reject any retribution for the day's events because they are "not as calamitous as a cataclysmic annihilation of the planet in consequence of collision with a dark sun . . . less reprehensible than theft, highway robbery," and a host of other crimes including "intelligence with the king's enemies, impersonation, criminal assault, manslaughter, wilful and premeditated murder" (p. 733). The passage concludes with yet another reference to food as a part of classical wholeness. Boylan's and Molly's tryst is "not more abnormal than all other altered processes of adaptation to altered conditions of existence, resulting in a reciprocal equilibrium between the bodily organism and its attendant circumstances, foods, beverages, acquired habits, indulged inclinations, significant disease. As more than inevitable, irreparable" (p. 733).

When the catechistic questioner asks why more abnegation than jealousy, less envy than equanimity, the catechistic answerer responds that Boylan's action was not directed at Bloom; thus the latter had no need to allow his overexercised and prideful ego to enter the violated bed with him. It is at this point that the issue of revenge is displaced into an appropriate epic rest with the repetition of the key word "satisfaction."

> In what final satisfaction did these antagonistic sentiments and reflections, reduced to their simplest forms, converge?
> Satisfaction at the ubiquity in eastern and western terrestrial hemispheres, in all habitable lands and islands explored or unexplored (the

land of the midnight sun, the islands of the blessed, the isles of Greece, the land of promise), of adipose posterior female hemispheres, redolent of milk and honey and of excretory sanguine and seminal warmth, reminiscent of secular families of curves of amplitude, insusceptible of moods of impression or of contrarieties of expression, expressive of mute immutable mature animality. [p. 734)

Bloom at the fundamental, the most hospitable of land forms or hemispheres, excretory, sanguine, and seminal, rounds out the day as exilic homecomer, the satisfied wanderer, Odysseus on rock-hard Ithaca, Monte Cristo on Sinbad the Sailor's treasure island.

Going to a dark bed there was a square round Sinbad the Sailor roc's auk's egg in the night of the bed of all the auks of the rocs of Darkinbad the Brightdayler.
Where?

●

[p. 737]

The exilic adventure is, in a sense, inscribed and signed off, but that is not the whole story, as Joyce himself recognized when right after the opening return depicted in *Finnegans Wake*—"by a commodius vicus of recirculation back to Howth Castle and Environs"— he situates the exilic hero back in Norman territory to refight the isolate wars of the peninsula, the pen, and the penis: "Sir Tristram, violer d'amores, fr'over the short sea, had passencore rearrived from North Armorica, on this side the scraggy isthmus of Europe Minor to wielderfight his penisolate wars" (p. 3). Continental crossings, with pen in hand—and I am not certain that Joyce's other pun ought to be entirely suppressed for my purposes—make up the subject of part two of this book. If I do not begin with the Norman-Irish Tristan, I do begin with the Irish Sterne, who sends both *his* Tristram and *his* Parson Yorick over the Channel in separate books to confront issues that are in substance and in essence at the heart of fictional activity.

PART TWO
EXILIC CROSSINGS

CHAPTER FOUR

Expatriated Adventurer: Sterne's
A Sentimental Journey

"The Novelty of my Vehicle"

Laurence Sterne propels his Parson Yorick to France after the opening sentences of *A Sentimental Journey* and never returns him.[1] The narrative gesture is comparable to one I have been charting throughout the first part of this book and will continue to chart in the second, the notion that fiction allegorizes its own potential, generates the "otherness" that becomes its action.

All fictional experience is a boundary crossing of sorts, a projection from familiar space into narrative space where consciousness is displayed as verbal territory. To cross over in fiction is not necessarily to get somewhere with a place name attached to it but to turn consciousness inside out, to make that which is perceived that which is imitated. Nowhere in the early development of the novel is the entire apparatus of fictional transport and translation, or verbal crossing, so tangibly brought to bear on the mechanics of fictional representation as in Sterne's *A Sentimental Journey*. To plunge into the French gap, which turns out to be exilic space for the narrator, Yorick, is not only to generate the immense comic spectacle that will give impetus to this particular novel but to create a generic arena where events and all varieties of relations—psychological, sexual, charitable, financial, and contractual—are imaginatively detailed and disposed.

When Parson Yorick begins and, in a sense, causes his sentimental crossing to France with a remark whose specific subject is never explained, "—They order, said I, this matter better in France—,"[2] he immediately sets the difference between explicit referential mimesis and narrative opportunity. If *A Sentimental Journey*'s first sentence barely misses out on the mimetic gist of a prior conversation, it serves immediately, and with stark power, as the novel's spatial and verbal radical. In the context of the eavesdrop, it performs what fiction does best, translate words into action. The Russian Formalist interest in Sterne earlier in this century focuses upon just such a notion: propositional reality is, in a sense, actionable. Any reader so "obtuse" as to try to gauge the zero degree point of Sterne's precise narrative angle into France—what exactly it is that is better ordered—has indeed come in too late, so to speak, to catch the direction of the conversation's fictional pretext. Instead of merely parleying information about contemporary France, Sterne's Yorick will literalize the figure of fictional potential; he will cross over to the other side, translating belatedness into the expatriated adventure, the fictional main chance.

About the opening matter ordered, then, we have to assume it addresses questions that might be best addressed by the disposition of the fiction that evolves from it: not only questions about the warp and weave of the social fabric but questions concerning central principles of narrative expression. The first line of *A Sentimental Journey*, its first rhetorical and representational gesture, inscribes the space for narrative projection just as the final sentence of the book literally delimits the fictional trajectory by marking a posterior, that is, ending with an all too palpable grope. What negotiates the in-between spaces of this short narrative, this commerce, this interchange, this high and low road of the heart's purchases, is the vehicle that effects its crossing. Sterne, at different times, has his Yorick refer to the *"Novelty of my Vehicle"* (p. 82) or the "novelty of the situation" (p. 290), which makes the figure for conveyance interchangeable with the novelistic matter conveyed.

To narrate in Sterne's fashion is always to make the linguistic properties of utterance spatial. The notion of difference that begins the novel and also determines its narrative range is described and metonymized in a nutshell by one of Sterne's favorite philosophers, David Hume: "any great *difference* in the degrees of any quality is call'd a *distance* by a common metaphor."[3] When Sterne had occasion to comment in one of his sermons on a narrative archetype that absorbed his attention before the writing of *A Sentimental Journey*, the biblical fable of the prodigal son, he saw in that narrative's resources not only its obvious didacticism but the spatial determinants of his future sentimental record. The progress of the fable turns exilic scope into consciousness: "by seeing the difference of so many various humours and manners,—to look into ourselves and form our own."[4] Essentially, Sterne's program for his fictional venture in *A Sentimental Journey* is the same as the prodigal son's, to see "new objects, or old ones in new lights."[5]

If the metaphor that measures difference is, by nature of curiosity and imaginative range, a figure of distance, Yorick notices that the French across the channel perceive things hyperbolically, a spatial figure which means leaping o'er the mark.[6] The Parisian barber insists that the periwig buckle he tries to sell Yorick would stand submergence in the ocean, whereas for the experimental Englishman, surrounded by ocean, a simple pail of water in the next room would do. Yorick's is a less grand figure but a better practical possibility: "the grandeur is *more* in the *word;* and *less* in the thing" (p. 159). Again, Sterne literalizes his narrative figure since Yorick has himself made just such a move to test the "thing" after uttering the word. But in Sterne's space-conscious novel there is yet another dimension to this metaphorical enacting and reification of cross-cultural difference. *A Sentimental Journey*, after all, is as extravagant in form as the French are in speech. Yorick, just as he abjures making love like the French by sentiments while doing precisely that, also partakes of the hyperbolic sublime while differentiating his expression from that of the French who profess more than they perform. In crossing to France to test the nature of a few words uttered in a conversation, Yorick has not simply gone to the next room to drop the periwig buckle in a pail of water but crossed the ocean, albeit a channel. He has hyperbolized the figure. No one reading into the literal action of *A Sentimental Journey* could think the confirming impulse a mere exercise in induction. The novel's narrative range, in a practical and generic sense, is extravagantly, or outlandishly, beyond borders. This comports with the potential subject of narration since it is the very nature of sentiment as a psychological and intellectual phenomenon to extract the greatest possible range of feelings from the most attenuated of actions.

"Happiness sometimes beyond her limits"

Sterne's novel not only begins with a hyperbolic leap across borders, a leap initiated by a novelistic pretext; it quickly turns to the matter of rights of articulation, surely the very question that faces all mimetic actions at their beginning. Yorick again acts out in his language the issue of authority—he gains his rights, validates his status by performing for real in the very invention of which he is a part. He will subject himself mimetically to the circumstances contained rhetorically in the opinion that he has just articulated—he will "look into these rights," subject himself to their provenance and their limits as an English citizen and as a novelistic surrogate. It is the force of observation performed on the illusion of possible action that confirms narrative authority.

Just as Sterne's first sentence supplemented topicality while establishing opportunity, Yorick's attempt to concretize his rights of articulation subjects him to the paraphernalia of local law while releasing him to the world of extended, imagined, or exilic boundaries. The sentimental traveler, motivated as much as fictional travelers like the prodigal son or Robinson Crusoe "out of *Necessity,* and the *besoin de* Voyager" (p. 82), casts off security for coming attractions or adventure. True authority, in the fictional sense, subjects the protagonist-narrator to a kind of spatial jeopardy. The record of life, as is evident from the earlier *Tristram Shandy,* is difficult enough in proximity to the familiar. Cast out, both the imagination and the self are perplexed by the confusions of severe difference. Yorick considers.

> It must have been observed by many a peripatetic philosopher, That nature has set up by her own unquestionable authority certain boundaries and fences to circumscribe the discontent of man: she has effected her purpose in the quietest and easiest manner by laying him under

almost insuperable obligations to work out his ease, and to sustain his sufferings at home. It is there only that she has provided him with the most suitable objects to partake of his happiness, and bear a part of that burden which, in all countries and ages, has ever been too heavy for one pair of shoulders. 'Tis true we are endued with an imperfect power of spreading our happiness sometimes beyond *her* limits, but 'tis so ordered, that, from the want of languages, connections, and dependencies, and from the difference in education, customs, and habits, we lie under so many impediments in communicating our sensations out of our own sphere, as often amount to a total impossibility. [p. 78]

It later follows that writing, which Yorick sees as a form of communication, is also easier within one's sphere, where the familiarity with local manners, gestures, customs, facilitates literary translation[7] or what Sterne calls *short hand.* "There is not a secret so aiding to the progress of sociality, as to get master of this *short hand,* and be quick in rendering the several turns of looks and limbs, with all their inflections and delineations, into plain words. For my own part, by long habitude, I do it so mechanically, that when I walk the streets of London, I go translating all the way; and have more than once stood behind in the circle, where not three words have been said, and have brought off twenty different dialogues with me, which I could have fairly wrote down and sworn to" (pp. 171–72).

Removed from one sort of "habitude" when he leaves England, Yorick discovers that "the balance of sentimental commerce is always against the expatriated adventurer" (p. 78)[8]—that is, he must purchase experience before he makes it his own. To have too little in his account is to devalue his fictional worth and delimit his narrative authority. Thus we hear Yorick's initial harangue against the French *droits d'aubaine* in which the self as legal entity is nullified abroad should a man die and the French king inherit his goods on the spot,[9] something not far from Sterne's mind given his own health when he wrote the book and Yorick's health represented in it. There is a special irony here in that *A Sentimental Journey,* in front of its readers just three weeks before its real author's death, becomes by circumstance a voice from an exilic boundary land more remote than Yorick's

France. Contemporary reviewers wasted little time in alluding to the death of Yorick-Sterne and to the play of his origin: "Our Sentimentalist, having lately made a journey to that country *from whose bourne no traveller returns,* his memory claims at least as much indulgence as our duty to the public permitted us to allow him when alive."[10]

Of course Yorick's outrage at the first matter ordered worse in France seems but a canard when we later realize he travels under riskier (and more real in the action's idiom) circumstances by carrying no passport—for that he can actually be arrested and his narrative progress stymied. The other prospect of falling dead and losing one's self to France is but a metaphoric projection even within the illusion of novelistic action. Like all "real" pieces of mimetic action in Sterne, the passport sequence raises more issues about Yorick's validity as narrator than it settles. The matter of proper credentialing paradoxically represents the novel's bona fides in two worlds: a mimetically legal one and a markedly literary one.

We learn only later in the novel that Yorick had withheld the information about his missing passport until it was "time the reader should know it, for in the order of things in which it happened, it was omitted; not that it was out of my head; but that, had I told it then, it might have been forgot now—and now is the time I want it" (p. 192). Yorick refers specifically to the fact that England and France were at war when he departed from his native land to test his proposition about matters ordered across the channel. Of course, a passport is required in such circumstances almost as a matter of state. Yorick uncredentialed is Yorick illegal.

But these larger affairs of nations do not stake their claim to priority in Sterne's imagination. As Yorick puts it after his conversation with the French barber about periwig buckles and national metaphoric habits of mind: "I think I can see the precise and distinguishing marks of national characters more in these nonsensical *minutiae* than in the most important matters of state" (p. 160). Yorick's narrative backtracking on the subjects of the missing passport and the then ongoing Seven Years' War constitutes Sterne's version of what might be called the ideology of novelistic information. To justify his delayed revelations he repeats the key word "order." That is, whatever Sterne introduces in *A Sentimental Journey* is there as much for narrative exigency—"now is the time I want it"—as for militant topicality. Indeed, the first true hint of Sterne's tactics depends upon his calculated silence on some issues—including the key topical issue dividing England from France in 1762—in deference to matters of narrative interest that turn on more intimate crossings of sentiment and consciousness.

For Yorick to keep his own counsel on a war then raging for six years suggests just how far Sterne has come from the novel's more historically conscious epic forebears, where national wars were primary subjects rather than temporal nuisances. Could one imagine, say, the Homeric *Iliad* beginning with a Greek protagonist remarking "—They order, I said, this matter better in Troy—," without any thought of the war then raging in its last year on the planes of Troas? Of course, Sterne had already discovered in *Tristram Shandy* the fictional virtue of readjusting topical representation to the scope of personal perspective when he reduced the great battlefield at Namur to Uncle Toby's freeze-framed psychological obsession, his little miniaturized acre on the Shandy estate.

In a novel purportedly about the state of things in France, Sterne's withholding of the passport from Yorick—a document that would have offered him mimetic authorization beyond "actual" borders—generically allows for Yorick's later reissue, so to speak, through the agency of a bibliophiliac French count who thinks him the famous court jester from *Hamlet*. Of course, the process of naming Yorick, issuing him his credentials for fiction, was literary long before the quixotic Count de B**** entered the lists in *A Sentimental Journey*. In Yorick's case, he had already lived and died in *Tristram Shandy* as an embodiment of literature's most immortal mortal joke, the "thingsake" from the grave, the deathhead *qui rit*. Sterne originally buried Yorick in 1748. The sign of his death in *Tristram Shandy* is a page of all ink and no lines, a black rectangle or literary grave in memoriam of Yorick's passing. But Sterne's Parson, like another of Shakespeare's clowns, Falstaff in *Merry Wives*, returns to what for him is a better time and place—the powers of the narrative and dramatic imagination are never quite ready to give the coup de grace to successful inventions. From any perspective—whether going or coming, whether sparking memories or simply staring blankly into Hamlet's face, whether beaten to a pulp in *Tristram Shandy* or jaunting through Europe in *A Sentimental Journey*—the comic Yorick keeps leaping out from the grave (or page) in generic distinction, say, to the tragic Hamlet who keeps leaping in.

Rendered by his new imprimatur as a literary figment, and already revived from his death years before in *Tristram Shandy,* Yorick travels under special auspices. In that hare-and-tortoise race writing runs with linear time and space, his record gives him life just as Sterne himself hoped his fictional crossing might deflect or postpone death by creating a supplementing necessity to which the exigencies of mortality must defer. To keep a pen stroke ahead is to keep a step ahead, and the jesting Yorick cannot die because Sterne has not yet finished off what he imagines for him.

Passports

The authorizing progress of the passport sequence bears some closer scrutiny because its fictional development touches on notions of the circulating, liberated self that Ian Watt and others have considered so crucial to the new subjective legitimacy in eighteenth-century fiction. It is only in Paris, after registering at the hotel, that the authorities, emissaries from the official French world, show up to question Sterne's unauthorized creation, his narrative intention. When the master of the hotel hears that the police are in pursuit of Yorick, he reacts as if Yorick carries the plague instead of papers. The hosteler represents in this scene and in a later one the scourge of hypocritical bourgeois legalism. The correspondent reaction of La Fleur, Yorick's servant *bonhomie,* is a kind of downclass heroic fortitude: "The master of the hotel retired three steps from me, as from an infected person, as I declared this—and poor La Fleur advanced three steps towards me, and with that sort of movement which a good soul makes to succour a distress'd one—the fellow won my heart by it; and from that single *trait,* I knew his character as perfectly, and could rely upon it as firmly, as if he had served me with fidelity for seven years" (p. 193).

Having tested the one pole of narrative projection, that of expatriation, Yorick now is in position to test another, the status of illegal alien. He began by assuming that his journey would give him certain rights of expression and now he moves about in alien terrain without the legal rights of circulation. The only alternative habitation for someone so deprived is the prison cell where the idea of imaginative traveling through projected space becomes as much a therapeutic necessity as an aesthetic challenge. Just such a notion occurs to Yorick after we hear of something else he had withheld after the novel's *propter hoc* first sentence but before Yorick's posthaste departure. Prior to his journey, his friend Eugenius slipped him some money and the two bantered that Yorick would probably say or do something that would get him into the Bastille where he might live rent free, a not altogether displeasing fate since Yorick's tastes are more expensive than his resources. Upon imagining the actual prospect of arrest, Yorick's joke comes home to roost. But with pen and paper in the Bastille he could still, perhaps, journey in ink, which is what he had begun to do earlier when writing his preface in a *desobligeant.*

It is at this point, a crucial one in the novel's inscribed space, that Yorick hears the sounds of a caged starling: "I can't get out—I can't get out" (p. 197). Like the memorable scene in *Robinson Crusoe* when Crusoe hears the wild parrot echo his own earlier laments, the sound of another voice for Yorick allegorizes his narrative situation. The starling galvanizes a change of heart in Yorick and later mimics the kind of authority and circulating powers *A Sentimental Journey* possesses as a celebrated novel. It seems that the captive is an English bird and would gain fame in the way novels do—by circulating around London in all houses and among all classes: "Lord D gave him to Lord E—and so on—half round the alphabet—From that rank he pass'd into the lower house, and pass'd the hands of as many commoners— But as all these wanted to *get in*—and my bird wanted to get out—he had almost as little store set by him in London as in Paris" (p. 205). That the starling doubles for Sterne, whose name means star, is clear from Yorick's protest, in case anyone should pass off one thing as another, "that that bird was my bird—or some vile copy set up to represent him" (p. 205). Quite naturally, Sterne works the starling in as the crest to his arms, an insignia or image of himself reprinted in the text. Given his death shortly after the publication of *A Sentimental Journey*, the starling's insignia literally signs him off at the same time it imprints him forever in the spaces of the book's pages.

Back in France, during the course of the novel's action, the starling's plea as prisoner silences Yorick's paean to the Bastille as a place for uninterrupted writing. He sings, instead, a new song to the strains of personal liberty. Many have argued that the politics of sentiment growing in England, at least, out of the 1688 Glorious Revolution reflect both latitudinal principles of toleration and antiabsolutist principles of liberty, an argument for which it is best to take the French way out and profess its force without actually repeating its performance. In any case, sentimentally or politically, once the soul feels deprived of liberty, the imagination projects a sense of confinement.[11] Yorick paints a verbal picture of the prisoner.

> I beheld his body half wasted away with long expectation and confinement, and felt what kind of sickness of the heart it was which arises from hope deferr'd. Upon looking nearer I saw him pale and feverish: in thirty years the western breeze had not once fann'd his blood—he had seen no sun, no moon in all that time—nor had the voice of friend or kinsman breathed through his lattice. [p. 202]

Yorick continues at length and concludes, before bursting into tears, with the remarkable sentence: "I saw the iron enter into his soul" (p. 203). The phrase penetrates to the center of Sterne's fictional effort, dehumanizing its sustaining symbol and immobilizing its driving impulse, the liberty of a character in sentimental fiction to put a soul in motion—one's own soul and one's own soul in relation to others.

To avoid the fate of the Bastille and the insult to his liberty, Yorick must petition for credentials. But even here he reenacts the exilic allegory of suffering on another man's stairs when he complains of the wait at the Count de C*****'s: "and as walking backwards and forward in the saloon, without a soul to commune with, was for the time as bad as being in the Bastile itself, I instantly went back to my *remise*" (p. 208). Governed by circumstances because he cannot seem to govern them, Yorick tries Count de B**** in Versailles whose confused handiwork grants him access and freedom of movement around Paris as "Yorick, the king's jester." Yorick therefore circulates like a kind of Cervantic hero, living in a world that, at least in its higher circles, will have access to him as if he were a character in a play or a book.

When he earns his passport from the Count, Yorick is no longer subject to conditions where either the droits d'aubaine or the king's police can put an end to him. He is an ongoing jest or, more permanently, an ongoing narrative *geste* or deed. His journey, his crossing, can now sustain him as part of its fiction—a mobile bagatelle, a series of stories and forms assembled, dismembered, redistributed, rejected for the emergent shape of that inner consciousness that finally determines the process of form in the novel. Of course, all the while Yorick has been passing through a host of way stations in the novel's development. First to arrive and first to depart Sterne's new narrative ground is the Bunyanesque narrative allegory—a collection of deadly sins accost Yorick just before he deals "sentimentally" with the Flemish lady; epistolary fiction similarly arrives with a flourish and departs casually or, to use a Sternean phrase, out of hand, when Yorick allows La Fleur to substitute the French corpsman's letter for one he ought to have written personally; the "Three Sons" folktale appears in the guise of a Franconian mourning a dead ass; the interpolated tale arrives with all the originality of a found manuscript but lingers only as the intentionally long-winded and open-ended adventure of the scribe's hat; the pastoral romance seems a mere blathering beast fable when suffered by the mad Maria; and the fabliau puts in its appearance only to be one-upped by a modern graft of the comedic proviso scene when the novel ends with what amounts to an interrupted clause in the contract with the genteel Piedmontese lady.

Interests of the Heart and Hand

Yorick's narrative crossing is Sterne's *ars roman*. He had already observed the potential for the novel one hour after Yorick's initial crossing to Calais.

> What a large volume of adventures may be grasped within this little span of life by him who interests his heart in every thing, and who, having eyes to see, what time and chance are perpetually holding out to him as he journeyeth on his way, misses nothing he can *fairly* lay his hands on. [p. 114]

Such a remark offers up an appropriate manifesto for that which is "novel" in Sterne. The witty injunction—"*fairly* lay his hands on"—allows for all interests of the heart, sentimental and sexual, so crucial to Sterne's sense of novelistic vitality from Corporal Trim's convalescence in *Tristram Shandy* to the tactile and charmingly manipulated amours of *A Sentimental Journey*. The texture of narrative for Sterne encourages a laying on of hands. [12] In a more important sense, the key word of the passage, *interests,* opens up the supplemental spaces required for action. Sterne repeats the word again when Yorick describes the Flemish lady's face, a description that marks the interior domain of his sentimental consciousness: "it was not critically handsome, but there was that in it, which in the frame of mind I was in, attached me much more to it—it was interesting" (pp. 93–94). Raymond Williams has an entry on *interest* in his *Keywords,* in which he points out that the word came into use as a term for concern or "the power to attract concern" right around the time Sterne was writing. The original sense of the word was, of course, economic, but even there the etymology suggests the perspective that allows for the word's development: from the Latin, *interesse,* to be between. [13] Narrative interest is the space of writerly duration, the legitimate time it takes to dwell in and on subjects that can be, in a sense, written upon. And the focus of narrative attention takes its position between things observed and things projected.

Within the context or space of generated "interest" Sterne's narrative crossing places him at odds with his contemporary traveler in the realms of fiction, Tobias Smollett, whose efforts are at best satiric or picaresque romances of the outland. According to Sterne, Smollett describes such places as the European Turin as if he were Othello marveling about cannibals in South America. Smollett, or Smelfungus, has the bravado but not the grace to understand the subtlety of representation or the mode of writing that best expresses the range, strength, and delight of all those seemingly empty journeys from Dan to Beersheba that fill the heart and head, if not the eye, with interesting things: "I pity the man who can travel from *Dan* to *Beersheba,* and cry, 'Tis all barren—so it is; and so is all the world to him who will not cultivate the fruits it offers" (p. 115). Instead, Smollett has found the style answerable to what Sterne had already rejected as writerly disobligation, the "vehicle" unsuitable for both sentiment and its narrative crossings. Yorick admits to a simple traveler who "never heard . . . of a preface wrote in a *Desobligeant*" that it "would have been better . . . in a *Vis à Vis*" (p. 85), that is, confronting, in a literal, almost etymological sense, an interesting face, be it the Flemish lady's or even the mute's at Montreuil, whose face, like a kind of Beckettian tramp's, had seen better days.

Before Yorick gains the grace afforded by the interest implicit in his sentimental confrontations, he loses face in another sense. He botches his first encounter with a man like him, a man of the cloth. The fictional traveler is suspicious in alien territory; he literally acts at cross-purposes. Yorick harbors a parochial conviction that he will get from France more than he will give to it—a notion that might prove desirable in the realm of foreign exchange but invidious in the realm of true sentiment. After the niggling response to the polite mendicant Monk, Yorick feels his "rights" have somewhat slackened. He says that he has much to learn from the supply of adventures in front of him: "I have only just set out upon my travels; and shall learn better manners as I get along" (p. 75). The observation is rich. He shall both learn better manners and learn them better. He offers here the prospect of sentimental adventure as *bildung,* surely one of the guiding principles of the novel as it developed into and through the next century. The action of fiction will increase the capacity of its actors to act fully. For Sterne this means that a better understanding of manners goes hand in hand with better expression. The very confrontations that forge experience in the novel also forge the consciousnesses capable of finer touches, finer discriminations, finer interests.

Having sensed from the first awkward encounter with the Monk that he has nowhere to go "novelistically" if he proceeds self-protectively, Yorick readies to confront sentiment head-on. For the purposes of coming to any fair comprehension of Sterne's narrative domain in *A Sentimental Journey,* it is important to understand some things clearly about the word *sentiment* and the seeming excesses and flourishes that are coded into its expressions. Sentiment is muscular, not effete; ideological, not eccentric. Around the word stand the shock troops of decades worth of moral, political, and even economic philosophy. [14] The root philosophical and, by implication, political idea behind the notion of sentiment is that there exists in the human order at large an impulse to act in conformity with mankind's essentially sympathetic nature. [15] And a look at the beating heart of *A Sentimental Journey* seems to confirm the passions of sentimental ideology: "'tis a quiet journey of the heart in pursuit of NATURE, and those affections which arise out of her, which make us love each other—and the world, better than we do" (p. 219). Yorick hopes "that if ever I do a mean action, it must be in some interval betwixt one passion and another" (pp. 128–29). It is as if mean-spiritedness in his world falls in the interstices of natural passions. Passion and sentiment do not reflect the psychological distinction between passion and reason, nor the moral one between passion and righteous action; rather, they are part of a system of expression that exists to make the human spirit bond or connect to the idea of the other, vis-à-vis, face to face. When passion is missing, matters are thrown into a kind of materialist, Hobbist arrears.

It is significant, in this sense, that the alternating subjects of sentiment in Sterne's novel, charity and sex, are constantly tested by the materialist challenge, specifically by personal gain, whether contribution, tip, purchase, bribe, or, in its fullest sense, personal credit. The first gesture of sentiment in the novel is Yorick's taking out his purse for charity in relation to the dilations of his heart; the first gesture of selfishness is putting his purse away in relation to the suspicion of another's motives. To move beyond the Hobbist ethic of self-protectiveness insists on behavior that allows for the accommodation of self-interest within a more natural system of social expression and exchange. Yorick walks with Mons. Dessein and observes: "It must needs be a hostile kind of a world, when the buyer (if it be but of a sorry post-chaise) cannot go forth with the seller thereof into the street to terminate the difference betwixt them, but he instantly falls into the same frame of mind and views his conventionist with the same sort of eye, as if he was going along with him to Hyde-park corner to fight a duel" (p. 89).

The world of exchange and negotiation has the potential to be one of suppressed material violence, but the sentimentalist aims to make the flow of resources a symbol of human bounty rather than human greed.[16] Yorick learns to let what money he has flow as freely as he can distribute it, and this is why he feels so miserable after initially determining to give nothing to the Monk at Calais. Yorick, of course, understands that he is nothing if not "equipped" for sentimental action, and to be equipped implies the ready availability of loose change for some encounters and hard cash for others. For instance, he senses immediately that to enter Paris without proper equipage is literally to sneak in, and this so depresses him that he confines his sentimental forays to that which he can purchase more cheaply from a *grisset*. The essence of the sentimental is to pay willingly for matters that contribute to the heart's fund. Sentiment becomes a kind of marketplace, the "great—great SENSORIUM of the world" (p. 278), not unlike the London Exchange in the *Spectator Papers*.

Yorick and Sterne discover in the course of *A Sentimental Journey* that the alien space, France, is an experimental arena for the practice of sentiment because the nation has refined its economic motives into

the economies of manners and language. The simplest material state-
ment in the book occurs when Yorick gives us his mini-discourse on
French expressions: *tant pis* and *tant mieux* (p. 122). The one is uttered
when little is to be gotten, the other when a great deal. What ultimately is to be gotten, of course, is the range of possible encounters
that constitute the experience registered and supplemented by fictional "interest." Yorick must make the trip to France to stand
between his subject and its best expression, at which time material
self-interest expands to include a social communion of motive force
and an imaginative exchange of feeling and passion. That otherness
which sets off the novel—the test of unexperienced territory and its
social articulations—is also the otherness that must be accommodated for the sentimental code to make personal sense. Expatriated
adventure makes the alien sympathetic.

Nowhere is Sterne's accommodation of sentimental interest better
represented than in the famous scene of the Franconian's dead ass, to
which Byron took such exception. The scene touches on a basic
Hobbist proposition when Yorick comments on the pilgrim mourning over his poor beast lying in the middle of the road: "Did we love
each other, as this poor soul but loved his ass—'twould be something" (p. 141). It would be indeed. But that's one of Sterne's points:
built into the sentimental code is the kind of verbal expression that
becomes self-expression. The code, in a sense, allows the loving of one's
own ass to near solipsistic distraction if certain other obligations have
been met. The emotional bond or inclination to pity the "other"
implies a kind of self-love, a perfectly acceptable and socially bonding
kind. The politesse of sentiment is an elaborate game of give-and-
take, all those negotiated and nuanced exchanges that profit the
human order. The heart, after all, is "for saving what it can" (p. 107)
even if this means spending more than it ought. We see this most
clearly in the mysterious riddle of the urbane beggar who only seeks
the charity of women he can talk up sexually. What is exchanged is
not so much the coin of the realm for the good of the needy, but excess
sexual energy for the good of the soul, something never very far from
the idea of "feeling" in Sterne.

Sterne often raises a distinctly Hobbist notion only to counter it with a distinctly delicate or sentimental response. While Yorick, as a stranger in a strange land, finds himself at the point of thinking "thy hand is against every man, and every man's hand against thee," the lovely Flemish widow's black-gloved hand, raised in mock horror to her forehead, appears in the text, virtually before she herself does, and with it the exclamation, "heaven forbid!" (p. 89). The particular symbol of the raised hand of natural hostility gives way to the hand that throughout *A Sentimental Journey* becomes the emblem of sexual good nature.

Because Sterne can be so funny on charting the behavioral delineations of the sentimental code, it is easy to think of him either as abjuring the predominant line of defense against the Hobbist view by secretly agreeing with the notion of "other" as enemy, or, as Byron charged, giving in to the excesses of sentiment by whining over a dead ass while starving his own relations. It takes a special kind of sentimentalist to chortle with pleasure at his own sly jokes about human suffering, to depict, for example, the woman of Montreuil begging only for the love of God because her dislocated hip provides no other secure footing. But Sterne is perfectly able to locate the comic in sentimentalism without either damning its hypocrisy or becoming its hypocrite. [17] It is really only in the nineteenth-century English novel that writers like Thackeray, Meredith, and Dickens begin to treat aspects of genteel sentimentalism as part of the hypocritical ideology of class power. In the *Old Curiosity Shop,* Dickens says of the downtrodden Kit:

It must be specially observed in justice to poor Kit that he was by no means of sentimental turn, and perhaps had never heard that adjective in his life. He was only a soft-hearted grateful fellow, and had nothing genteel or polite about him; consequently, instead of going home again in his grief to kick the children and abuse his mother (for when your finely strung people are out of sorts they must have everybody else unhappy likewise), he turned his thoughts to the vulgar expedient of making them more comfortable if he could. [18]

In the mid-eighteenth century, Sterne was not yet at the point of employing the novel as a bludgeon against the philosophical and class values that sustained it. Rather, he knew how to radicalize the surface of the sentimental ethic, letting it go in all directions, testing its management on two continents, falling every so often into the comic breach, that place where the material and sexual impulses of sentiment become too strong for their perfectly decorous expression. Sentiment both generates and postures, like the book's title which is both substantive and slightly parodic. Sterne's title, as titles so often do, forecasts and absorbs the project at hand. The noun *sentiment* is buried in its adjectival form. *Sentiment* as a substantive directs the journey, but *sentimental* as an adjective qualifies it, adds a syllable of rococo or affected flourish. And *journey* is both the inward expanse and the call to narrative inscription. Centripetally Yorick "feels"; centrifugally he is part of the errantry of the expatriate fiction, ranging its full sentimental course and participating in its full sentimental crossing.

A Class Act

There is another important constituent of sentimental action that shapes the disposition of events in Sterne's novel and suggests that the sequences of narrative crossing are not limited to the spatial terrain of national borders. Class lines and boundaries are also to be crossed, and both the etiology of sentiment and the etiology of fiction in the eighteenth century treat narrative event as a class act. [19] It is in this sense that the novel as a form has been said to be the creation of the expanding genteel order in the century, or, perhaps in a more intriguing variation, the genteel order was the creation of the novel. There are mannered obligations in eighteenth-century fiction that virtually depend on equality or parity of rank, order, degree, class. When class relations change, so do the obligations attendant upon behavior and its representation in fiction.

Sterne, of course, is not alone here. There are examples scattered through the fiction and drama of the period from the shifting sexual rights attendant upon the gentrification of a Moll Flanders or the humble servant Pamela to the various downclass and upclass sexual escapades in *Tom Jones*—watching Molly Seagrim perform *flagrante* is a laughing matter for Tom, whereas toying with his beloved Sophia's muff turns him to genteel jelly—to the sexual hesitancies and effusions of *She Stoops to Conquer*. Sex surfaces across class lines but recesses into mannered discourse within the ranks of the genteel, a class comprising the well educated, the well dressed, and the well off (or any combination thereof). Sterne understands as well as any eighteenth-century writer that matters ordered are also matters ranked.

Yorick, who makes his narrative crossing in late May when everyone's spring juices are flowing, learns to perform in full accord with the quality of the occasion, whether he encounters ladies of degree, grissets of the middling bourgeois, the surrogate genteel (ladies' maids), or pastorally possessed peasants. In each case he changes the negotiated territory of sexual commerce, including appropriate degrees of fore- and afterplay. The least detailed liaisons in the narrative, though not necessarily the least sexually complete, occur at the very top of the scale, and the silliest at the very bottom. Yorick projects one affair forward with the Italian Marquesina di F***, but his other forays into the world of the blood aristocracy seem more focused on earning his strained budget a free meal than in gaining him sexual favors. As for his undifferentiated and undifferentiating passion for the hapless Maria, the lovely loon is more interested in goats and dogs than in sentimental admirers.

Women of all classes may represent the urgency of desire—Yorick conceives of "every fair being as a temple, and would rather enter in, and see the original drawings and loose sketches hung up in it, than the transfiguration of Raphael itself" (pp. 218–19)—but for the sentimental traveler it is as Hume writes: "The skin, pores, muscles, and nerves of a day-labourer are different from those of a man of quality: So are his sentiments, actions, and manners."[20] Sterne, for the most part, accommodates Hume's organic ideology of sentiment. Though Yorick protests that the "sons and daughters of service part with liberty, but not with Nature" (p. 247), sex among the lower orders is like the little carnal dance La Fleur performs in the kitchen of the Count de L***'s auberge in Amiens or the Schnitzler-like circle of lust traveled by the bouquet La Fleur delivers to the Count de B****'s maid. The true exercise of sentimental desire belongs neither to the lower orders who, at best, ape its manners poorly nor to the aloof remnants of the blood aristocracy who have older and haughtier rites of pride to sustain them. Sentiment belongs to the genteel, the class to which the novel also belongs.

The novel's genteel allegiance seems apparent from the opening scenes when Sterne draws two men of the cloth (Yorick and the Monk) and one woman "of the better order of beings" (p. 107) into a conspiracy of gracious exchange, both benevolent and sexual. While intently but decorously holding the Flemish lady's hand, Yorick wonders what his earlier mean-spiritedness to the Monk "in case he had told it her, must have planted in her breast against me" (p. 98). He must transform his original boorishness to its opposite, graciousness, because such behavior is the only appropriate mode of sexual exchange that will "play" with a woman of degree. Yorick, in essence, performs with the Monk in a highly wrought fictional adventure for the benefit of the Flemish lady—they exchange snuff boxes, an action of genteel indulgence. Yorick says that all the while "I had never quitted the lady's hand" (p. 104), as if his new sense of gracious benevolence gives freer play to the ardor of his grip.

Still learning at this point in the novel, Yorick protests that the particular quality of his brief relation with the Flemish lady has nothing to do with one of the possible reasons for his exilic jaunt, nothing to do, that is, with the French notion of making love by sentiments.

> —To think of making love by *sentiments!*
> I should as soon think of making a genteel suit of cloaths out of remnants. [p. 111]

Sterne's figure here is an interesting one in that the metaphor substitutes class status for desire while Yorick performs a version of the very thing he abjures.[21] Of course one of the characteristics of a new kind of class mobility in the eighteenth century is the struggle of everyone to compose his or her remnants into a suit or dress of genteel dimension. Bernard Mandeville remarks early in the century: "The poorest Labourer's Wife in the Parish, who scorns to wear a strong wholesom Frize, as she might, will half starve her self and her Husband to purchase a second-hand Gown and Petticoat, that cannot do her half the Service; because, forsooth, it is more genteel."[22] It will not take long for Yorick to realize that mere sex, if that is his end, is more serviceable downclass, but, forsooth, more intense by sentiments. When the participants share in genteel desire, the nuance can be as titillating as the caress.

It is only upon entering Paris that Yorick gets the chance to cultivate less fine but broader sexual fields, to pick up the remnant instead of the highly fashioned product. On his desultory way to visit Mme. de R***, he whiles away some time with a tradeswoman grisset who, naturally enough, sells gloves—as always, hands are "feeling" objects in *A Sentimental Journey*. During one of the book's discourses on manners we even hear of a law in the time of Molière requiring any abbé who happened to be standing behind a grisset in the theater to raise his hands in the air for the entire performance. The law's intent was less to prevent a possible theft than to impede a more probable grope. The scene with Yorick and his grisset is only slightly subtler. Yorick feels the course of his heart's action right through to his fingertips: he takes the grisset's pulse and gets to forty in his count when the grisset's husband comes in from the back parlor: " 'Twas no body but her husband" (p. 166). For a variety of reasons, one of them having to do with the deflected passion of salique law into trade, *nobody* is precisely who arrives, a mere cipher in the less than genteel order. Yorick counts another twenty beats, the husband bows, and the grisset says that "Monsieur is so good . . . as to give himself the trouble of feeling my pulse" (p. 166). The husband, like a sad sack out of a René Clair comedy, simply puts on his hat and walks out. The result is less the titillating comic mystery of the hand-holding encounter with the Flemish lady than something closer to bourgeois triangle farce. As if to emphasize the inequality of the brief interlude, Yorick puts money into the grisset's hand after purchasing a pair of gloves that do not fit.[23] He has paid for more than he has gotten in terms of quality, but gotten more than he has paid for in terms of gratification.

In his next significant sexual encounter, Yorick crosses another class line. This time he pays first and, ultimately, gets most. At a book stall he slips a crown to a *fille de chambre*—"I never gave a girl a crown in my life which gave me half the pleasure" (p. 189)—and soon works himself into a position to put his hand in her pocket which contains the sentimental Crebillon novel *Wanderings of the Heart.* Though it's not his heart that does the wandering, he says: " 'Tis sweet to feel by what fine-spun threads our affections are drawn together" (p. 190). Yorick's observation touches as much on senti-ment's sexual fabric as on its psychology. Later, in his rooms, when he puts his hand in the fille de chambre's lap, a lap holding the purse she made for the crown he had given her—one might say, in advance—the excitement is so great that threads and buckles seem to unravel or pop off articles of clothing for the mere joy of it.

We have to take Yorick's word that nothing more than an acciden-tal tumble occurs, though from a later reckoning it appears that the Parson and the fille de chambre spent two full hours in the room. For the second time in the novel, the hotel master acts as bourgeois conscience, asking Yorick to leave the premises. His complaint is not so much that Yorick indulged himself with a fille de chambre, but that he did so at the wrong time of day and with a girl for whom the hotel master did not pimp. A cleverer remedy (*tant mieux*) occurs to the hotel master—he will share in the profits of his guest's libido. So another grisset, this one on the payroll, enters the scene to sell Yorick some lace. Yorick agrees to see her, planning a kind of sneaky re-venge, but ends up paying her instead for what he might have us believe about his "other" relation with the fille de chambre: "I have only paid as many a poor soul has *paid* before me for an act he *could* not do, or think of" (p. 243).

A Sentimental Journey comes to its literal and inscriptive end with an encounter that sets the narrative journey in motion again toward another boundary as Yorick and a Piedmontese lady return the sexual stakes to parity. The lady requests a room at the inn when a boulder in the road between St. Michel and Madane prevents stage passage, and finds that she is unable to occupy that room because Yorick, on a first-come, first-served basis, had the "right to do the honours of it" (p. 286). The "gentleman would do anything to accommodate matters" (p. 286), says the innkeeper, which articulates the basis of sexual negotiation in the sentimental code, assuming negotiation has something substantial to settle. The result, after a sufficient amount of wine to stir the senses and a two-hour negotiation—it takes two hours for Yorick to do almost anything, perhaps because "it fares better with sentiments, not to be in a hurry with them" (p. 285)—produces a settlement fit for "posterity" (p. 288). Posterity, or a variant thereof, is precisely where it ends. All points are worked out but the sexiest one, how to undress, which Sterne prefers to leave to the reader less delicately trained for his particular fictional realm than he: "and that I leave to the reader to devise; protesting as I do it, that if it is not the most delicate in nature, 'tis the fault of his own imagination—against which this is not my first complaint" (pp. 289–90).

The final scene of *A Sentimental Journey* inverts the strategy of the novel's opening. There discourse initiated action; here action terminates discourse. Yorick, supposedly during sleep time (beyond the sentimental hour), is allowed no utterances in bed but prayer, though he moans an "O my God!" at the evening's titillating proximities. The lady, wide awake for the same reasons but still negotiating, claims a breach of both decorum and contract; Yorick insists his "ejaculation" is covered by the prayer clause in the contract. When corking pins start to fall from the contraption dividing the sleepless sleepers, Yorick's hand gropes toward its inevitable resting place; it meets, we must assume, the fille de chambre's voluminous "end," inserted for decorum's sake between the two sentimental travelers. Given Sterne's impulse to literalize proximity, the impulse that initiated his narrative crossing into France, one more mimetic matter is ordered by an impulsive gesture just before Yorick crosses out of France. Yorick and Sterne sign off, and the narrative motion and expatriate adventure are ended.

So that when I stretched out my hand, I caught hold of the *fille de chambre*'s

END OF VOL. II

CHAPTER FIVE

The Lone Exile: James's
The Ambassadors and *The American Scene*

"Pierced, betimes, by the sharp outland dart"

The transition from Laurence Sterne to Henry James is not as odd as it might seem. James, who in an early journey through France called himself a "sentimental traveller," writes of the visit to Paris by his fictional latecomer, Lambert Strether in *The Ambassadors:* "he has come so far through his total little experience that he has come out on the other side."[1] The kind of experience of which James speaks, as I have argued for Sterne's Parisian crossing, is rendered as much by the process of fiction as by its action; "the other side" is neither a complete narrative mystery nor a simple transcontinental romp, but an imaginative passage, a projection of the reality that supposedly inaugurates it. In that complex relation between novelistic mimesis—human events, activities, motives, manners, expressions, desires, fears—and the illusionistic space in which mimesis takes place, the notion of crossing to "the other side" literally perpetuates the metaphor that grants fiction its imaginative domain.

Late in *The Ambassadors* Maria Gostrey puts a question to Lambert Strether about his exilic crossing: " 'Where *is* your 'home' moreover now—what has become of it?' "[2] In their next conversation she asks the question again and then answers it: " 'To what do you go home?' " Strether responds, " 'I don't know. There will always be something.' 'To a great difference,' she said" (2:325). Maria means difference not merely in terms of the situation that awaits Strether in America but in terms of what has.penetrated and absorbed Strether's mind in Europe.

Difference is a form of illusion that James constantly portrays in his fiction and in his autobiographical and travel writing. In *The Middle Years,* he writes of a return to Europe (in this instance to England).

> Not to be denied also, over and above this, is the downright pleasure of the illusion yet again created, the *apparent* transfer from the past to the present of the particular combination of things that did at its hour ever so directly operate and that isn't after all then drained of virtue, wholly wasted and lost, for sensation, for participation in the act of life, in the attesting sights, sounds, smells, the illusion, as I say, of the recording senses.[3]

"Going again" provides a mimetic overlay to having gone before, just as returning to a difference becomes part of the experience of having left in the first place. In *The American Scene,* James speaks about what coming home means in terms of a different kind of illusion, a national romance.

> Nothing could be of a simpler and straighter logic: Europe had been romantic years before, because she was different from America; wherefore America would now be romantic because she was different from Europe. It was for this small syllogism then to meet, practically, the test of one's repatriation; and as the palpitating pilgrim disembarked, in truth, he had felt it, like the rifle of a keen sportsman, carried across his shoulder and ready of instant use.[4]

If exile enchants the ground of native territory, refamiliarization always writes its new romance. James is a pilgrim again—he does the land's history over. His return is an opportunity to confront territory made new and wild for its reinscription, something that seems to happen for James whenever Americans are on the move, going or coming. He even writes of the Europeanization of the American as "one's having been so pierced, betimes, by the sharp outland dart as to be able ever afterwards but to move about, vaguely and helplessly, with the shaft still in one's side" (*American Scene,* p. 223). In the preface to *The Ambassadors,* James sets up the scene of Strether's Parisian adventure with a similar image: "the *situation* clearly would spring from the play of wildness and the development of extremes" (1:xii). To approach territory anew as a rifled pilgrim, or bedarted exile, and seek from it deliverance is, in a way, to make it originary, whether upon the virgin shores of America or in the refined historical spaces of Paris. Of Strether's outland European mission, James writes that he was "launched in something of which the sense would be quite disconnected from the sense of his past and which was literally beginning there and then" (1:9).

In *The Ambassadors,* Lambert Strether goes to a Europe he had known just over a quarter century before; in *The American Scene,* James returns to an America after just under a quarter-century absence. Of his own exile from home James wrote that he considered himself a native of two continents and an outcast from both: "I saw, moreover, that I should be an eternal outsider."[5] At the same time, to move in any direction is to experience something of a homecoming. He writes of the beginning of his quarter-century European exile that by returning to the Paris of his youth he was "restored to air already breathed and to a harmony already disclosed."[6] To be in Paris for James is to increase the range of his sensations, to add to the present that exilic supplement he always carries, that "whole perfect Parisianism I seemed to myself always to have possessed mentally,"[7] a prospect not so different in its effect, though different in its timing, from that of Strether's in *The Ambassadors.*

To read *The Ambassadors* next to *The American Scene* is to get a special insight into the mind of the novelist, equal in many ways to the insights produced by the prefaces James provided for the novels themselves. *The American Scene* is the product of an admitted exilic consciousness—*Return of the Native* is the title James would have chosen had not Hardy already appropriated it. James's American return invites its own visionary record: "I was to return with much of the freshness of eye, outward and inward, which, with the further contribution of a state of desire, is commonly held a precious agent of perception" (p. xxv). The impulse is the same in the preface to *The Ambassadors* when James writes of Strether's experience in Paris: "The answer to which is that he now at all events *sees;* so that the business of my tale and the march of my action, not to say the precious moral of everything, is just my demonstration of this process of vision" (1:vi).

"Seeing" in *The American Scene,* as it does in all James's fiction, combines vision as the mimetic record of places, events, people, institutions, manners, and vision as the aesthetic record of formal comprehension extending beyond the mere incremental march or succession of things sighted. James claims he is "fresh" as an "inquiring stranger," and not so disoriented as to cease to see as an "initiated native" (p. xxv). His exilic bias grants him the privilege of fresh enchantments within familiar boundaries, grants him, that is, those special visionary coordinates on imaginatively primed ground. What is most intriguing about the way James "sees" in *The American Scene* is that his vision is comparative and double. For example, upon his return back to the East after he has been in the Far West, James reimposes the very kinds of distinctions he makes in his novels between America and Europe, just as he will later transpose similar distinctions to the temporal relation between the New North and the Old South. Coming back into New York State, James writes of

> the absurdest sense of meeting again a ripe old civilization and travelling through a country that showed the mark of established manners. It will seem, I fear, one's perpetual refrain, but the moral was yet once more that values of a certain order are, in such conditions, all relative, and that, as some wants of the spirits *must* somehow be met, one knocks together any substitute that will fairly stay the appetite. [p. 147]

The substitute supplies for the imagination what is wanted; James in this instance is not so much describing actual phenomena as creating those which he can then "see." When he does go south in *The American Scene,* he makes another substitution that has already appeared, under comparable imaginative circumstances, in *The Ambassadors.*

> On the one hand nothing could "say" more to the subject long expatriated, condemned by the terms of his exile to a chronic consciousness of

grey northern seas, than to feel how, from New York, or even from Boston, he had but to sit still in his portentous car [to become aware of] the gradual soft, the distinctively demoralized, conversion of the soul of Nature. This conversion, if I may so put it without profanity, has always struck me, on any southward course, as a return, on the part of that soul, from a comparatively grim Theistic faith to the ineradicable principle of Paganism; a conscious casting-off of the dread of theological abstraction—an abstraction still, even with all Puritan stiffening—in the interest of multiplied, lurking, familiar powers; divinities, graces, presences as unseen but as inherent as the scents clinging to the folds of Nature's robe. [pp. 303–04]

This passage, of course, recalls the moment in *The Ambassadors* when Strether senses something "Pagan" in the young man, Chad Newsome, transposed from a gray, stern, material New England to a relaxed, bright, sensual Paris: "What could there be in this for Strether but the hint of some self-respect, some sense of power, oddly perverted; something latent and beyond access, ominous and perhaps enviable? The intimation had the next thing, in a flash, taken on a name—a name on which our friend seized as he asked himself if he weren't perhaps really dealing with an irreducible young Pagan" (1:156–57). But there is in the move south for James in *The American Scene* something else that touches on the supplementary power of places in his fiction. As he moves even farther south through the Carolinas toward Florida, James writes: "Every breath that one might still have drawn in the South—might if twenty other matters had been different—haunted me as the thought of a lost treasure" (p. 461). The difference, of course, is the residue of slavery and the Civil War, but the airwaves of impressions James receives are like the impressions of an older Europe for James and for so many of his characters, impressions of history, of care, of texture, of scale. And the phrase, "a lost treasure," is one of those aesthetically material images that haunts James's imaginative sensibility from the artifacts in the *Spoils of Poynton* to the jewel of Paris in *The Ambassadors* to the eponymous *Golden Bowl*.

The Lone Exile

Powers Plenipotentiary

Exilic action, as Maria Gostrey implies, is the illusion, and perhaps even the pathos, of a "great difference." In this sense, the action of *The Ambassadors* portrays what James calls a disparity so complete between New England America and France as that "between a life led in trees, say, and a life led in sea depths, or in other words between that of climbers and swimmers—or (crudely) that of monkeys and fish."[8] James works the very notion of difference into the generic constituencies of the novel's plot. Consider the following narrative action:

> A new and aggrandizing culture to the west fulminates after one of its glorious products has been lured to a refined and ancient civilization somewhat to the east, whose energies reside more in present intensities than promised futurities. The action focuses on the last stages of an ongoing struggle, a stalemate almost, between the impatience of the newer culture and the wiles of the older. In a burst of energy the forces from the emergent culture resolve to retrieve their abducted prize even after it appears that the supposed victim has been transformed into a half-willing captive. The older civilization puts up a game display of its virtues before ultimately relinquishing both its abductee and its cause, though the precise moment of relinquishment has not yet arrived when the present action ceases.
>
> In the midst of the retrieval mission, the chief proponent for the emergent western culture undergoes a severe crisis of conscience, entertaining grave doubts about the values embodied, indeed, that he himself embodies, in perpetuating the cause of the forces that have marshaled him for the repatriation of its absconded human "property." Doubts concerning what might be called the grounds of the action become literal when the marshal for retrieval actually sets up dilatory residence in the alien land, shifting allegiance from the dominant will of the homefront to the ethos of the supposed antagonist culture. The original mission is, in a sense, fulfilled, but only at considerable cost to its participants, especially the waivering hero, who, toward the end of the action, seems no longer motivated by events as they occur sequentially, but experiences things, as it were, under revision, as if life has moved beyond that realm where destiny follows choice.

One more detail: the supposed victim from the west has been ensnared, and, in a way, captivated, by Paris.

Obviously, this narrative paradigm or mythos "belongs" to *The Ambassadors*. But in narrative legend Paris is as much a person as a place, and there is nothing in the sequence I have described that does not conform point for point to a plot as old as the dusty hills of Mycenae and the undulating plains of the Troas, the abduction of Helen by Paris that sets off the action of the Homeric *Iliad*. The renegade victim from the emergent West is male in James's case, Chad Newsome of Woollett, Massachusetts. Chad, whose epithet for himself at one point is "the lone exile" (2:32), finds that he has been made over by Paris just as Helen of Troy, loved by Paris, temporarily gives up the role of Spartan *hausfrau* to take on, as femme fatale, the name of the rival city and culture that most elegantly displays her.[9] Both exiles become, in a sense, voluntary; they cross to a zone of opportunity that readily serves as a metaphoric space for the state of their altered consciousnesses.

The idea of the transforming space is an enduring one in imaginative literature, especially if attendant upon its occupation is the cultural rupture that occurs when different civilizations or societies seem to want to "time" things in different ways, when marvelous but spent civilizations try to give pause to the orders that will efface them. For James, Paris is the same lure and threat to the ethos of America that Troy was for the Greeks. Paris is otherness, and for those who do not have it in their blood or being to acclimatize to it, it is even further "other" than its location in the west of Europe. The tricks of metaphoric analogy and the transports of epic memory project James's scene farther east and farther back into a forbidden and lustful past. Paris is "the vast bright Babylon" (1:89) that sustains the notion of the overrefined, alluring place where the material, enterprising world can be, at least, well lost.

As the brightest jewel of Catholic Europe, Paris evokes in its Babylonian image the traditional Protestant horror of the city as Church, the old temptress herself, the Whore of Babylon; and when

James begins the second half of his novel, the program for European salvation, in the very confines of Notre Dame Cathedral, the scene calls up a passage from the earlier sequence in the old feudal city of Chester: "The Catholic Church for Waymarsh—that was to say the enemy, the monster of bulging eyes and far-reaching quivering groping tentacles—was exactly society, exactly the multiplication of shibboleths, exactly the discrimination of types and tones, exactly the wicked old Rows of Chester, rank with feudalism; exactly in short Europe" (1:41).

Strether, through the course of the novel, finds himself estranged from Waymarsh and the new American mission when he discovers himself on Paris's side. There is something there "more acute in manners, more sinister in morals, more fierce in the national life," and he later finds himself, he was "amused to think, on the side of the fierce, the sinister, the acute" (2:271). The best place for him in Paris is, indeed, the apartment of its most alluring temptress, Madame de Vionnet, who seems to have just the right collection of things to reflect a lost epic order that made up a "vista, which he found high melancholy and sweet—full, once more, of dim historic shades, of the faint far-away cannon-roar of the great Empire" (2:125).[10] As James writes of Strether in his "Project" for *The Ambassadors,* Madame de Vionnet "gratifies some more distinctively disinterested aesthetic, intellectual, social, even, so to speak, historic sense in him" (p. 392). Her Paris for Strether is, in a certain sense, comparable to what James in *The American Scene* calls "the epic age" (p. 383) of the Old South, beset, if not by Baron von Haussmann's city planners, then by northern carpetbaggers who pillage a land, after its four epic years, "disinherited of art or of letters" (p. 386).[11]

In his eulogy for James, Ezra Pound recognized the epic, national proportions of many of the novels: "In his books he showed race against race, immutable; the essential Americanness, or Englishness or Frenchness—in *The American,* the difference between one nation and another; not flag-waving and treaties, not the machinery of government, but 'why' there is always misunderstanding, why men of different race are not the same."[12] Though in *The Ambassadors* James sets his novel's epic proportions deliberately and arranges them with considerable force, the result is not an array of structural parallels in the manner, say, of Joyce's absorption of the Homeric *Odyssey* into *Ulysses* but a model for action that conforms to the comparison James draws himself to *Antony and Cleopatra,* a play that with a few adjustments mirrors the identical exilic plot: Egypt is to Rome what Troy is to Greece what Europe is to America. [13]

The larger *casus belli* of such a plot always stems from the alienation of native affection and the rage that alienation inspires. Strether and his friend Waymarsh starkly frame the situation for *The Ambassadors* in reference to Chad's fellow exile, the young American Little Bilham: " 'Why don't he go home?' " asks Waymarsh. " 'Well, because he likes it over here' " (1:108), answers Strether. A similar question might be asked and a similar answer rendered for Helen of Sparta and Antony of Rome, be they in Troy or Alexandria: " 'Why don't they go home?' 'Well, because they like it over here.' "

There is, of course, more to what Richard Blackmur, in a nice phrase, calls the "sensitized deep form" [14] of *The Ambassadors* than the rudiments of its international epic plotting. As James wrote of his novel to Hugh Walpole, "it *is* probably a very *packed* production, with a good deal of one thing within another." [15] Much has been written about these "things," about James's refinement of novelistic language, about his scenic richness, about his conversant intellect, about his portrayal of well-imagined and imagining beings. But even if for the moment we limit matters to the realm of plot, *The Ambassadors* comes more firmly packed than I have so far suggested. For example, James enfolds another classically derived action within the exilic adventure. Consider the following:

A family scion prompted by desires of an initiatory nature, predominantly sexual, finds himself in conflict with obligations that are of a familial and financial nature. He strives to achieve a balance between promptings and obligations that will allow him his moment in the sun, his prime time, before resumption of conventional responsibilities. During the interval of readjustment, an older male delegate, materially aligned with the family interests, finds himself exposed to a world of charged sensibilities. He moves from the brink of male menopause to the brink of sexual infatuation. Forces from and of the family seek to rescue both scion and *senex* advisor from the lure of prompting enticements. Both rescuers and enticers gauge the best strategic means to negotiate and compromise so that most may be gained or least be lost. Actors and actresses in this scenario act or do not act in relation to benefits that in one way or another accrue to their credit or discredit in both a material and ethical sense.

I have described, very roughly, a pattern of action generally applicable to *The Ambassadors* that is also a standard variant of comic plotting available from Greek new comedy to contemporary jet set farce. Chad Newsome is the young, wayward scion; Lambert Strether a "belated" (1:xiii) *senex* adventurer and convert.[16] The intricate and calculated way James combines his comic and epic plots is one of the glories of *The Ambassadors*. The diagram below outlines the relation of the parts to the generic whole.

Comic Mission

Book I American Dispensation: Mrs. Newsome of Woollett; Strether's arrival in Europe as agent for Chad's return

Book II Arrival of primary Ambassador (Strether) on Parisian scene

Book III Strether and surrogate American: Little Bilham in Chad's apartment

Book IV Crucial negotiation with Chad for his American return

Book V Gloriani's garden epiphany (first "super-sensual hour")

Book VI Strether's first promise to Madame de Vionnet ("I'll save you if I can")

A legitimate question to ask of James's venturings into epic and comic plots is what appeal would such schemes have for him? And part of an answer involves his understanding of what might be called the concentric pressures operating on individual characters in distinction to the eccentric appeal of the exilic or international imagination. But these pressures and appeals are difficult to separate, and James's adaptation of traditional plots, melding nationally and socially determined obligations with the finer tuning of individual consciousnesses, gives his work real dimension. T. S. Eliot remarked that James's characters are constituents of a greater social entity, which can be more or less true of any fiction but which is surely true of action on the scale James presents it. [17] Thus the intensely personal and complex drive to absorb qualities one lacks or discard qualities one abhors is often frustrated by defenses and loyalties that one carries as part of a national baggage. It is as Ralph Touchett says in *Portrait of a Lady:* "Ah, one doesn't give up one's country any more than one gives up

Epic Salvation

Book VII   European Dispensation: Notre Dame of Paris; Strether as agent for postponement of Chad's return

Book VIII   Arrival of secondary Ambassador (Sarah Pocock) on Parisian scene

Book IX   Strether and surrogate American: Mamie Pocock in Sarah's hotel

Book X   Crucial negotiation with Sarah for Chad's remaining in Europe

Book XI   Rural seat epiphany (second "super-sensual hour")

Book XII   Strether's second promise to Madame de Vionnet that he will ask Chad "never to forsake her" one's grandmother. They're both antecedent to choice, elements of one's composition that are not to be eliminated" (1:125).

Cross-Purposes

Initially, Strether has two jobs to do in America's cause, neither of which is very subtle but both of which are empowered by his portfolio as Ambassador from Woollett. Strether is reminded of his national burden when he sees his friend Waymarsh, a Connecticut Yankee in the west of Queen Victoria's realm. Strether, "for his part, felt once more like Woollett in person" (1:29). His first job is to present the details of his mission to Chad, the business proposition that Mrs. Newsome offers her son in regard to taking on the advertising department of the home enterprise, what James, emphasizing his version of progressive America, calls in the "Project" for the novel "the bustling business at home, the mercantile mandate, the counter, the ledger, the bank, the 'advertising interest,' [all of which] embody mainly the special phase of civilization to which he must recall his charge" (p. 396). Strether's second job is not to have his first fail to take effect; that is, he must not only inform Chad but reform his exilic propensities, return him to the native material fold. The payoff for Strether is Mrs. Newsome's hand in marriage.

Strether's American mission, the ostensible purpose for his crossing, is tied to the letter of economic and familial law, but it was only after he performed its first part, laying the ledger on the table, that he began to realize that the second part of his mission, making it work, had much less to do with the possibility of his failing Mrs. Newsome at home than with betraying his new international self. The fact that Strether considered himself "a perfectly equipped failure" (1:44) in America is precisely what Mrs. Newsome counted on to ensure against his failing her in Europe. But ambassadors exist so that they might make compromises, and the question for Strether is what kind of compromises he has already made and what kind he can afford to keep making.

Strether begins with good intentions toward his American mission. He wishes to get matters over with quickly, virtually blurting out his demands—a middle-aged "now see here!"—to a polite Chad. James calls Strether's quick pitch a "night-attack" (1:143), which is efficient but not very ceremonious.[18] Later, Strether's much vaguer but more compelling commitment to save Madame de Vionnet requires, if nothing else, time to contemplate options. The buying of time against the enterprise of repatriation is represented in the figuration E. M. Forster projected as the novel's hourglass pattern, and the figure is wonderfully descriptive of action as temporal purchase. Strether no longer serves as the material agent for a family factory, but as a barterer for Europe's historical, epochal, and epic time, the slow, steady accretions of what culture needs to save itself. It is in this sense that the quality of the European experience alters everything for him, makes him imaginatively exilic. His situation in Paris is not altogether different, at least structurally, from the prototypical temporizing epic *salvator,* Achilles, whose refusal to act on behalf of the aggrieved home forces in the *Iliad* seems vaguely echoed in *The Ambassadors* when Strether says of himself " 'the hero has taken refuge in his corner. He's scared at his heroism—he shrinks from his part' " (2:179). Wronged families always want action; individual conscience takes time. Achilles sulks and makes of his tent a little Troy; Strether stalls and forces the home front to dispatch a second wave of ambassadors joined by Waymarsh as a kind of Agamemnon.

Strether's subtle shift in allegiances when "exposed to the action of another air" (1:xii) is his special fate—it singles him out like Achilles, like Antony, as he will learn when the second, more loyal, more national ambassadorial mission, headed by the matriarchal surrogate, Sarah Pocock, arrives to consider whether it is even worthwhile to bother retrieving *him.* Some Americans, like Waymarsh, are homeward bound in whatever direction they move; others are more comfortably exposed to "another air." In the conflict of cultural values that makes up the implicit action of the novel, Maria Gostrey acts to repatriate Americans who deserve it and to provide a European

itinerary for those who have the capacity to appreciate the "outland";
she is an agent of the border police against interlopers: "I'm—with
all my other functions—an agent for repatriation. I want to re-people
our stricken country. What will become of it else? I want to discour-
age others" (1:36).

Strether, even at the beginning of his European experience, is
intrigued by what he calls, picking up a mock-epic cadence, "the
enemy's country" (1:163). In a conversation with Maria, he begins to
doubt what it means to be a "good American." He complains before
he knows what he intends: " 'Oh hang it,' " and we hear immediately:
"It represented, this mute ejaculation, a final impulse to burn his
ships. These ships, to the historic muse, may seem of course mere
cockles, but when he presently spoke to Miss Gostrey it was with the
sense at least of applying the torch. 'Is it then a conspiracy?' " (1:132–
33). If so, it is a conspiracy at the expense of America, balanced
cleverly by James in the comic plot when Waymarsh conspires with
America against an increasingly Europeanized Strether. As Strether
moves through Europe by moving from Maria Gostrey to Madame de
Vionnet, his friend Waymarsh gets re-Americanized by deserting
Miss Barrace for the new American ambassador, Sarah Pocock. Exile
is a *chiasmus* or narrative crossing.

It is precisely when the other or "alien" race gets under Strether's
distinctly American skin in *The Ambassadors* that the complex and
imaginatively textured European experience has the effect of reducing
his perceived social, indeed, racial obligations to America and to the
values James sees as nationally disposed. On the other hand, James,
by his own testimony in the preface to his eponymously titled *The
American,* embarked on an enterprise in which he realized that his
fiction still staked its American claim in the very teeth of its greater
European resource. James's dilemma was equivalent in some ways to
that of Maria Gostrey as go-between in *The Ambassadors* when she
says: " 'I bear on my back the huge load of our national consciousness,
or, in other words—for it comes to that—of our nation itself' "
(1:18). [19]

Since consciousness is actionable in James's fiction, it is clear that

James's American load, like Maria's, is one that he might be tempted, at any given time, to jettison, but could not, for various reasons, manage to do. Many of his characters, including Strether, operate under the same strain.[20] James makes this clear early and late in *The Ambassadors*. He writes in the preface that the most notable thing about Strether is his nationality: "Possessed of our friend's nationality, to start with, there was a general probability in his narrower localism; which, for that matter, one had really but to keep under the lens for an hour to see it give up its secrets" (1:xi). Strether's nature and his localism bespeak New England denial, which makes for a natural conflict when the sexual juices of the plot begin to flow and the resonances of the international theme begin to sound. When Maria Gostrey senses that in his walk with her he is indulging in something he does not think right, Strether concludes that he must be displaying enjoyment. She describes his reluctance to enjoy himself as his failure; he attributes it to " 'the failure of Woollett. *That's* general' " (1:16). Though he is capable of joking about it, Strether still takes a kind of pride in his localism even later in the novel. It is not so much his American citizenship he gives up as the credentials for the particular ambassadorial mission upon which he was "launched." He says to Little Bilham in regard to his admiration for Mamie Pocock: " 'I've been sacrificing so to strange gods that I feel I want to put on record, somehow, my fidelity—fundamentally unchanged after all—to our own' " (2:167).

This tension that marks the design of the novel, its local obligations and international longings, seems confirmed with Strether's first understanding of Chad's Parisian liaison, an understanding not as mistaken as his second concerning its virtuousness: "Was there in Chad, by chance, after all, deep down, a principle of aboriginal loyalty that had made him, for sentimental ends, attach himself to elements, happily encountered, that would remind him most of the old air and the old soil?" (1:213). There is an interplay of phrasings in *The Ambassadors* that identifies American contingents whatever Europeanized values they might imbibe. At one point while Strether is struggling over the issue of just exactly what happens to the American consciousness saturated in the splendors of Europe, Maria Gostrey says of the most dandified of the Americans, Little Bilham, the very object of Strether's plea in Gloriani's garden for that Pagan intensity presumably missing in America, " 'Oh he's all right. He's one of *us!*' " (1:125), meaning that he, like them, is an American, pierced by the outland dart, but, also, that he, like them, is simply American. Later, Chad uses the same phrase of himself, " 'Oh I'm all right!' " (1:161) to suggest that he has lost the sense of neither his origins nor his obligations. In *The American Scene,* when James worries about the character of America and the state of its progressivism, he hears the voice of the Demos, the spirit that makes the people and the land "different" in ways that Europe will never know. America is an "enormous family of rugged, of almost ragged, rustics—a tribe of sons and daughters too numerous to be counted and homogeneous perhaps to monotony." James's own response picks up the very idiom of the place: "Oh, the *land's* all right!" (p. 20). Americans can never go entirely wrong because they are vague about their deficiencies. The surface their imaginations rarely penetrate is an amiable one; the despondency of cultural paralysis is "foreign" to them. Chad in his person makes this argument for *The Ambassadors,* and what James says in *The American Scene* about the amiability of the American rich applies to the young Mr. Newsome: "The amiability proceeds from an essential vagueness; whereas real haughtiness is never vague about itself—it is only vague about others" (p. 115).

Matriarchy and the Wash of Gold

It is of great importance to *The Ambassadors* that so much of its represented action is controlled by an unrepresented figure, Mrs. Newsome, who sits invisibly powerful at home, judging, in a sense, all that goes on abroad. Strether begins, as he later notes of Jim Pocock, by serving "essentially a society of women" (2:83); he takes his marching orders, as Maria Gostrey puts it, in such a way as to receive " 'at the point of the bayonet a whole moral and intellectual being or block' " (2:239). When he lingers too long in Europe, supposedly in the swim with Madame de Vionnet, whose commerce with Strether, negotiated almost spiritually from the Cathedral of Notre Dame, seems to Sarah Pocock "hideous" (2:205), Sarah asks, " 'what is your conduct but an outrage to women like *us?* ' " (2:199).

The sets of differences that mark Americans and Europeans are located, for the most part, in images of women, who, like the controlling deities of the *Iliad*, are influential, determinate, and national. If the *Iliad* has its stern, unattached Athena behind the Greek cause and the wife-goddess Hera behind the Trojan, *The Ambassadors* boasts of Mrs. Newsome, the ever-absent, ever-present doyenne of the American factory, and, on the Continental side, Marie de Vionnet, with the image of the Catholic Mary, Notre Dame, in the background. Strether's switch in allegiances from the "moral swell" of Woollett to the "pathos" of Madame de Vionnet determines the fate of his consciousness: "It marked for himself the flight of time, or at any rate what he was pleased to think of with irony and pity as the rush of experience; it having been but the day before yesterday that he sat at her feet and held on by her garment and was fed by her hand. It was the proportions that were changed, and the proportions were at all times, he philosophised, the very conditions of perception, the terms of thought" (2:48–49). National and social proportions turn to aesthetic ones, the projection or the "performance of 'Europe' " (2:105). Utility gives way to intensity. Actresses such as Madame de Vionnet play Cleopatra or, more affecting yet, the deserted Dido of the *Aeneid*.

In Europe, as Chad's experience and, subsequently, Strether's bear out, women tend not to negotiate from positions of familial power but to persuade as the transmitters, the molders of behavior that is "wonderful," as Miss Barrace keeps putting it, that is culturally and perhaps even sexually awesome. In *The American Scene*, James distinguishes between the American and the European woman: "she had been grown in an air in which a hundred of the 'European' complications and dangers didn't exist" (p. 348). The American woman is, for James, the very symbol of utility in an aggrandizing social economy. In *The Ambassadors*, Waymarsh says of Mamie Pocock, " 'her full beauty is only for those who know how to make use of her' " (2:107), and in *The American Scene* James says of the American woman: "It has been found among them that, for more reasons than we can now go into, her manner of embodying and representing her sex has fairly made of her a new human convenience, not unlike fifty of the others, of a slightly different order, the ingenious mechanical appliances, stoves, refrigerators, sewing-machines, type-writers, cash-registers, that have done so much, in the household and the place of business, for the American name" (p. 347). When Strether refuses to identify the utilitarian item of Woollett manufacture in *The Ambassadors* marketed by the factory presently controlled by the will, if not the effort, of Mrs. Newsome, it may be because he doesn't have to. The item is the "new convenience" of American matriarchy.

In the larger view of the action, Strether's delay in rescuing Chad Newsome becomes a political or ideological affront, an assault on the matriarchal home front. And the politics might even be conceived as internecine even if, and when, the absconded American heir returns home and struggles with his sister for the future. As Chad says of Sarah's probable motives, she wants him in her own American sphere because "'when you hate you want to triumph, and if she should get me neatly stuck there she *would* triumph'" (2:221). American battles are fought in different ways and on different turf than exilic ones in a European theater.

Chad's European performance, and soon Strether's, are anathema to the new set of American representatives in France, led by the family's vice-regent, Sarah Pocock, who seems to prefer events like the circus to the theatrical or salon life of Paris. Hers is the arena of the Demos. When James analyzed the features of the American family in *The American Scene,* he sensed a certain arriviste quality: "family life is in fact, as from child to parent, from sister to brother, from wife to husband, from employed to employer, the eminent field of the democratic demonstration" (p. 325). For James the "active Family" is "a final social fact," the People, he calls them, who enjoy every easy convenience of being American.

> That's their interest—that they *are* the people; for what interest, under the sun, would they have if they weren't? They are the people 'arrived,'

and, what is more, disembarked: that's all the difference. It seems a difference because elsewhere (in 'Europe,' say again), though we see them begin, at the very most, to arrive, socially, we yet practically see them still on the ship—we have never yet seen them disembark thus *en masse*. [p. 327]

It is almost as if James in this passage from a book describing his return home to America remembered the American arriviste family of *The Ambassadors* depositing itself on the shores of an older, refined European civilization.[21]

Family democracy, the source of the comic enterprise in *The Ambassadors,* runs completely counter to the image of the imperial European lure who so intrigues first Chad and then Strether in the figure of Madame de Vionnet. Marie's effort is, finally, anti-American; she seeks to hold for the present what has been her past. About the future she is almost inarticulate. One of James's complaints against the newness of America in *The American Scene* is the land's perpetual repudiation of the past, "so far as there had been a past to repudiate" (p. 53). James's distrust of the speed of American production plays upon a different sense of "production," an imaginative and aesthetic one: "There we catch the golden truth which so much of the American world strikes us as positively organized to gainsay, the truth that production takes time, and that the production of interest, in particular, takes *most* time" (p. 153).

In *The American Scene,* time is money, and it cannot buy European experience: "expensive as we are, we have nothing to do with continuity, responsibility, transmission, and don't in the least care about what becomes of us after we have served our present purpose" (p. 11). James does not condemn the existence of money so much as wonder at what it purchases—what connection expense has to value as the basis for America's "accommodation of life."

This basis is that of active pecuniary gain and of active pecuniary gain only—that of one's making the conditions so triumphantly pay that the prices, the manners, the other inconveniences, take their place as a friction it is comparatively easy to salve, wounds directly treatable with the wash of gold. What prevails, what sets the tune, is the

American scale of gain, more magnificent than any other, and the fact that the whole assumption, the whole theory of life, is that of the individual's participation in it, that of his being more or less punctually and more or less effectually "squared." To make so much money that you won't, that you don't "mind," don't mind anything—that is absolutely, I think, the main American formula. [pp. 236–37]

The best trick in James's anti–Gilded Age rhetoric here is the set of quotation marks around "mind," as if the lack of caring is also the lack of thinking, a notion perhaps behind Strether's wish at the beginning of *The Ambassadors* that his old friend Waymarsh, "the exile from Milrose" (1:49), would not be the first "note" of Europe for him. Waymarsh, who goes through Europe on the forward incline, sees his exilic experience as a conspiracy to keep him away from newspapers, "an elaborate engine for dissociating the confined American from that indispensable knowledge" (1:78), which rendered him his sense of an established order. Progressive, future-rendering America needs "new" information; it does not thrive on what constitutes tradition. The real old Europe belongs to that lost historical sense that Madame de Vionnet represents for Strether—a Europe of refinement and almost forlorn vestigiality. In Paris he feels "odd starts of the historic sense, suppositions and divinations with no warrant but their intensity" (2:274).

When Strether first arrives in Europe he is still enmeshed in a system of values that turns on money. He cannot quite understand what Maria Gostrey means when she says that she doesn't "do" Europe with American travelers for money but for national necessity. Bewildered, Strether responds: " 'You can scarcely be said to do it for love.' He waited a moment. 'How do we reward you?' " " 'You don't!' " (1:18), returns Maria. It is as if Strether has not yet seen that the European venture will involve something other than cash flow, that it will involve the separation of his pleasure from the financial and social ordinance that supports it. In a telling Jamesian figure that reinforces the impending abandonment of the American mission, Strether seems glad at the prospect of some free time in England before encountering Waymarsh: "he was like a man who, elatedly finding in his pocket more money than usual, handles it a while and idly and pleasantly chinks it before addressing himself to the business of spending" (1:5). Paradoxically, the more he spends toward "change," the less he will rely on his substantial American line of credit. Indeed, Strether uses the phrase "disinherited beyond appeal" (2:144) for the latter stages of his deteriorating relations with Mrs. Newsome.

When Strether stops hearing from Mrs. Newsome entirely, he loses his credit but gains validity, a more imaginative resource. This makes an earlier discussion between Strether and Maria Gostrey of great interest. Strether says of Mrs. Newsome that she is high-strung, nervous. Maria puts it epigrammatically: " 'You mean she's an American invalid?' " (1:57). Strether says he would not put it quite that way, but she is American to the core and would consent to being, in a sense, *invalid,* to remain an American. The substance of what happens in the novel turns on Strether's invalidation of the material mission in order to appreciate, in all senses of the word, the European supplement.²² He faces with equanimity what Chad calls the sharpest of sharp facts about his predicament: " 'you give up money. Possibly a good deal of money' " (2:220). To do so is to give up, as exile, one version of America.

Meanwhile, Chad, whom Strether on Marie's behalf begs to remain in Europe, takes up on his own behalf the American material obligation. As Little Bilham puts it, Chad "has his possible future before him" (1:285). Sooner or later he will terminate his exilic adventure and go home. His language reveals the direction in which he points: " 'But I'm coming around—I'm not so bad now' " (1:157). Chad comes around to America and to an American idiom; he uses "bad" as his sister might use it, as the uxorious Jim Pocock might use it, as the American Family entire might use it in relation to Europe. To be able to use the word that way is to have made the American circuit. And Strether does not remain oblivious to the turning force of egoism in Chad, the certainty that no matter what else happens he will act as is best for him, which is to say best for him as an American. James can be devastating on Chad when the mood strikes him, and his language picks up the metaphor of turnarounds that so marks the action and the novel's plot: "Chad was always letting people have their way when he felt that it would somehow turn his wheel for him" (2:278).

Coming Out

Chad's readiness at the end of *The Ambassadors* to leave the place that initiated him may resolve the conventional comic plot of the novel but leaves the international one in arrears. Strether much prefers his first impression of Chad, his first startling image of what might happen in the exilic place. Europe has made Chad anew, almost completely refashioned him, at least to Strether's eyes: "Chad had been made over. That was all; whatever it was it was everything. Strether had never seen the thing so done before—it was perhaps a speciality of Paris" (1:150). This sort of initiatory scene has always been a part of Western civilization ever since the Renaissance invention of the grand tour. When James writes in *The Middle Years* of his own return to Paris in the 1870s he remembers what the original crossing meant to him, a memory that appears to partake of both Chad's and Strether's European experience, with its metaphors of sexual *tristesse* as well as "quickening" glory.

> To return at all across the years to the gates of the paradise of the first larger initiations is to be ever so tempted to pass them, to push in again and breathe the air of this, that and the other plot of rising ground particularly associated, for memory and gratitude, with the quickening process. The trouble is that with these sacred spots, to later appreciation, the garden of youth is apt inordinately to bristle, and that one's account of them has to shake them together fairly hard, making a coherent thing of them, to profit by the contribution of each. [pp. 9–10]

The imaginative and sexual quickening is a process that Strether is slower than Chad or, for that matter, than James to register.[23] This is so even after Strether attributes to Madame de Vionnet Chad's transformation in Paris: "he had created for himself a new set of circumstances" (2:93–94). Little specific is either said or meant, partly because Strether avoids some of the obvious details, but what is always implied, in addition to the imposition of a smoother texture over a rougher native surface, is sexual familiarity. Maria Gostrey says of Chad that "'two quite distinct things that—given the wonderful place he's in—may have happened to him. One is that he may have got brutalised. The other is that he may have got refined'"(1:69). What Maria really means to say is that *one* thing may have happened to Chad, but that one thing strikes particular viewers in *two* ways. It is when Strether begins to understand that the notion of brutalization is not really possible except to an aggrieved American mind that allegiances begin to shift. Brutalized could mean, in another context, libertinized or, as Strether says himself, "Paganized." He would have done well to have kept that possibility—even if differently conceived—in mind; it would have saved him some sexual surprises. Of refinement there could be no doubt in Chad's case, though even here James makes it clear—and Strether sees this only later—that Chad never abandons his rougher American egoism. He has merely learned to display himself with more skill during his Parisian hiatus. From a literal course in painting, he had graduated to what James calls "initiations more direct and more deep" (1:92). Initiations are part of the exilic experience narrative creates and records.

What Strether sees in Chad, of course, is what James primes him to see as part of his own narrative adventure, a "transformation unsurpassed" (1:137). Chad has experienced the "rupture of an identity," and what Strether says of him might be what he belatedly desires for himself and what generally takes place in the fictional invention of mimetic being: "You could deal with a man as himself—you couldn't deal with him as somebody else" (1:137). The somebody else Strether envisages in Chad is a version of the somebody else Strether might have been. Strether later comes to realize that he has invested too much in Chad's newer consciousness without admitting its sexual implications for himself, a bad investment in that when Chad tries to assuage his accumulating guilt for readying to leave Marie, Strether has to assume the full debt with only a recent comprehension of its total nature.

One of the calculated ironies of *The Ambassadors* is that Chad tends to clear out of town just as Strether, in one way or another, moves in. This pattern occurs often enough in the novel to make one think that more than social spaces are negotiated; Chad seems to be giving everything over, including the image of the place and the woman who performs the initiating rites. Chad's American career promises a future in advertising, and his first advertising campaign is the selling of his options in Marie de Vionnet to Strether. Chad virtually offers her to Strether at their first introduction in Gloriani's garden, and when he leaves town toward the end of the novel, he does so to leave Strether alone with Marie, adding later an excuse about picking up "some news of the art of advertisement" (2:315) in London. But, of course, Chad gives Strether only the "performance" of Madame de Vionnet; her person he keeps for himself. She is a European supplement that ought not place too severe a tax on Strether's developing imagination. Maria keeps warning Strether—she tells him that Chad is not free and assumes Strether knows what she's talking about. The same is true about Little Bilham's famous description of the affair as a "virtuous attachment" (1:180). Little Bilham means it is neither debilitating nor vulgar. Strether wishes it to mean *innocent*, which is precisely the word he uses later.

But this is to pick up Strether's own initiatory path somewhat down the road. If we look to his and Maria Gostrey's recollection of how Strether started, we can begin closer to the beginning and mark the initiation ceremony, both spatial and sexual, that still interests the two of them at the end of the novel, "the curiosity felt by both of them as to where he would 'come out.' They had so assumed it was to be in some wonderful place—they had thought of it as so very *much* out. Well, that was doubtless what it had been—since he had come out just there. He was out, in truth, as far as it was possible to be, and must now rather bethink himself of getting in again" (2:321–22).

Strether begins his exilic progress as a "belated" (1:xiii) adventurer, a trait he never quite loses: "he was for ever missing things through his general genius for missing them" (2:185). Strether says of himself, " 'I don't get drunk; I don't pursue the ladies; I don't spend money; I don't even write sonnets. But nevertheless I'm making up late for what I didn't have early'" (2:50–51). He is always a little vague as to exactly what it is he is trying to make up: "what I want is a thing I've ceased to measure or even to understand" (2:233). What he does do is register an almost continuous sense of difference and contrast: what he wants is what he lacks. Maria Gostrey senses as much immediately. She is more than Strether's "guide" to Europe, his Baedecker of civilized consciousness. She is also the pattern for a different kind of indulgence of the immediate, something that Strether never quite practices but comes around to expressing during the key scene in Gloriani's garden. Maria Gostrey is what Strether isn't; she has those "qualities and quantities that collectively figured to him as the advantage snatched from lucky chances" (1:9).

Strether is an unlikely participant in the drama that is about to beset him, and if, as Miss Barrace says, he is supposed to perform in it as "'the hero,'" he shrinks from the action that might make it momentous for him, sexual choice. In the "Project" for the novel, James says he did not want to represent every woman in the book to have "made up" to his hero (p. 414), nor would he solve any narrative problem with a purely sexual choice in Strether's case, though he was not above complicating the narrative texture with sexual intrusions. James does admit, however, that he allows most of the women in the novel to appear agreeably affected by Strether. Strether does not seem all that grateful. When Madame de Vionnet says in public that all women love Strether, he assumes that "to say such things to a man in public, a woman must practically think of him as ninety years old" (2:102). The fact is, despite his stirrings of new youth, that is the way he thinks of himself. There is, and could be, a large sexual component acted out in Strether's part, but James resists forcing his actor to act it. Strether prefers separating his imaginative ecstasies from his sexual latencies. The best he can do is feel his blood stir in the company of Parisian power. He equates place and fate as if something is bound to happen because Paris, especially old Paris, is the revolutionary arena with its "smell of revolution, the smell of the public temper—or perhaps simply the smell of blood" (2:274). Strether's reference to the revolutionary Paris comports with his own rebellion from the clutches of Woollett, and the smell of blood, no matter how it flows, is for him the sign of vitality lacking in the "secret" repression of his New England "prison-house" (1:66).

The strength of James's decision not to have Strether consciously traffic in sexual matters is tested by the opportunities the novel provides him with two women with variants of the same name, Maria and Marie. He militantly misses twice, even feeling uneasy at the challenge: "he had a horror, as he now thought of himself, of being in question between women" (1:273). The irony of this situation mirrors part of the novel's chiastic structure: "it was others who looked abstemious and he who looked greedy; it was he somehow who finally paid, and it was others who mainly partook" (2:186). It is not as if there are no full experiences for Strether in Paris, but he sees the fullest, Marie de Vionnet, more as an aesthetic and historical artifact than as the possessed Dido she appears at the end. Surely, Strether does not understand that for the likes of Dido or Helen of Troy or, indeed, Cleopatra, to whom he directly compares Marie, aesthetics and sexuality are indistinguishable.

Strether's reaction is not so much to proclaim the separation of aesthetic appreciation and physical desire as to ignore the intricacies of the combination. His reaction to any one piece of life's puzzle that confronts him in Europe during the few months of his mission is that it is too confusedly connected to the whole of the impression to make any distinct sense: "'I can't separate—it's all one'" (2:233). Two things can be said about such a view. First, the experience is really imaginative and aesthetic and, as such, must be taken whole; and second, the experience is intensely sexual and any concentration on one of its parts would reveal the single piece of the puzzle upon which Strether resists focusing until it is forced upon him. Then he considers it a catastrophe. James as artist knows more than Strether admits as hero about the state of his frustration. In the "Project" for *The Ambassadors*, James carefully chooses a word that has both aesthetic and sexual connotations in reference to Strether: "disenchanted without having known any great enchantments, enchanters, or, above all, enchantresses" (p. 375). James recognizes that one basis of failure in life, as it was in his famous story, "The Beast in the Jungle," is missed sexual opportunity. Maria Gostrey asks a blunt question of Strether about Marie de Vionnet: " 'Are you really in love with her?' " Strether offers the bizarre answer: " 'It's of no importance I should know . . . It matters so little—has nothing to do, practically, with either of us' " (2:228). But, to be fair to Strether, James is not entirely certain how gained sexual opportunity transfers from private circumstance to the integrity of the imagination.

Parisian Supplements

Strether's resistance to what James in all his international novels advertises as a key ingredient of the exilic adventure leads to an initiatory scene that is itself belated in *The Ambassadors,* coming as it does so near the end of the action, the scene of the rural retreat when Strether witnesses evidence of the liaison whose likelihood he had so long denied. Ironically, his own intimacies with Madame de Vionnet made others think he was "as much in the swim [with her] as anybody else" (2:272), and long before the country scene, Strether says of Madame de Vionnet that "she thus publicly drew him into her boat" (2:94). He uses the metaphor as an analogue for his passionate interest in her case—though even he is not exactly sure where the passion lies—but his language also suggests a switch from his transatlantic mission to an inland waterway: "He took up an oar and, since he was to have the credit of pulling, pulled" (2:94–95). The credit he loses after wasting the price of Mrs. Newsome's steamship ticket he assumes from Madame de Vionnet's rowboat. Sarah and Waymarsh naturally see him as "launched in a relation," though Strether protests that he "had never really been launched at all" (2:94). The metaphor builds to its finest irony in the rural scene when Strether discovers for certain that the sexual relationship between Chad and Marie de Vionnet is neither virtuous in his sense of it nor innocent in anyone's. He discovers the lovers rowing in a small boat, or, to put it another way, he discovers how embarrassing it is to think one's self in someone's boat when another already occupies the only vacant seat.

Strether's own reverie-like metaphor for the day of the country retreat places him in the midst of a landscape painting that he remembers he would have liked to purchase. And the image of the small boat coming around the bend in the river provides a double shock; Chad was not only sitting in the boat Strether had already appropriated metaphorically, but he was also in the picture of the day Strether had just worked so hard to draw up. Before the country discovery, Strether had refused to talk about Chad on the last two occasions of visiting Marie de Vionnet. This, he said, gave him the sense with her of "fulness and frequency" (2:249). Clearly, Chad had been, in a symbolic way, sexually displaced, even if Strether was unaware of it.

Before his awakening Strether describes the scene as a pastoral idyll: "a land of fancy for him—the background of fiction, the medium of art, the nursery of letters; practically as distant as Greece, but practically also well-nigh as consecrated. Romance could weave itself, for Strether's sense, out of elements mild enough" (2:245). When sex enters this rural seat, it does so like the figure of Death in Arcadia, "a marked drop into innocent friendly Bohemia" (2:262). Strether's explanation for the coincidence is that of life imitating art: "queer as fiction, as farce, that their country could happen to be exactly his" (2:257). But that is the point all along to which his sensitized exilic ambassadorship has taken him. Whether one sees the whole as a comical farce or a queer fiction or an inexorable drama of need and lack, Strether comes imaginatively to a point beyond which his self-limiting capacities will not allow him to act. He finds himself having rejected the sharp facts of Woollett but excluded from the vivid facts of Europe. For the remainder of the action there is a certain pathos in an imagination at its prime served by a prime that will not be his.

If, as James says, Strether lacks both enchantment and enchantresses before Europe, his own tastes betray his problem. He purchases during one of his walks a complete set of Victor Hugo's works. Hugo, the romancer of Paris, is to Strether what Amadis of Gaul was to Don

Quixote. Both models ease the move from the sterile plain to the land of verdant romance. Strether is, of course, needful. As James writes of him: "He would have issued, our rueful worthy, from the very heart of New England—at the heels of which matter of course a perfect rain of secrets tumbled for me into the light" (1:xi). One wonders if James has Cervantes's romance-seeking "Knight of the Rueful Countenance" somewhat in mind, especially when in the Gloriani garden scene he describes Strether's epiphany "with the light, with the romance of glory" that "had the consciousness of opening to it, for the happy instant, all the windows of his mind, of letting this rather grey interior drink in for once the sun of a clime not marked in his old geography" (1:196–97). And Paris is an appropriate exilic geography: "wherever one paused in Paris the imagination reacted before one could stop it" (1:96). The city is the happy hunting ground for former moralists, a "symbol for more things than had been dreamt of in the philosophy of Woollett" (1:xiv).

For Strether, whose imagination is primed, Paris is a field for his projections. James's commentary on this matter in his preface is among the fullest he provides for the book: "It was immeasurable, the opportunity to 'do' a man of imagination" (1:viii).[24] Though he admits it is an imagination in "the minor scale," James immediately goes on to say that minor scale or no, at least the substance of what Strether comes to see and say in the episode set in Gloriani's garden ought to enjoy the advantages of the major

> since most immediately to the point was the question of that *supplement* of situation logically involved in our gentleman's impulse to deliver himself in the Paris garden on the Sunday afternoon—or if not involved by strict logic then all ideally and enchantingly implied in it. (I say "ideally," because I need scarce mention that for development, for expression of its maximum, my glimmering story was, at the earliest stage, to have nipped the thread of connexion with the possibilities of the actual reported speaker.) [1:viii–ix]

This is fascinating: the major imaginative proclamation about vision is recorded by James as an enchanting supplement to the action of the story, but a supplement that denies the possibilities inherent in it for the one who imagines it. What James calls the supplement therefore belongs to the full life of the novel, if not the missed opportunity for its represented character. As for Strether, he is a part-time worker in the Jamesian enterprise: "it had only been his charming office to project upon that wide field of the artist's vision—which hangs there ever in place like the white sheet suspended for the figures of a child's magic-lantern—a more fantastic and more moveable shadow" (1:ix). The supplement in the artist's world is the primary phenomenon, not an epiphany born of middle-aged male crisis.

This is the essential reason that Strether does not even consider giving in to the temptations of Europe and remaining there as cosmopolitan exile to indulge what might remain for him of sexual life. That strikes him as a violation of both moral and imaginative form. He says to Chad, aghast when the young man suggests that Strether stay in Europe while he goes home to mother: "'to go back by yourself, I remaining here?' Again for an instant their eyes had the question out; after which Strether said: 'Grotesque!'" (2:35). *Grotesque* is an intriguing choice of words. The complete plot reversal, so classically worked out, takes on distorted form if Strether should make his impulses the same as his imaginings. What Strether has is what he has fervently argued for, the illusion of freedom; the freedom itself is secondary for him. To choose a course of action that involves, indirectly or not, choosing a woman is to bend Strether's imagination out of shape.

What is of greater moment for James as narrator is the coursing of Strether's imaginative powers into the exilic stream of the narrative so that the arrangement of mimetic instances represents, in a special way, the processes involved in making up a life. As I have been arguing throughout, narrative both imitates action and allegorizes it: "There is the story of one's hero, and then, thanks to the intimate connexion of things, the story of one's story itself" (1:x). In the latter sense, neither Strether nor Bilham matter to what James calls the supplement in the garden. And the substance of what was said, insofar as it touches on the plot of this story, matters less to James than the power that it reveals for the telling of any story, or the painting of any picture, or the composing of any symphony. The supplement, that is, serves the enterprise in which Strether and Bilham have come to us more than it could or might serve the older and younger men who participate in it.

If the Parisian supplement ends up confusing Strether practically, it at least stimulates him imaginatively. But to experience its benefits he must postpone the material mission at hand. In other words, the action mirrors the aesthetic issue in the book, and, reflexively, the aesthetic issue necessitates the particular form that the action takes. Thus the process begins early when, upon Strether's arrival in Paris, he learns that Mrs. Newsome's letters seem to have been held up. The delay opens supplemental space and time that allows Strether the experience that he will then, in order to buy time for a new mission, record in copious letters back to America in the hope that these, too, will effect delay: "Wasn't he writing against time, and mainly to show he was kind?" (2:46). His ambassadorial portfolio includes padded reports whose service is not to accomplish the mission that gained him his portfolio but gain time for the mission that will lose him his credentials. For it is a fact of his new Parisian life that he has been cut off from home; the letters stop—Mrs. Newsome utters only a "sacred hush" (2:47). By this time Strether is aware that his actions constitute imaginative time, which has as its emblem that epiphany in Gloriani's garden, what James called in his "Project" for the book "snatching a little super-sensual hour" (p. 393). Later, when Strether boasts that Chad's turn toward Woollett is "stayed by his own hand," he "had the entertainment of thinking that if he had for that moment stopped the clock it was to promote the next minute this still livelier motion" (2:59).

The reflex of delay, to which Strether finds himself at least psychologically susceptible from the beginning, is also the reflex of a double consciousness, material and imaginative: "He was burdened, poor Strether—it had better be confessed at the outset—with the oddity of a double consciousness. There was detachment in his zeal and curiosity in his indifference" (1:5).[25] Detachment from the zeal of his

American mission "creates" the time for curiosity to graft onto an original indifference about the lure of the exilic European experience. At the center of all relations is the figure of chiasmus or crossover. Strether soon has a zeal for what he had been curious about and an indifference toward that material comedy from which he had detached himself.

Strether wonders about his new interest in what he considers the "livelier" motion of the action, and his curiosity has a narrative dimension, one that any inventor of plots might contemplate: "Did he live in a false world, a world that had grown simply to suit him?" (2:81). His is not an idle question for, in a certain sense, the cultivation of the imagination after a long dormancy is *only* for him. In fact, it occurs to Strether that part of his problem is that he invests too much of what he sees in his estimation of other people's conception of reality. That Chad's change, for example, is not noticed by others in the same way he notices it may actually be the menace of the real, as Strether puts it, against the vain or imagined. Later he gets petulant about the possibility: "If they were *all* going to see nothing!" (2:88). There may be little to see, in terms of the new Woollett delegation to Paris. At best, the American contingent wishes to appropriate Chad's refinements for New England; in other words, the supplementing forces of the exilic experience are themselves put *en exil.*

Strether does not easily give up on the issue of what he has seen and requests that Sarah at least convey to Mrs. Newsome the tenor of the European situation. Sarah marks the aesthetics of his vision, "'that what you speak of is what *you've* beautifully done'" (2:201). And when Strether, in frustration, realizes that his picture of Madame de Vionnet's effort on Chad's behalf is aesthetically uninteresting to the materialist will of Woollett, he virtually begs Sarah for his supplemental image of Marie de Vionnet, if not of Chad: "'Ah dear Sarah, you must *leave* me this person here!'" (2:203). She cannot be taken from him, at least in the way he sees her. And he sees her as a piece of exquisite work, the "perfection of art" (2:276), with "such variety and yet such harmony" (2:300), "so odd a mixture of lucidity and mystery" (2:115), part of Europe's performance, "like Cleopatra in the play, indeed various and multifold" (1:271).

It is very important for Strether that Madame de Vionnet not only be kept for him in the special way he sees her, but that the pathos in her life that answers to its details of her relation with Chad be kept from him: "while he had himself been enjoying for weeks the view of the brilliant woman's specific action, he just suffered from any characterisation of it by other lips. 'I think tremendously well of her, at the same time that I seem to feel her "life" to be really none of my business'" (2:204). Even toward the end, when he realizes "that a creature so fine could be, by mysterious forces, a creature so exploited" (2:284), it still seems "as if he didn't think of her at all, as if he could think of nothing but the passion, mature, abysmal, pitiful, she represented, and the possibilities she betrayed" (2:286). It is one thing to say that Strether is simply naively self-protective here, and quite another to say that he knows, after all, that an imaginative view of these things is the best he can make of his present capacities. His steamship ticket may return him to America, but his sensibility, as James implies, has made him a permanent exile; he has crossed over to the land of "difference," and he has "come out on the other side."

CHAPTER SIX

Stereoscope: Nabokov's *Ada* and *Pale Fire*

False Passports

Of all novelists who have lived in exile and written its traumas and its imaginative opportunities into the texture of their fiction, Vladimir Nabokov reigns, in his way, supreme. As the poet John Shade puts it in *Pale Fire,* the old exile "suffocates and conjures in two tongues."[1] The agonies and ecstasies of the exilic state for Nabokov—what he calls, borrowing a line from Melville, the life of a flower exiled by a weed—are emotionally and aesthetically connected to the retrospective imagination, to the search and Proustian *recherche* for the nostalgic source that locates the wonder and combinatory powers of the creating mind.

When Nabokov writes in *Speak, Memory* of his long-cherished exilic recollections of Russia, he means those that he associates with the special memories of his youth.

> Nowadays, the mental image of matted grass on the Yayla, of a canyon in the Urals or of salt flats in the Aral Region, affects me nostalgically and patriotically as little, or as much as, say, Utah; but give me anything on any continent resembling the St. Petersburg countryside and my heart melts. What it would be actually to see again my former surroundings, I can hardly imagine. Sometimes I fancy myself revisiting them with a false passport, under an assumed name. It could be done.[2]

Nabokov goes on to say he shall never do it—"I have been dreaming of it too idly and too long"—but the exiled writer, no matter where he is, travels with a false passport all his life. Or, to put it another way, his passport may be false in the eyes of literalists like the border police, but valid enough in the realm of memorial retrospect. An exile's passport is the license to travel, like Blake's mental technician, inside the head. Such travel could take place, must take place, and does take place for Nabokov under a variety of names in a variety of places.[3]

To comprehend more fully the effect and resonance of exile in Nabokov's life and art, it makes sense to begin at the place where Nabokov begins: with the origin of imagination in the familiar and marked domain of childhood. The exilic imagination in its maturity tries to recapture not only remembered space but nostalgic time. Whenever Nabokov writes, as he does so often, of the loss of Russia, he separates it from any notion of real material loss, the loss, say, of a family fortune, and turns instead to family memories: "the nostalgia I have been cherishing all these years is a hypertrophied sense of lost childhood, not sorrow for lost banknotes" (*SM*, p. 73). At home, or *in time,* a child's first imaginative efforts are phenomena "of orientation rather than of art, thus comparable to stripes of paint on a roadside rock or to a pillared heap of stones marking a mountain trail" (*SM*, p. 217). To move into the world of art is to project into a world of possibilities, a world beyond those traditional boundary markers setting out the contours of familiar territory.

In Nabokov's early, partially autobiographical novel, *The Gift,* Fyodor Cherdyntsev, the émigré poet and novelist, contemplates the supplementing powers of the imagination and draws a comparison with those extraordinary moments of childhood when "he could see all sorts of distant and interesting things, just as, when a little boy, his father used to lift him by his elbows thus enabling him to see what was interesting over a fence."[4] The word *interesting* is pivotal here in the sense of focusing originary perspective.[5] Recall and vision, a rush of orienting memories and extravagant projections, position the imagination. Nabokov always relies on positioning to measure the poetic or artistic moment. He notes that "in a sense, all poetry is positional: to try to express one's position in regard to the universe embraced by consciousness, is an immemorial urge. The arms of consciousness reach out and grope, and the longer they are the better. Tentacles, not wings, are Apollo's natural members" (*SM*, p. 218).

For the child "all forms of vitality are forms of velocity, and no wonder a growing child desires to out-Nature Nature by filling a minimum stretch of time with a maximum of spatial enjoyment" (*SM*, p. 301). This gesture remains in essence what Nabokov offers as formal design in his later fiction, whether accomplished by sequences of exquisitely formulated sentences or by the splendor of invented kingdoms and reformulated continents. Artistic positioning begins at the boundary or meeting place between that which already exists as accessible information or sensation and that which requires the projection of images: "There is, it would seem, in the dimensional scale of the world a kind of delicate meeting place between imagination and knowledge, a point . . . that is intrinsically artistic" (*SM*, pp. 166–67). When Nabokov grappled later in his career with the difficulties of capturing America imaginatively for *Lolita,* he worried about his own positioning: "My private tragedy, which cannot, and indeed should not, be anybody's concern, is that I had to abandon my natural idiom, my untrammeled, rich, and infinitely docile Russian tongue for a second-rate brand of English, devoid of any of those apparatuses—the baffling mirror, the black velvet backdrop, the implied associations and traditions—which the native illusionist, frac-tails flying, can magically use to transcend the heritage in his own way."[6]

Perhaps because Nabokov's sensibility encouraged it, he began to consolidate from his knowledgeable world his imaginative world, what he called his "unreal estate," even before he needed it. Looking back upon his childhood, he writes of his first memory of returning to Russia once from abroad: "In result, that particular return to Russia, my first *conscious* return, seems to me now, sixty years later, a rehearsal—not of the grand homecoming that will never take place, but of its constant dream in my long years of exile" (*SM*, p. 97). Later, in England, Nabokov felt himself able to deal with the condition of exile when his imagination freed itself to present his homeland to him complete; he crammed himself full of Russian literature for "fear of losing or corrupting, through alien influence, the only thing I had salvaged from Russia—her language" (*SM*, p. 265). He writes of the immense relief he experienced at Cambridge when he also finally felt at home in England, and "this state of harmony had been reached at the very moment that the careful reconstruction of my artificial but beautifully exact Russian world had been at last completed" (*SM*, p. 270). There could be no clearer example of the exilic projection serving as exilic supplement, a replica serving as replacement.

Politically, Nabokov tried to think in similar ways—to make the supplemental reconstruction of Russia his memorial reality so he could beneficially accommodate his exilic perspective. Nabokov writes in an essay on the tenth anniversary of the 1917 Russian Revolution that the best of what remains to be imagined about the homeland is precisely what can be imagined in exile.

> In that particular Russia which invisibly surrounds, quickens, and supports us, nourishes our souls, adorns our dreams, there is not a single law except the law of love for her, and there is no power except that of our own conscience. We may say everything about her, write everything, for we have nothing to hide, and there is no censorship to limit us—we are free citizens of our dreams. Our far-flung state, our nomadic empire has its strength in this freedom, and someday we shall be grateful to the blind Clio for the way in which she allowed us to taste this freedom and in emigration to understand thoroughly and develop a deep feeling for our native land.[7]

The gratefulness, of course, reserved itself for intellectual and literary memory because time took its toll on the political element of that dream. Nabokov writes in the 1962 foreword to the English translation of *The Gift* of that saving Russian remnant whose memorial status becomes almost mythical in exile, "at present as much of a phantasm as most of my other worlds."

> The tremendous outflow of intellectuals that formed such a prominent part of the general exodus from Soviet Russia in the first years of the Bolshevist Revolution seems today like the wanderings of some mythi-

cal tribe whose bird-signs and moon-signs I now retrieve from the desert dust. We remained unknown to American intellectuals (who, bewitched by Communist propaganda, saw us merely as villainous generals, oil magnates, and gaunt ladies with lorgnettes). That world is now gone. Gone are Bunin, Aldanov, Remizov. Gone is Vladislav Khodasevich, the greatest Russian poet that the twentieth century has yet produced. The old intellectuals are now dying out and have not found successors in the so-called Displaced Persons of the last two decades who have carried abroad the provincialism and Philistinism of their Soviet homeland. [p. ii]

What Nabokov carries abroad is the consciousness of where he has been. In *Speak, Memory,* he describes his exilic experience upon settling in New England and wonders

what I am doing in this stereoscopic dreamland? How did I get here? Somehow, the two sleighs have slipped away, leaving behind a passportless spy standing on the blue-white road in his New England snowboots and stormcoat. The vibration in my ears is no longer their receding bells, but only my old blood singing. All is still, spellbound, enthralled by the moon, fancy's rear vision mirror. The snow is real, though, and as I bend to it and scoop up a handful, sixty years crumble to glittering frost-dust between my fingers. [pp. 99–100]

In aesthetic terms, the stereoscopic blood song of memory in fancy's rear vision mirror is so strong it seems to enter even when not exactly invited. In *The Gift,* Fyodor considers the layering of reaction to the sighting of a face and the distant, former home place takes strange, if irrelevant, hold. Merely by looking at a person the many valences of art and exile enter in.

You look at a person and you see him as clearly as if he were fashioned of glass and you were the glass blower, while at the same time without in the least impinging upon that clarity you notice some trifle on the side—such as the similarity of the telephone receiver's shadow to a huge, slightly crushed ant, and (all this simultaneously) the convergence is joined by a third thought—the memory of a sunny evening at a Russian small railway station; i.e., images having no rational connection with the conversation you are carrying on while your mind runs around the outside of your own words and along the inside of those of your interlocutor. [p. 175]

Zembre on the Minder

If we turn now to the way Nabokov constructs the special worlds and special places of his fiction, we begin to see the centrality of exilic projection as a principle of narrative design. To bring into imaginative scope what Nabokov calls in *Ada* the "whereabouts and whenabouts" of memorial space is to draw on the alliance between exile and nostalgia, a key alliance in his fiction and one, as Van Veen says in *Ada,* that measures "the blood current coursing through my brain, and thence through the veins of the neck heartward, back to the seat of private throes."[8] Van knows the process well; he is a psychiatric writer of what Nabokov calls "physics fiction," visionary treatises on mental landscapes embedded in the texture of time: "Time is a fluid medium for the culture of metaphors" (p. 537).[9] He theorizes that the present lasts at best a tenth of a second, during which time the impostor space makes its only impression on the eye. Futurity is at best a guess. Time is what one desires and "to give myself time to time Time I must move my mind in the direction opposite to that in which I am moving" (p. 549). Van has a special term for past as a product of memory—he calls it a construction, a "Deliberate Present" as opposed to the "Specious Present" of living life as unreconstructed "nowness" (p. 549). And he asks a question whose answer approximates the form, shape, and temporal overlap of *Ada,* not only as childhood chronicle, but as exilic space-romance, a narrative genre that transverses inconvenient space and collapses oppressive time: "Has there ever been a 'primitive' form of Time in which, say, the Past was not yet clearly differentiated from the Present, so that past shadows and shapes showed through the still soft, long, larval 'now'?" (p. 539).

Van goes on to expound on the process of imaginary spatialization, which is at the heart of the exilic imagination and which implies transforming geography into a species of temporal metaphor: "Not for the first time will Space intrude if I say that what we are aware of as 'Present' is the constant building up of the Past, its smoothly and relentlessly rising level. How meager! How magic!" (p. 551). Van had already proposed an illustration in which memorial nostalgia actually becomes physical reconstruction, the imagined restoration of an original town named Zembre on the river Minder—a natural enough space-place—that during the decades of the Industrial Revolution experienced a bad case of urban sprawl. The architectonics here provide a parallel for the deliberate present of exilic reconstruction.

> Today, after years of subtle reconstruction, a replica of the old Zembre, with its castle, its church, and its mill extrapolated onto the other side of the Minder, stands opposite the modernized town and separated from it by the length of a bridge. Now, if we replace the spatial view (as seen from a helicopter) by the chronal one (as seen by a retrospector), and the material model of old Zembre by the mental model of it in the Past (say, around 1822), the modern town and the model of the old turn out to be something else than two points in the same place at different times (in spatial perspective they *are* at the same time in different places). The space in which the modern town coagulates is immediately real, while that of its retrospective image (as seen apart from material restoration) shimmers in an imaginary space and we cannot use any bridge to walk from the one to the other. [p. 545]

The imaginative, retrospective space, the one that admits of no real bridge to real state, is, of course, the space of Nabokov's supreme fictional supplements, Humberland in *Lolita*, Zembla in *Pale Fire*, and the North American Estoty on the planet Antiterra of *Ada*. Of *Lolita*, for example, he writes: "It had taken me some forty years to invent Russia and Western Europe, and now I was faced by the task of inventing America."[10] Nabokov does so before he writes *Lolita*, but he also does so between parts one and two of the novel. The transition from part one to part two is a neat Nabokovian fold that first brings the object of obsession into the sphere of the obsessed and then widens the sphere to an inscriptive or mental place, an exilic territory. As Lolita comes to Humbert, part one ends: "You see, she had absolutely nowhere else to go."[11] Humbert and his Lo, after a couple of compulsory text-dividing blank pages, initiate the trajectory that makes up much the rest of the book: "It was then that began our extensive travels all over the States" (p. 147). Humbert, the maniac of the map, seems to sense that he is nothing but itinerary: "She had entered my world, umber and black Humberland" (p. 168).

Nabokov also rewrites America in *Ada* by projecting it as exilic space. Backing up a century in its putative time scheme while still allowing its inhabitants to live as if in a different version of the twentieth century, *Ada* provides the perfect reconstructive supplement for the cosmopolitan Russian genius-cum-exile. It is as if the circumstances for exile never existed in Russia, indeed, as if centuries of worldwide geopolitical contingencies are rearranged for the benefit of the imagining mind. Not only does Nabokov's exilic event, the Russian Revolution, fail to occur, but most of the historical conditions for centuries past that might have proven threatening to the aristocratic, liberal Western world are altered on Antiterra. What remains is a world of extended European and American civilization that has marginalized rather than centralized violence and political uprootedness. *Ada* takes place primarily on a continent called Amerussia, leaving European and Asian Russia for the hordes of Tartary (as if these throwbacks from the realm of darkness held Russia in her hyperborean prehistory and never lost her). Home for *Ada* in the nineteenth and twentieth centuries is an amalgam of the Yukon, French and British Canada, and northern America, where culture's separate imprints produce a fictionally unified country, Estoty, coincidentally served by virtually interchangeable languages, Russian, French, and English, Nabokov's native and exilic tongues.[12]

The temporal-spatial axis of *Ada*'s world is based on a complicated conceit where, in a reversal that befits the exilic reconstruction, history as we might know it from perusing the front pages of the *New York Times* or *Pravda* is represented only by a bizarre and remote projection on a planet or plane called Terra, accessible only to presumed lunatics and visionaries. Terra, of course, is a place where Russia still is Asian and European, where "Russian peasants and poets had not been transported to Estotiland. . . .they were dying, at this very moment, in the slave camps of Tartary" (p. 582). Since the inhabitants of Antiterra deal with Terra only as a fantasy, facts get garbled, but experts (or madmen) have a sense of what its history looks like—the English Empire has broken up into small pieces, somebody called Athaulf the Future has thrown Europe into a terrible turmoil, Tartarian Russia is called, as far as Van mishears or misconstrues, the Sovereign Society of Solicitous Republics. Like many exiles whose imaginative spirit strikes home no matter where their bodies, Nabokov undermines the devalued homeland by keeping his characters well out of it.

The represented world of Antiterra—the pun is idyllic as well as nostalgic—denies the reality of Terra precisely because its historical fantasy is too terrible. Antiterra, which Van seems to require as an intermediate world to his true desire, the young girl Ada at Ardis, takes on personal dimension, which is why it exists aesthetically. It is also known by family names that center Van's chronicle, making it sound slightly mad and demonically supplemental: Demonia, Vandemonia, Desdemonia. As is the case for Kinbote's evocation of Zembla in *Pale Fire,* a symptomatic kind of artistic insanity lurks in the full geographical supplement. Van Veen seems to sense as much—it is not just Terra that projects a mad world: "He also gave a minute's thought to the sad fact that (as he well knew from his studies) the confusion of two realities, one in single, the other in double, quotes, was a symptom of impending insanity" (p. 232). Antiterra is the verbal and visual imposition that allows him to make *Ada* out of his artistic treatise, *The Texture of Time.* The entire planet becomes that memorial space, a Neverland,[13] "where artists are the only gods" (p. 521). Indeed, the only named god is the appropriate figure for an exilic place filled with and by what Nabokov calls "word dreams": God Log, a parodic form of the word, or logos. Again, as in *Pale Fire,* Nabokov adds an exilic signatory to the imaginative Shakespearean compact among lunatics, lovers, and poets.

For Van, Antiterra makes over the historical rift by literally remembering over it or remembering it over. We can gain a sense of the two worlds of the novel by listening to a distinction Van makes early between the supposedly real Antiterra and the fantastic Terra, a "distortive glass of our distorted glebe" (p. 18).

Ved' ("it is, isn't it") sidesplitting to imagine that "Russia," instead of being a quaint synonym of Estoty, the American province extending from the Arctic no longer vicious Circle to the United States proper, was on Terra the name of a country, transferred as if by some sleight of *land* across the ha-ha of a doubled ocean to the opposite hemisphere where it sprawled over all of today's Tartary, from Kurland to the Kuriles! But (even more absurdly), if, in terrestrial spatial terms, the Amerussia of Abraham Milton was split into its components, with tangible water and ice separating the political, rather than poetical, notions of "America" and "Russia," a more complicated and even more preposterous discrepancy arose in regard to time—not only because the history of each part of the amalgam did not quite match the history of each counterpart in its discrete condition, but because a gap of up to a hundred years one way or another existed between the two earths; a gap marked by a bizarre confusion of directional signs at the crossroads of passing time with not *all* the no-longers of one world corresponding to the not-yets of the other. It was owing, among other things, to this "scientifically ungraspable" concourse of divergences that minds *bien rangés* (not apt to unhobble hobgoblins) rejected Terra as a fad or a fantom, and deranged minds (ready to plunge into any abyss) accepted it in support and token of their own irrationality. [pp. 17–18]

The language here boasts of word modules such as "sidesplitting," which, like Nabokov's imp Split, makes exilic imagining into a "preposterous" temporal-spatial rupture. The mitosis of the supplement (a fabulous birth if not strictly Caesarean) allegorizes the joke of projection, spatialized in the figure of the landscape trompe l'oeil, the "ha-ha," where space is an aesthetic surprise, the projection that at once seems an illusion and a prospect, a disjunct and an adjunct, a joke and a doubling. Beyond Nabokov's delicate spatial magic, however, is the process of exilic imagining at its most robust. Van's throwaway for the governor of Amerussia, Abraham Milton, hints at a mythic territory that is both originary and structuring, since Abraham begins and Milton records the great founding and exilic experiences of Western tradition.

Exilic Desire

Having artfully and laboriously constructed, named, and overlapped two worlds in *Ada,* one the exilic idyll, the other a newsreel artifact, an "actuality" as a fantasy of the remote, Nabokov also augments the spaces of the nostalgic supplement, associated, as is so often the case in his writings, with the sexual fixations of youth: *"One* wonders if *any* art could do without that erotic gasp of schoolgirl mirth" (p. 500). If this sounds either perilously or generatively close to the center of the earlier *Lolita,* one should not be surprised. Very little of *Lolita* as well makes sense without an understanding of the allegorization of nostalgia as original nymphette desire and the subsequent displacement of desire into the spatial diaspora of lust. The pathos of *Lolita* is that Humbert's inscription of desire is all exilic velocity without the imaginative innocence left behind on the Riviera of his youth. In the beginning was the original nymph, Annabel on the beach.

> I leaf again and again through these miserable memories, and keep asking myself, was it then, in the glitter of that remote summer, that the rift in my life began; or was my excessive desire for that child only the first evidence of an inherent singularity? When I try to analyze my own cravings, motives, actions and so forth, I surrender to a sort of retrospective imagination which feeds the analytic faculty with boundless alternatives and which causes each visualized route to fork and refork without end in the maddeningly complex prospect of my past. [p. 15]

When Nabokov has Humbert say that "in a certain magic and fateful way Lolita began with Annabel" (p. 16), he is saying that the girl and the book derive from the same retrospective overplus. The difficulty for Humbert Humbert is that his world, like his name, is indeed double; it comprises both the America of his odyssey and the Nabokovian "elsewhere" of nostalgia reflected erotically in *Lolita*. Even Humbert recognizes the "maddeningly complex prospect" where the projection of his own childhood desire both sustains him and imposes upon him, so "that the search for a Kingdom by the Sea, a Sublimated Riviera, or whatnot, far from being the impulse of the subconscious, had become the rational pursuit of a purely theoretical thrill" (p. 169).

From the experience of reading *Lolita* it would appear that there are two entirely different circuits of an American odyssey taking place. One is a criss-cross country ramble of perversion and pathos: "We had been everywhere. We had really seen nothing. And I catch myself thinking today that our long journey had only defiled with a sinuous trail of slime the lovely, trustful, dreamy, enormous country that by then, in retrospect, was no more to us than a collection of dog-eared maps, ruined tour books, old tires, and her sobs in the night—every night, every night—the moment I feigned sleep" (pp. 177–78). The other journey is an authorial reconstruction by the Nabokovian exile in awe of the territory he inscribes, the wordsmith who marvels at Painted Canyons because, in a way, he has painted them, who delights in places like Crystal Chamber, Conception Park, and Shakespeare, New Mexico, because he can, after a fashion, admire their aesthetic resonance, admire his having imagined them. Perhaps that is why Nabokov later in *Pale Fire* named a hurricane Lolita and in *Ada* named one of his imagined places on an imagined American mainland Lolita, Texas. The book, in a sense, derives the land. Lo may have been oblivious to the landscape, but Humbert finally saw something out in the West, the traditional literary place for exilic wandering and resettlement, and, in this instance, a place that seems to exist as an inspiration for the writing of it.

> Distant mountains. Near mountains. More mountains; bluish beauties
> never attainable, or ever turning into inhabited hill after hill; south-
> eastern ranges, altitudinal failures as alps go; heart and sky-piercing
> snow-veined gray colossi of stone, relentless peaks appearing from
> nowhere at a turn of the highway; timbered enormities, with a system

of neatly overlapping dark firs, interrupted in places by pale puffs of aspen; pink and lilac formations, Pharaonic, phallic, "too prehistoric for words" (blasé Lo); buttes of black lava; early spring mountains with young-elephant lanugo along their spines; end-of-the-summer mountains, all hunched up, their heavy Egyptian limbs folded under folds of tawny moth-eaten plush; oatmeal hills, flecked with green round oaks; a last rufous mountain with a rich rug of lucerne at its foot. [p. 158]

Though Humbert's verbal diorama here has the feel of a made-up spectacle, it is at least nominally descriptive of a real America. It is in *Ada* that Nabokov takes the next inevitable step and makes America up as part of a new geography for an Amerussian continent, a geography conforming to the desire and dementia of exilic consciousness. The same "maddeningly complex prospect" that faces Humbert is also structuring in *Ada;* the place and the girl sustain the back action of the novel. Nabokov even provides a book reviewer who mistakenly thinks that Van's *Letters from Terra* (described, by the way, right after a series of letters from the girl, Ada) is "a fancy novel about a girl called Terra" (p. 343), as if all Nabokov's books within books are about the twin supplements of nostalgic place and ardent desire.

There are always two actionable phenomena going on in Nabokov's fiction, described similarly in *Lolita* and again in *Pale Fire:* the viewing of action with open eyes, where events play out in the present, and the viewing of that same action on the nether lids, where present action plays out, almost in a theatric sense, actionable desire. As is the case with the homeland, the desire for the object of love grows in proportion to the distance placed between it and the disorienting, displaced mind. For example, in *Pale Fire* Charles Kinbote recreates, while in exile, emotions attendant upon his Queen Disa that never existed within the borders of his own imagined Zemblan kingdom.

He dreamed of her more often, and with incomparably more poignancy, than his surface-life feelings for her warranted; these dreams occurred when he least thought of her, and worries in no way connected with her assumed her image in the subliminal world as a battle or a reform becomes a bird of wonder in a tale for children. These heart-rending dreams transformed the drab prose of his feelings for her into strong and strange poetry, subsiding undulations of which would flash and disturb him throughout the day, bringing back the pang and the richness—and then only the pang, and then only its glancing reflection—but not affecting at all his attitude towards the real Disa. [p. 209]

Love seems more necessary as an exilic and literary solace than as a represented experience. As we remember years before from Nabokov's *Despair:* "To begin with, let us take the following motto (not especially for this chapter, but generally): Literature is Love. Now we can continue."[14] The actual experience of love for Nabokov entails an imaginative fecundity that results in an unending compulsion to supplement. As he says in a passage from *Speak, Memory* about his love for his wife, Véra: "I have to have all space and all time participate in my emotion, in my mortal love, so that the edge of its mortality is taken off, thus helping me to fight the utter degradation, ridicule, and horror of having developed an infinity of sensation and thought within a finite existence" (p. 297).

It is a recurring condition of Nabokov's imaginative life that what seem the intrinsic velocities of consciousness and memory also seem the velocities of love, maddening velocities when beyond the merely nostalgic "erotic gasp of schoolgirl mirth." Love follows the course of the exilic imagination, both centripetally and centrifugally. In that same passage on the immensity of his love for his wife, Nabokov describes love's dimensions and the riot of its explosion inside his heart and brain. The process resembles the emergence of a literary consciousness but lacks the curtailing, reining, proportioning principles of aesthetic design.

Whenever I start thinking of my love for a person, I am in the habit of immediately drawing radii from my love—from my heart, from the tender nucleus of a personal matter—to monstrously remote points of the universe. Something impels me to measure the consciousness of my love against such unimaginable and incalculable things as the behavior of nebulae (whose very remoteness seems a form of insanity), the dreadful pitfalls of eternity, the unknowledgeable beyond the unknown, the helplessness, the cold, the sickening involutions and interpenetrations of space and time. [p. 296]

Love represents at various times and in various places the two great frozen territories of exilic supplements: paradisal memories and hellish, eternal voids. In *Ada,* to know the one is to experience the other: "Eros, the rose and the sore" (p. 367); or the "horror and ardor of Ardis" (p. 451). Ada's name in Russian means, as she is fond of letting us know, Hades: "I know there's a Van in Nirvana. I'll be with him in the depths *moego ada,* of my Hades" (p. 583). Too much of love in the supplemental state is always degenerative, even unreciprocated love as in Queen Disa's letter to the captive Zemblan king from Villa Paradisa in *Pale Fire,* which gets translated from "I want you to know that no matter how much you hurt me, you cannot hurt my love" to the Zemblan "I desire you and love when you flog me" (p. 205). [15]

Love may induce consciousness for Nabokov, but it also induces pain. In *Ada,* the recapturing of childhood is the recentering of actual, fervent, and abundant desire at the still point of the Antiterrestrian globe, the ancestral estate, Ardis, of both hero and heroine, which means " 'the point of the arrow'—but only in Greek, alas" (p. 225). The estate is cupidic, directional, bullseyed, and, beyond the ecstasy of the primal point of contact, piercing and painful.

Ada, spoken with *ardor* by Van, gathers emotions around her—she is desire at its most desirable time, paradisal love in the paradisal place. Ada's Van is described as "her Adam" (p. 406), while her name seems born of the originary name as well, with two syllables of the first generating male principal in her. Van retains the pelvic consonant of Eve to start him off—but, then, she is the one with "a pink scar between two ribs" (p. 120) and he is the one who gets pregnant: "When in early September Van Veen left Manhattan for Lute, he was pregnant" (p. 325). The split narration in the novel produces a form: "Vainiada" (p. 409). And the collaborative effort of the book is the sexuality of childhood revisited. In Ardis, as "lovers *and* siblings," Ada cried, "we have a double chance of being together in eternity in terrarity. Four pairs of eyes in paradise!" (pp. 583–84).

As is invariably the case with love, the promiscuous pain begins when Ada and Van are forced by the disjunction of time to leave the paradisal world. Edenic exile is the first nostalgic plot. Like Anna Liffey and HCE in *Finnegans Wake,* where primal love also turns promiscuous, Ada ends up loving "only males and, alas, only one man" (p. 416). Van ends up leaving Ardis for relentless immersion in various Venus Villas scattered through the novel like the western motels in *Lolita*. The run of action in *Ada* touches, as had *Lolita,* on the debasing horror that constitutes the unfulfilled retrospective imagination as Van wanders the world in desperate search for the lost idyllic embrace. The weed surely exiles the flower as the botanical Ada recedes in time and Van's lust-rage succeeds her.

Time for Van loses its texture when exile extends beyond the Edenic Ardis of the novel. Ardis, in fact, takes up most of the time chronicled in the book as if inconsequential time requires fewer words. The technical trick resembles the explanation Kinbote provides in *Pale Fire* for concentrating on his and Shade's houses at the expense of the much larger Wordsmith College: "It is probably the first time that the dull pain of distance is rendered through an effect of style and that a topographical idea finds its verbal expression in a series of foreshortened sentences" (p. 92).

So much of Veen time, as Nabokov calls it, is spent at the point of the arrow, at the originary, cupidic home because Van sees the primal, death-defying, madness-thwarting ecstasy and agony of original love.

> What, then, was it that raised the animal act to a level higher than even that of the most exact arts or the wildest flights of pure science? It would not be sufficient to say that in his love-making with Ada he discovered the pang, the *ogon'*, the agony of supreme "reality." Reality, better say, lost the quotes it wore like claws—in a world where independent and original minds must cling to things or pull things apart in order to ward off madness or death (which is the master madness). [pp. 219–20]

The Elysian or futuristic supplement, of which Van is eschatologically wary, is a recapitulation of memorial desire: "The transposition of all our remembered relationships into an Elysian life inevitably turns it into a second-rate continuation of our marvelous mortality" (p. 586). All time is a riot of pastness, and even the future palatial domain of the older Van and Ada is named Ex, meaning both "out of" and "former," as if the two properties of the exiled mind unite in the previous place of love.

Nabokov realizes that the places the imagination makes for the range of its exilic experience in *Ada,* Paradise and Hell, seem to originate, as Genesis, too, implies, in a myth of excess desire: "One can even surmise that if our time-racked, flat-lying couple ever intended to die they would die, as it were, *into* the finished book, into Eden or Hades, into the prose of the book or the poetry of its blurb" (p. 587). And that is precisely what happens as Van eases into blurb prose to return himself to Ardis at the end of the novel. His is an alluring parody of *Ada*'s own retrospective romance. The supplemental domain is "the writer's magic carpet" where the perfect reconstruction is forever Ardis, the girl within the grove, "the Ardors and Arbors of Ardis—this is the leitmotiv rippling through *Ada,* an ample and delightful chronicle whose principal part is staged in a dream-bright America" (p. 588). Here lovers forever attempt to reimage and rehear, perhaps in stereoscope, the sounds and accents of an exilic spot, what Nabokov calls their "hopeless, rapturous sunset love."[16] Van and Ada "spend their old age traveling together and dwelling in the various villas, one lovelier than another, that Van has erected all over the Western Hemisphere" (pp. 588–89). The last paragraph of the parodied blurb, like the state of exile itself, is a remembered idyll supplemented by a glut ("much, much more"), the very shape of plot in Nabokov's nostalgic, botanical, lepidopterous imagination.

> Not the least adornment of the chronicle is the delicacy of pictorial detail: a latticed gallery; a painted ceiling; a pretty plaything stranded among the forget-me-nots of a brook; butterflies and butterfly orchids in the margin of the romance; a misty view described from marble steps; a doe at gaze in the ancestral park; and much, much more. [p. 589]

"Mirror, mirror on the wall"

Van Veen, as already noted, confesses to the insanity lurking in the confusion of nostalgic and temporally linear worlds. Nabokov witnessed the phenomenon even as a child when his maternal grandfather, like Humbert Humbert, stopped time in the Riviera of his youth. In *Speak, Memory,* Nabokov describes his mother's creation of a nostalgic mirage adjusted to the pathology of the old man's desire.

> As he gradually regained consciousness, my mother camouflaged his bedroom into the one he had had in Nice. Some similar pieces of furniture were found and a number of articles rushed from Nice by a special messenger, and all the flowers his hazy senses had been accustomed to were obtained, in their proper variety and profusion, and a bit of house wall that could be just glimpsed from the window was painted a brilliant white, so every time he reverted to a state of comparative lucidity he found himself safe on the illusory Riviera artistically staged by my mother. [p. 59]

This is a relatively harmless mirage, but matters get more complicated when other of Nabokov's "characters" negotiate illusory space as a way of deflecting experiential anguish. In *The Gift,* Nabokov narrates instances where "if, according to the Swabian code, an insulted actor was permitted to seek satisfaction by striking the *shadow* of the offender, in China it was precisely an actor—a shadow—who fulfilled the duties of the executioner, all responsibility being as it were lifted from the world of men and transformed into the inside-out one of mirrors" (p. 215). In later Nabokovian fiction, the mirror substitutes are not in every sense desirable shadows, and the victims in mirror worlds take upon themselves a burden of violence not even intended for them. Such is the nature of the action in Nabokov's mad exilic narrative, *Pale Fire,* with its world of mirrors and "zemblances," its revolutionaries in glass factories, its projected assassin, Jacob Gradus, reflected from his ancestral source, a mirror-maker image of himself, Sudarg of Bokay, and its poem that begins with the violent crash of waxwing against windowpane and ends with a bungled assassination in which the wrong Shade or shadow stands in for a hanging judge.

The violence done to and by the mirror images in *Pale Fire* is nowhere better depicted than in the climactic scene at the end of the action. Two or possibly three sets of characters are loosed within the narrative's New Wye and Zemblan reflections. The result is not only a moment of violence but a narrative crisis. A lunatic imagines himself to be in pursuit of a judge named Goldsworth, though he shoots a poet named Shade, who teaches at Wordsmith College. [17] Instead of the judge—the harshest of critics—he kills a poet, a wordsmith, thus completing a chiasmus, or cross up. Not only is Goldsmith crossed with Wordsworth, but poetry in the larger sense is crossed by lunacy, which is what *Pale Fire* is all about. Furthermore, the denouement is interpreted by an annotator, an exilic lunatic, who imagines himself as the implicit text of the action when he "wears" the manuscript of "his" dead poet's poem like a bulletproof vest. The manuscript, not the poet, becomes an "inviolable shade" (p. 294). Charles Kinbote, putative Zemblan king, takes the madman's double dip into literalization to avoid, perhaps, another imagined assassin after the first one hit the wrong man: "I circulated, plated with poetry, armored with rhymes, stout with another man's song, stiff with cardboard, bullet-proof at long last" (p. 300). The poem whose subject did not contain enough of Kinbote's story to please him now contains all of him; whereas the man who wrote the poem admits, willy-nilly, a final reflection upon his life that ends up killing him: "I was the shadow of the waxing slain / By the false azure in the windowpane" (p. 33).

Without treating the crisis of *Pale Fire* solely as a police procedural—who did what to whom?—it is enough to say that the crossings of the denouement reflect the relation of supplemental to contingent worlds in the exilic state. Narrative for Kinbote is an extenuation of circumstances. When Kinbote's Zemblan empire, from which he claims he is exiled, is translated to New Wye, the remote, romance kingdom becomes confused with another supplemental world appropriately named by Kinbote as New Wye's Arcady. The Myth of Arcadia represents the final intrusion: Death is let loose in poetic spaces. Death's appearance produces a special and unnerving kind of penetration. Kinbote has to account for Shade's New Wye death in terms of the Zemblan supplement, so he says, as if the band of assassins known as the Shadows compose a kind of mirror faculty, that Gradus "has colleagues in Arcady too" (p. 180). He spirits the poet's immortal poem to a hiding place with other Zemblan artifacts while intoning a self-serving Arcadian lament: "My work is finished. My poet is dead" (p. 300).

Death is a contingency for the contingent world, a fate that strong-minded exilic fabulists admit less readily than local chroniclers. At the very beginning of *Pale Fire*, presumably before Kinbote gets his hands on it if we grant that the dedication to Véra and the epigraph are not his, Nabokov reveals the subjective impulse to close off death from life, to avoid the invasions of violence that can shatter insular visions and obliterate domestic security. For its epigraph, *Pale Fire* sports an anecdote about Samuel Johnson and his famous cat, Hodge. Upon hearing the story of a lunatic walking the streets of London and shooting cats, Johnson says, Boswell records, and Nabokov cites: "But Hodge shan't be shot: no, no, Hodge shall not be shot." The power of Johnson's concerned mind cannot admit the seepage of contingency into his own reality. This does not so much make the story of the cat-killer a fiction and Johnson's conviction about Hodge a certainty; rather, it makes Johnson's insistence on Hodge's insularity a symptom of his own anxious imaginative power. Perhaps Hodge is not marked for this particular cat-killer, but there will be some contingencies that even Hodge can't dodge.

In similar fashion, despite the elaborate lengths to which Kinbote goes to seal off his supplemental projection—covering himself with the fair-copy cards of Shade's poem, writing its last line, coaxing the pathetic lunatic, Jack Grey, to admit to the Zemblan scheme, taking refuge with his anxious dementia in the vaults of variants—his very language hints that he is the "ego" that violates Arcady. Of possible lunatics in the neighborhood, Kinbote claims he knows no local madmen personally, but he mixes his pronouns, his allusions, and his sly references to Gradus while ventriloquizing what others say of Kinbote's presence in Appalachia: "'Even in Arcady, am I,' says Dementia" (p. 237). In the doubling that takes place in the seepages of *Pale Fire*, the killer and his object become linked, just as the word *Kinbote* breaks down etymologically into "kingly destroyer." If Gradus is, like Kinbote, demented, then Kinbote is, like Gradus, an assassin. Kinbote will repay in kind for the violation of his royal, almost divine, sanctity, and Nabokov even manages to mirror his own Russian experiences into Gradus's several reflections, bringing exilic dementia a bit closer to home.

> All this is as it should be; the world needs Gradus. But Gradus should not kill kings. Vinogradus should never, never provoke God. Leningradus should not aim his pea-shooter at people even in dreams, because if he does, a pair of colossally thick, abnormally hairy arms will hug him from behind and squeeze, squeeze, squeeze. [p. 154]

When the supplement becomes too perverse in Nabokov's fiction, when the imaginer doubles as assassin-god, the powerful, mirroring mind of art becomes its own worst enemy. Of the meaning of his own name, Kinbote comments to Shade: " 'Yes, a king's destroyer,' I said (longing to explain that a king who sinks his identity in the mirror of exile is in a sense just that)" (p. 267). Kinbote's head hurts at the end of *Pale Fire* when his dazzling Zembla jostles for space in his brain with the migraines that are driving him crazy. Causes confuse effects as Kinbote reverts to a kind of mock-clarity without supplemental potential, symptom without vision: "I may pander to the simple tastes of theatrical critics and cook up a stage play, an old-fashioned melodrama with three principles: a lunatic who intends to kill an imaginary king, another lunatic who imagines himself to be that king, and a distinguished old poet who stumbles by chance into the line of fire, and perishes in the clash between two figments" (p. 301).

What happens here is not simple; it is not merely a moment of sanity in which Kinbote, inadvertently punning on the key and generative word *fire,* sarcastically provides the actual or imaginatively unadorned plot of the novel; it is also a point where, knowing the wealth of what has gone before in the texture of the commentary, the reader can correctly imagine the poverty of literalness if that is all the projecting imagination has to offer. The orchestrative Kinbote, the misreader, the mad editor who covers himself with Shade's poem, is the exilic artist. When Kinbote comments on the line from Pope's *Essay on Man* struck from Shade's poem, "The sot a hero, lunatic a king," he claims not to know its source and says, without exploring its implications, that Shade struck it because of possible offense to a certain king, not to a certain lunatic. Similarly, when Kinbote forces his own name into the ellipsis of Shade's variant line "Poor old man Swift, poor—, poor Baudelaire" (p. 167), he inserts himself between a mad prose writer and a mad poet, surely hoping to share the genius of the company rather than the agony of lunacy.

The literal, as Nabokov well knew, is a none-too-wholesome refuge for art. Those who are committed literalists, whose sole motivation is thirst for revenge or appetite for destruction, are those "for whom romance, remoteness, sealskin-lined scarlet skies, the darkening dunes of a fabulous kingdom, simply do not exist" (p. 85). Gradus is such a figure; so, too, Sybil Shade, who stands in the mind of the visionary Kinbote with the figment Gradus, as a kind of denier. She is a "domestic anti-Karlist" (p. 74). For Kinbote, the Zemblan king, Sybil is also a "domestic censor," responsible for erasing the traces of Zemblan material from Shade's poem, thus barring the king-commentator from the vision of his history that he imagines Shade has imagined for him or along with him. Gradus is far worse. For creatures such as he, whether conjured or real, artistic power, mental power, even political power are preferably brought to one dead level: "People who knew too much, scientists, writers, mathematicians, crystalographers and so forth, were no better than kings or priests: they all held an unfair share of power of which others were cheated" (p. 152).

Kinbote makes it clear that the literalist, assassinating impulse, cannot even imagine the creative impulse when he says of Gradus: "We must assume, I think, that the forward projection of what imagination he had, stopped at the act, on the brink of all its possible consequences; ghost consequences, comparable to the ghost toes of an amputee or to the fanning out of additional squares which a chess knight (the skip-space piece), standing on a marginal file, 'feels' in phantom extensions beyond the board, but which have no effect whatever on his real moves, on the real play" (p. 276). Ghosts can be the shadows of *Pale Fire,* the supplementing images in the book and products of the imagination's most potent forces, but Gradus, among his other failings, is less a ghost with an afterlife than a corpse masking a mechanical man. He has no life left in him. After an affair with his blind and dropsical mother-in-law, he tries several times to castrate himself "and now, at forty-four, was quite cured of the lust that Nature, the grand cheat, puts into us to inveigle us into propagation" (p. 253).

In the absolute form of Kinbote's dementia, Gradus exists in Kinbote's own head, a migraine-like double whom he would annihilate with a reflexive bear hug: "At times I thought that only by self-destruction could I hope to cheat the relentlessly advancing assassins who were in me, in my eardrums, in my pulse, in my skull" (p. 97). But in the nostalgic aesthetics of Zembla, Kinbote distinguishes himself from the fretting, soporific Gradus: "How much happier the wide-awake indolents, the monarchs among men, the rich monstrous brains deriving intense enjoyment and rapturous pangs from the balustrade of a terrace at nightfall, from the lights and the lake below" (p. 232). "Monarchs" is plural at this point, as if the kingdom of Kinbote's imagination multiplies sovereign exiles rather than subtracts lost principalities. And it is testimony to the power of the imagining mind in opposition to the literal mind that Gradus the assassin, in Kinbote's version, hits the wrong man. In a way, what he does is take the literal in John Shade down with him, thus succeeding in burying one poet while inadvertently releasing the ghost of Zembla, a more restrained "project" than Kinbote's, "a minute but genuine star ghost of my discourse on Zembla and her unfortunate king" (p. 82).

Shade's poem, whose failing from Kinbote's perspective is its admission of too much that did not memorialize him, becomes a double or a Zemblan supplement only when it is no longer a rival or a Zemblan assassinator. Kinbote must squeeze its body to free its vision. An assassin is thus drawn to New Wye purely by the mechanical, literal nature of Shade's art, the line-to-line movement of the poem, "the very mechanism and sweep of verse, the powerful iambic motor" (p. 136). Kinbote's observation on Gradus's presumed movement comes in a note on lines 131–32, Canto I, lines that repeat with a difference the violent opening lines of the poem: "I was the shadow of the waxwing slain / By feigned remoteness in the windowpane" (p. 37). The art of assassination, in this sense, is the literal collision of Shades and Shadows, and for every ghost that flies a body falls.

Stygian Soaks and Lethean Leaks

There are two supreme fictions at work in *Pale Fire,* fictions that are based in one way or another on the exilic projections of narrative art and the farcical seepages of Nabokovian wit. Even in the spookiest of otherworld visions, communications through dreams with the dead, the imagination finds itself subject to domestic embellishments, accidental details—like puddles on the basement room floor—that seem to seep into projected worlds. Kinbote comments on a passage in John Shade's poem, "Pale Fire": "We all know those dreams in which something Stygian soaks through and Lethe leaks in the dreary terms of defective plumbing" (p. 231).

In *Pale Fire,* the visionary may get enmeshed in domestic pipings, the magical may touch the pedestrian, romance may surface as parody, but the Stygian experience possesses the remnants of its original, the *Aeneid*'s descent. Like the Roman Aeneas, Kinbote means to project from his present circumstances a full history of past wonder and future poetic promise. His domestic lot as "exiled prince" is a one-man *translatio imperii,* and he requires a history that is providential, just as he insists that the afterlife, "Independence Day in Hades" (p. 226), is not some chaotic "science fiction yarn" but has a real end, a *telos*.

Kinbote's past and envisioned simulacrum, his Zemblan unreal estate, is most manifest when, at the moment of the poet Shade's death in the narrative, Charles clutches the bundle of index cards that make up the manuscript of "Pale Fire": "I was holding all Zembla pressed to my heart" (p. 289). Though the scarcity of reference to his supplemental kingdom disappoints Kinbote, he reinvests himself in Shade's narrative by getting underneath it, becoming its Avernian or

Stygian spectacle. As Kinbote says of the variants of "Pale Fire," the supplementary stuff upon which his imagination works: "Actually, it turns out to be beautifully accurate when you once make the plunge and compel yourself to open your eyes in the limpid depths under its confused surface" (p. 14).

In the last phrase of his own index, and thus in the last words of *Pale Fire,* Kinbote describes Zembla as "a distant northern land" (p. 315); its imaginative, literary, or, if anyone insists, real location, places it in the traditional region of literary magic lands and afterworlds. The Avernian spaces of the *Aeneid* are "up toward the frozen North" (6:22), and the very name, Zembla, is itself a kind of blank, icy, fantasy or poetic trope, a place named by Shade's favorite poet, Alexander Pope, in the *Dunciad* and in the *Essay on Man.* Zembla for Pope is a figuration, a poetic shorthand, the place for the no place, like the actual place names Kinbote remembers from his northern homeland: Embla Point, Emblem Bay, the Gulf of Surprise. [18]

Pale Fire is steeped with examples of its own supplemental vision-making, rendered in language that reflects back on the narrative's and poem's title. The first mention of the phrase "pale fire" comes with an image of Shade standing next to his incinerator burning the index-card drafts of a poem like "wind-borne black butterflies" (p. 15). [19] Kinbote, too, is a fireside imaginer of sorts—he even offers a parable of the Zemblan creation when, if we believe his fantasy, he falls asleep in front of a farmer's fire during his revolutionary escape while "shadows of his lost kingdom gathered to play around his rocking chair" (p. 140). To sleep, perchance to dream: such a state is something like the imagined death or death-in-life that allows poetry its Lethean vision or Kinbote's supplement its exilic splendor—"even the most demented mind still contains within its diseased mass a sane basic particle that survives death and suddenly expands, bursts out as it were, in peals of healthy and triumphant laughter when the world of timorous fools and trim blockheads has fallen away far behind" (p. 237). [20]

Kinbote says that if "I were a poet I would certainly make an ode to the sweet urge to close one's eyes and surrender utterly unto the perfect safety of wooed death" (p. 221). Here the unreal estate is a kind of Asphodel, and, as a recent commentator on the common gaffe in the transcription of Wordsworth's *Immortality Ode*—"fields of sheep" for "fields of sleep"—points out, the editor may slip into woolly pastoral memories but the poet meant "phantom underworld of the Greeks."[21] As Shade might say, "Life Everlasting—based on a misprint!" (p. 62). In the most famous of underworld descents, of course, the exiled Aeneas reascends through one of the gates of sleep, the one made of ivory.

> There are two gates of Sleep, one said to be
> Of horn, whereby the true shades pass with ease,
> The other all white ivory agleam
> Without a flaw, and yet false dreams are sent
> Through this one by the ghost to the upper world.
> Anchises now, his last instructions given,
> Took son and Sibyl there and let them go
> By the Ivory Gate.
>
> [Book 6, 893–900, trans. Fitzgerald]

In a sense, Aeneas's experience remains unavailable to him or to anyone else except through retelling as a dream, and a potentially false dream in the bargain. Commentators on the descent guess that the gates of ivory have something to do with voicing a vision, as if the hero can only tell his supplemental tale by whistling through his teeth. Nabokov has something of the same notion in mind when he has Kinbote describe his path of escape through a secret tunnel from his fantasy palace at Onhava (which means far away). The big lie passes out through an underworld tunnel. As he exits the world of his self-romance and enters the public theater, moving from fantasy to performance, Charles Rex appropriately meets a deformed statue of "Mercury, conductor of souls to the Lower World" (p. 133). The rest of *Pale Fire* consists of getting someone, namely Shade, to believe in the substance of this vision.

Kinbote's adventure makes poets of the dispossessed, exiles out of kings. Whether he invents the entire sequence or not, dozens of Charles's dispersing retainers appear in royal garb, supposedly to confuse the rebels taking power. The gesture is as imaginative as it is strategic. Exiles by the number assume the guise of kingship to ease the anguish of having no kingdom to call their own. Of course, the signifying king, the king who later wishes his friend John Shade would call the poem about him *Solus Rex*, [22] is in every sense all alone after Zembla.

The narrative of Kinbote's exit from Zembla is itself the longest supplement or annotation in *Pale Fire;* it is also the most irrelevant note to anything in Shade's poem. Kinbote says slyly, as if he knows he has put one over, "I trust the reader has enjoyed this note" (p. 147). Later, he recalls the language of the note at the crucial moment when he has to transfer its rudiments to the whole of his exile; he emerges from his New Wye closet after secreting Shade's manuscript in the hope that it will testify to his vision: "I exited as if it had been the end of the secret passage that had taken me all the way out of my enchanted castle and right from Zembla to *this* Arcady" (p. 295). Kinbote speaks metaphorically here of what he had recorded as actuality; but the exilic fable in *Pale Fire* suggests that his "actuality" is, in fact, all metaphor.

Supplemental places have to be imagined and articulated because, like Aeneas's vision of the "plot" for a future imperial Rome, they do not exist in reachable form. Another of Nabokov's northern exiles, Professor Pnin, mentioned in *Pale Fire* as head of Wordsmith's Russian Department, experiences in a more direct way the Virgilian dream through the gates of ivory. In the novel bearing his name, *Pnin,* the professor finds it difficult to portray and memorialize his supplemental world, his lost Russia, until he replaces his rotten teeth, which become an emblem of the very subject that stymies him. He first goes "into mourning for an intimate part of himself," a teethscape memory of old "familiar rocks," or coves and caves of a "battered but still secure kingdom." With his new ivories, what he calls his "new amphitheater of translucid plastics," Pnin feels like "a fossil skull being fitted with the grinning jaw of a perfect stranger." But soon the dentures give him imaginative life: "It was a revelation, it was a sunrise, it was a firm mouthful of efficient, alabastrine, humane America." At this point the freedom from the throbbing pain of exile, old teeth, allows him to begin work on a "dream mixture of folklore, poetry, social history, and *petite histoire*,"[23] exactly the kind of material that exits through Kinbote's passageway from palace to theater to New Wye's Arcady.

The Prince and the Sibyl

For Nabokov's domestic poet, who happens to be a real Shade—Zembla has only "fugitive poets" with names like Amphitheatricus—the reascent from the world whose borders he has struggled to cross is less voiced than written out: "The pen stops in mid-air, then swoops to bar / A canceled sunset or restore a star, / And thus it physically guides the phrase / Toward faint daylight through the inky maze" (p. 64). But for Kinbote the only way out of the supplement is through Shade's poem—he must make all experience a kind of vision, a kind of dream of his own history. There is even the hint in *Pale Fire,* as there is in the *Aeneid,* that the supplement is a part of history without actually being history, that it is the most unabashedly made-up part of the hero's exile, possessing the poetic reality of dreams, what Kinbote calls the "rich streak" of the imagination's "magical madness." Shade asks Kinbote—or, at least, is reported to have asked—how he knows that all this intimate stuff about the Zemblan king is true, and Kinbote replies that the issue is not authenticity so much as another kind of truth: "My dear John . . . do not worry about trifles. Once transmuted by you into poetry, the stuff *will* be true, and the people *will* come alive. A poet's unified truth can cause no pain, no offense" (p. 214). He doesn't exactly answer Shade's question, but he does imply that the project, in all senses, is more important than the verification of its particulars. He is a king in search of a laureate, but, like Aeneas, he is also an exiled hero in search of his own vision.

The envisioned space can easily become a home place for the discomfited mind, a mind imaginatively exiled until it fixes new boundaries for itself, which is one of the things the Avernian descent in the

Aeneid does; it marks out the future city limits of an Imperial Rome on a then empty field. In *The Gift,* Nabokov's most autobiographical narrative, he writes movingly of the act of poetic inspiration as the crossing of boundaries toward new imagined homelands, confusing the rivers of forgetfulness and vision: "That river is not the Lethe but rather the Styx. Never mind. Let's proceed: And now a crooked bough looms near the ferry and Charon with his boathook, in the dark, reaches for it, and catches it, and very . . . slowly the bark revolves, the silent bark. Homeward, homeward! I feel tonight like composing with pen in hand. What a moon!" (p. 87). Or what pale fire!

Even locally tethered narrative imaginations in *Pale Fire* desire the control over space and time that the otherworld or underworld supplement brings. John Shade's poem is, after all, actively, outwardly about the otherworld, though its fullest supplementary projection, the Institute of Preparation for the Hereafter—"I really could not tell / The difference between this place and Hell" (p. 56), says Sybil Shade—is more parodic than visionary. Still, I.P.H. provides a place where the weak imagination learns in primer fashion what the strong imagination, less damned than freed to circulate, projects in narrative: "How not to panic when you're made a ghost: / Sidle and slide, choose a smooth surd, and coast, / Meet solid bodies and glissade right through, / Or let a person circulate through you" (pp. 53–54). The spatial, almost tactile, irrational ("smooth surd") and the verbal license to "coast," with its hint of territorial borderlands and crossings, provide both the narrative estate for the Nabokovian supplemental world and the opportunity for the kind of interpenetration or seepage that rules the action and counteraction of *Pale Fire:* "let a person circulate through you."

At the time Shade seeks out I.P.H. (his relation to life or *"L'if"* is as conjectural as his relation to death), he feels the need as powerfully as does Kinbote to cross borders and escape. It is only later that his attitude is wait-and-see: "Life is a great surprise. I do not see why death should not be an even greater one" (p. 225). Though Shade's journey in "Pale Fire" is as much in the realm of doubt as in the realm of supplementary projection, it is no less pressing and pressuring an imaginative quest. In fact, his first poetic act in early life is a transporting epileptic funk, "An icy shiver down my Age of Stone, / And all tomorrows in my funnybone," that distributes him "through space and time" (p. 38). Later he turns classical tourist and modulates into a calmer otherworld to contemplate meetings "With Socrates and Proust in cypress walks, / The seraph with his six flaming wings, / And Flemish bells with porcupines and things" (p. 41).

Shade's interest in these imaginative projections has much to do with the path he senses his daughter has taken before him in Avernian depths: "A blurry shape stepped off the reedy bank / Into a crackling, gulping swamp, and sank" (p. 51). And his "survey / Of death's abyss" is as much motivated by misery as is Kinbote's supplemental vision; the poet a grief writer whose "vision" at his second crossing "reeked with truth. It had the tone, / The quiddity and quaintness of its own / Reality" (p. 60). Though Kinbote is quick to distinguish between the imaginative sunburst of his own romance supplement and the absurd, small, personal, painful details of Shade's daughter's death that has been emphasized and showcased, "expanded and elaborated to the detriment of certain other richer and rarer matters ousted by it" (p. 164), there is an Aristotelian "whatness" about Shade's otherworldly art, an art that, like Kinbote's commentary, creates word-worlds as supplements for the remotely possible.

If Kinbote questions Shade's loyalty to his Zemblan theme, Shade is well within his aesthetic rights to reject the grafting of Kinbote's "whole marvelous" supplement upon the body of his Appalachian descent. But it is surely a grand part of the exuberance of *Pale Fire* as a whole that the poet Shade and the commentator-cum-exiled king, Kinbote, whether separable figures within a fictionally represented world or figments of each other in a mad farce, possess different kinds of supplemental imaginations, or, in a Nabokovian sense, capable imaginations.[24] Shade is the imaginative skeptic; Kinbote the quixotic self-mythographer. From Kinbote's perspective, Shade leaks all the sorry fireside contingencies of domestic pathos; from Shade's perspective, Kinbote soaks up all moon-mad Zemblamania. But the fireside poet and exiled romancer join forces against debunkers and blatant literalists. When Shade complains that a certain Mrs. H. ought not apply the word *lunatic* to a poet who "peels off a drab and unhappy past and replaces it with a brilliant invention," that big bear of a Zemblan schizoid, Charles Kinbote, also rumbles to the defense: "We are all, in a sense, poets, Madam" (p. 238). Perhaps the implicit connection between Kinbote's Zemblan *romaunt* and Shade's stuffed domestic owl enters the narrative in the form of a sister art and a maiden aunt, Maud Shade, "A poet and a painter with a taste / For realistic objects interlaced / With grotesque growths and images of doom" (p. 36). Here is the pale fire of the imagination, what Nabokov calls the coal dust of realism joining the fading coal of romance in a region where the exile and the artist, both "just half a shade," share domain with the living and dead.

Shade is, in a way, Kinbote's Virgil or wished-for Virgil, capable of fulfilling him, including all the sudden glories and *lachrymae rerum* in his life: "We are absurdly accustomed to the miracle of a few written signs being able to contain immortal imagery, involutions of thought, new worlds with live people, speaking, weeping, laughing" (p. 289). But such projections tend to be mediated and, as in the Virgilian supplement, actually barred by a Cumaean sibyl who speaks for the poetic voice of Apollo and only painfully, grudgingly grants access to the desired vision. For Shade in *Pale Fire,* his Sybil is an ally, a wife of forty years, but for Kinbote, Sybil is a terror who does what she can to ensure the ignorance of the exile and extend the agony of his as yet unmemorialized historical displacement. It is only her gratefulness after Kinbote's seeming heroism during the fatal episode at the end that allows Charles Rex the official rights to the poem he has already stolen.

We see Sybil as the protectress of the grove or garden, just as she is in the Virgilian epic: "Straw-hatted and garden-gloved, she was squatting on her hams in front of a flower bed and pruning or tying up something" (p. 86). It is at this time, as Kinbote recalls, that she provided the information that Shade had "begun a really big poem." But henceforth she blocks all vision whenever she can; she literally pulls down shades on Shade: "for he never pulled down the shades (*she* did)" (p. 87).

In a more important and more crucial sense for the aesthetics of *Pale Fire,* Shade's poem, and Kinbote's commentary upon it, Sybil's role is to make the imaginer fall short of his potential, the full possibilities of vision. It is, fittingly, Shade who comes to this conclusion. When he writes of the poet's expansive sense of time and place, that habit of mind aligning the stuff of the communal experience with the powers of supplementing invention ("Coordinating these / Events and objects with remote events / And vanished objects"), he also writes of "Making ornaments / Of accidents and possibilities" (p. 63). With the last syllables of his line ringing in his ear, Shade then writes of entering the house to talk to his wife, only to be rudely interrupted: "Sybil, it is / My firm conviction—'Darling, shut the door'" (p. 63). Her interruption stymies the very kinds of transformation poetry makes possible—she is, as Shade retrospectively realizes, but a fragment of possibility ("sybilitis"), coming a syllable short.

After Shade's death, when Kinbote wrests control of the editing rights of "Pale Fire" from Sybil, he makes sure that he has enough syllables in reserve to round out the poem and his record in it. Kinbote not only supplements the poem with his commentary, but he recasts its first line as its yet unwritten last. The circle he closes keeps Sybil out, as he squeezes into his own Cumaean spectacle. For the exilic imaginer, it is a closure that inscribes both vision and madness. Projected space has become sovereign space, and Shade's first line becomes Kinbote's last. The fated waxwing, whose death in one sense images the violence of reflected worlds but in another sense images an afterlife or the possibility of freeing the imagination, revives: "I / Lived on, flew on, in the reflected sky." The bird in the reflection plummets as a mirror image of its own contingent fate or flies on as a life-after-death supplement. In this way, the opening lines of Shade's poem replay the imaginative trope of *Pale Fire*—the image or illusion of projection and its attendant "eschatological shocks." Kinbote the exile flies away with the poem when Shade the domestic poet, in the language of the criminal world, is "offed."

The waxwing—Icarian in its sudden death, Daedalian in its continued flight—falls as literalist but soars as exilic imaginer. And it is Kinbote the conjurer, for better or worse, as he himself observes, who has the last word, thereby reserving Shade's unfinished narrative for his own exilic flight. By supplying a last and enclosing line, Kinbote performs the final rite of imaginative projection, enacting the metaphoric notion that the poet may die a bit every time a poem is finished but that the imagination is immortal. If the sovereign exile, Solus Rex, rules on within the spaces of "Pale Fire" by appropriating it for commentary, Kinbote at the very least allows his Virgil, John Shade, the unintended luxury of writing his own epitaph.

Epilogue

When Henry James writes of the process of narrative composition in his preface to *The Ambassadors,* he notices that his retracing of the means by which he devised the action produces a new illusionistic thrill, a duplicate of the invention, what he calls "adventure *transposed*—the thrilling ups and downs, the intricate ins and outs of the compositional problem."[1] James's phrase allegorizes writing as a version of the experience it projects, as "a real extension, if successful, of the very terms and possibilities of representation and figuration."[2]

Any assessment of narrative action has to account for the paradoxical and sometimes downright contradictory principles of mimesis and allegory that govern it. Though we are given to assume that the primary circumstances and motives behind, say, realistic or naturalistic representation conform in some way to recognizable beings, places, institutions that exist in the world, what we actually experience in narrative is a mirage for which we provide wider social, political, economic, psychological contexts. The ease with which we extend such provisions experientially may determine the degree to which we would call a narrative real or natural, but, like Glendower beckoning the spirits, the mere calling it so does not make it so.

As much as a narrator would have his hearers or readers believe in the legitimacy or authenticity of events narrated, the effect of representation is linked to that power of imagination which prides itself on making *made-up* things project into a different aesthetic dimension— in the broadest sense, allegorizing them. André Gide has his Edouard Molinier, a novelist within a generatively named novel, *The Counterfeiters,* express indignation that anyone would think his task merely to reproduce, in a Balzacian manner, the civil records of France: "What have I to do with the *état-civil? L'état c'est moi!* I, the artist; civil or not, my work doesn't pretend to rival anything."[3]

I have indeed been arguing throughout this book that narrative performs not only as an experiential rival but as an aesthetic substitute or supplement. Exilic imagining in this sense is both the mirror and the "other" of narrative process; mimesis becomes an alien (or allegorical) phenomenon that establishes fictional sovereignty on fictional ground. From Defoe's *Robinson Crusoe* to Nabokov's *Pale Fire,* exilic space is the metaphoric terrain of projected adventure, and exilic time a resource for narrative repatriation.

In Marcel Proust's *Remembrance of Things Past,* one of the narrator's many observations on the imaginative state of mind that serves as a kind of narrative field theory for the novel provides what is, in effect, the central aesthetic argument for what I have called the property of exilic imagining. The narrator speaks of what it is like to conjure up the image of one place while rooted in another, and he concludes that aesthetic reality or aesthetic space mirrors the relation between desire and projection: "Even from the simplest, the most realistic point of view, the countries for which we long occupy, at any given moment, a far larger place in our actual life than the country in which we happen to be."[4] This would hold whether one is in one's own country dreaming of another or in another dreaming of one's own. Furthermore, as it does for Proust's narrator and for such memorialists as Nabokov's Van Veen, the remark also holds for those physically at home in a given place but temporally exiled from an earlier experience of it. The place in time has *become* exilic ground, inhabitable only through the approximations of narrative remembrance.

It is precisely the metaphoric lines that exile plots along both a temporal and a spatial axis that make it so dominant a condition in narrative and so prominent an emblem for the narrative imagination. Alain Robbe-Grillet, after some extended theorizing on the formal program for the postmodernist New Novel, says what I would want to say about the essence of narrative representation generally: "For of course an *elsewhere* is no more possible than a *formerly.*"[5] The narrative imagination inhabits exilic domain where absence is presence, or, to put it the other way around, where presence is absence. Narrative and exilic imaginers evoke powers of verbal re-creation and powers of memorial nostalgia that forge what Wordsworth calls those lawless tales taking place in the "here, nowhere, there, and everywhere at once."

Notes

Preface

1 In his study of the history of exile, funded, in part, by a committee of the United Nations, Paul Tabori defines an exile as someone who conceives of his or her displacement as temporary even "though it lasts a lifetime" (*The Anatomy of Exile: A Semantic and Historical Study* [London, 1972], p. 27). Tabori's study is useful in its compilation of material relating to all aspects of exile, though the thrust of his study points toward the massive displacements of individuals and populations in the twentieth century.

2 *The American Scene*, ed. Leon Edel (Bloomington, Ind., 1968), pp. 52–53.

3 Ibid., pp. 229–30.

4 *Pale Fire* (New York, 1962), p. 95. For the relations of exile to contemporary intellectual and political life, to the myths of nationalism, and to the notion of secular estrangement, see Edward Said's powerful and moving essay, "The Mind of Winter: Reflections on Life in Exile," *Harper's*, September 1984, pp. 49–55. Said speaks here (as he does in the opening chapter, "Secular Criticism," of his book *The World, the Text, and the Critic* [Cambridge, Mass., 1983]) of the debilitating personal and cultural strains of exile that attend what he calls the salutary "executive value" of exilic perspective. For a general essay on literature and exile which covers an immense amount of temporal-spatial territory in a few pages, see Harry Levin, "Literature and Exile," in *Refractions* (Oxford, 1966), pp. 62–81.

5 *Speak, Memory: An Autobiography Revisited* (New York, 1966), p. 250.

6 *The Gift* (New York, 1963), p. 187.

7 Ibid., p. 37.

8 For a brief but important essay on the nexus of language in the aesthetics of exile, see George Steiner's "Extraterritorial," in *Extraterritorial: Papers on Literature and the Language Revolution* (New York, 1971), pp. 3–11.

9 For the Hegelian critic Georg Lukàcs in his *Theory of the Novel*, the modern sense of alienation and homelessness is the dominant epic residue of the nineteenth- and twentieth-century novel; and even for the non-Marxist historian-mythographer

Oswald Spengler in his *Decline of the West,* the condition of rootlessness marks the drift of the West to a condition characterized, in part, by urban nomadicism.

Introduction

1 Conrad, *A Personal Record,* in *The Works of Joseph Conrad,* Dent Collected Edition (London, 1946; reprint of Dent Uniform Edition, 1923), p. 121.

2 *Lord Jim,* in *Works,* p. 111.

3 Ibid., p. 229.

4 *Ulysses* (New York, 1961), p. 687.

5 *Metamorphoses,* 8, 183–89, trans. Frank Justus Miller, Loeb Library (Cambridge, Mass., 1916; rev. 1977), 1:419.

6 *Ada or Ardor: A Family Chronicle* (New York, 1969), p. 264.

7 *Either/Or,* trans. David F. Swenson and Lillian Marvin Swenson (New York, 1959), 1:64. Franz Kafka makes a similar point, roundabout, in a parable entitled simply "On Parables." His is a particularly Kafkaesque version of the apostle Mark's argument that only at the very highest and almost inarticulable levels of wisdom literature do parables and fables convey meaning in any significant way different from meaning already assimilated or experienced. Kafka seizes on the metaphoric phrase "Gehe hinuber" (go over or across), which ought to suggest the function of imaginative transfer but rarely does so: "When the sage says: 'Go over,' he does not mean that we should cross to some actual place, which we could do anyhow if the labor were worth it; he means some fabulous yonder, something unknown to us, something too that he cannot designate more precisely, and therefore cannot help us here in the very least. All these parables really set out to say is that the incomprehensible is incomprehensible, and we know that already. But the cares we have to struggle with every day: that is a different matter" (*Parables and Paradoxes* [New York, 1961], pp. 10–11).

8 In the *New Science,* Vico argues that it is at the boundary that metaphorical extension takes over in defining institutions because metaphor is best equipped to transfer properties close at hand to properties distant: "When man understands he extends his mind and takes in the things, but when he does not understand he makes the things out of himself and becomes them by transforming himself into them" (*New Science,* trans. Thomas Goddard Bergin and Max Harold Fisch [Ithaca, 1970], p. 88). Points and places of origin for Vico are those at which metaphor begins to solidify strangeness into institutional form.

9 "Geography and Some Explorers," in *Last Essays, Works,* p. 13.

10 Though Kierkegaard's parable is conceived in spatial terms, there is a temporal component implied in it. Projection as repetition assumes continuity as well as contiguity. "Repetition," says Kierkegaard cryptically, "is reality" (*On Repetition: An Essay in Experimental Psychology* [Princeton, 1941], p. 6). In Paul

Ricoeur's recent speculation on temporality in fiction, "Narrative Time," he argues the similar point that narrative, as the result of its spatial projection in time, is "reconnected to anticipation, and anticipation rooted in retrospection" (*On Narrative*, ed. W. J. T. Mitchell [Chicago, 1981], p. 174).

11 *Ada*, p. 333.

12 The idea of the boundary is important not only in the romance of science fiction but in Gothic romance. There the outlandish, by the operation of a different moral and dimensional physics, crosses back to the familiar. The Gothic is a narrative mode in which the ordinary soul is under constant threat by its vaguely human antitype, a soul perpetually, restlessly, in exile, but intent on penetrating into domestic circumstance. Incursions of the boundless and timeless into the quotidien are rather like border raids into settled territory.

13 These lines are from Auden's "A Happy New Year," a poem marking the divides of time as well as the boundaries of space. Edward Mendelson points out that Auden uses the word *property* "in the deeper Latinate sense that derives from *proprietas*, that which is proper to a thing and makes it itself, not something else instead" (*Early Auden* [New York, 1981], p. 126).

14 *Despair* (New York, 1966), p. 37.

15 *Speak, Memory*, p. 40.

16 Benjamin, "The Image of Proust," in *Illuminations*, ed. Hannah Arendt, trans. Harry Zohn (New York, 1969), p. 205. J. Hillis Miller discusses Benjamin's essay in *Fiction and Repetition in Seven English Novels* (Cambridge, Mass., 1982) and comments on Proust that his homesickness for the "home from which he was exiled [was] not the likeness of ordinary longing for home. To it apply exactly those phrases used by Walter Pater to describe 'aesthetic poetry': 'The secret of the enjoyment of it is that inversion of home-sickness known to some, that incurable thirst for the sense of escape, which no actual form of life satisfies, no poetry even, if it be merely simple and spontaneous'" (p. 12).

17 Charles Bernheimer, *Flaubert and Kafka: Studies in Psychopoetic Structure* (New Haven, 1982), p. 151.

18 *The Castle*, trans. Wila and Edwin Muir, additional material trans. Eithne Wilkins and Ernst Kaiser (New York, 1974), p. 449.

19 Dante employs the same psalm verse for the turn in the *Commedia* from Hell's seas to Mount Purgatory, and Joyce employs it, remembering Dante, when Bloom and Stephen leave the house at Eccles Street for the parodic parting of the waters in the Jew's garden at *nostos*.

20 *Paradiso*, trans. Charles S. Singleton (Princeton, 1973), p. 191.

21 *Under Western Eyes*, in *Works*, p. 209.

22 For information on just how old the punishment of exile is, see E. Balogh, *Political Refugees in Ancient Greece* (Johannesburg, 1943). Balogh describes some of the old tribal rituals that allowed an exile from one community to approach a

designated place at the border of another (a tree, a rock, a stream) and await the communal decision on admittance. In his discussion of the scapegoat in *Violence and the Sacred,* trans. Patrick Gregory (Baltimore, 1977), René Girard points out how criminals in ancient time were cast out beyond tribal frontiers, either to kill themselves because they were no longer a part of the community or to remain marginal, as it were, for a space of time (pp. 298 ff.).

23 *Tristia* 1.1.55–61, trans. Arthur Leslie Wheeler, Loeb Classics (Cambridge, Mass., 1924), pp. 6–7.

24 Ibid., 4:10.115 ff., pp. 204–05.

25 Reintegration in this sense is comparable to the liminal rituals Victor Turner describes in primitive societies, whereby members of the group "betwixt and between the positions assigned and arrayed by law, custom, convention, and ceremonial" are disguised as aliens, sometimes monstrous, sometimes wild, until they are reformed and reincorporated into the community: "It is as though they are being ground down to a uniform condition to be fashioned anew" ("Liminality and Communitas" in *The Ritual Process: Structure and Anti-Structure* [Chicago, 1969], p. 95).

26 *Daniel Deronda* (Harmondsworth, 1967), chap. 3, p. 50. As much as home might have meant to her, Eliot argued that she was to get her own novelistic bearings only when she and George Lewes bolted to Germany. See U. C. Knoepflmacher, "On Exile and Fiction: The Leweses and the Shelleys," in *Mothering the Mind,* ed. Ruth Perry and Maxene Brownley (New York, 1984), pp. 102–21.

27 The Middle English word *elenge* partakes of the same meanings: miserable, solitary, lonely, strange.

28 In Gibbon's description of it, the second city of the Roman Empire, Byzantium (later Constantinople; later still, Istanbul) almost managed literally what Rome accomplished figuratively in relation to Troy: "Before Constantine gave a just preference to the situation of Byzantium, he had conceived the design of erecting the seat of empire on this celebrated spot, from whence the Romans derived their fabulous origin. The extensive plain which lies below ancient Troy, towards the Rhoetean promontory and the tomb of Ajax, was first chosen for his new capital; and, though the undertaking was soon relinquished, the stately remains of unfinished walls and towers attracted the notice of all who sailed through the straits of the Hellespont" (*The Decline and Fall of the Roman Empire,* ed. J. B. Bury [London, 1909], 2:146).

29 *The Life and Strange Surprizing Adventures of Robinson Crusoe,* ed. J. Donald Crowley (London, 1972), p. 128.

30 *Ulysses,* p. 109.

31 The word *supplement* has a particular critical currency these days because of the use to which Jacques Derrida puts it in *Of Grammatology,* trans. Gayatri Spivak (Baltimore, 1976). Whether the supplement fills a void or substitutes for some-

thing else, Derrida makes this one crucial point: in either case it is "alien to that which, in order to be replaced by it, must be other than it" (p. 145). Though Derrida does not name the underworld, he implies that such a place is the final supplement: "Imagination is at bottom the relationship with death . . . the power that allows life to affect itself with its own re-presentation. The image cannot represent and add the representer to the represented, except in so far as the presence of the re-presented is already folded back upon itself in the world, in so far as life refers to itself as to its own lack, to its own wish for a supplement. . . . In that sense imagination, like death, is *representative and supplementary*" (p. 184).

32 Poe, "The Purloined Letter," in *The Collected Works*, ed. Thomas Olive Mabbot (Cambridge, Mass., 1978), 3:993.

33 *The Analogy of the Faerie Queene* (Princeton, 1976), p. 777n.

34 *Ulysses*, p. 41.

35 Ibid., p. 216.

36 For a complex but rewarding study of allegory in literature and *as* literature, see Paul de Man, *Allegories of Reading: Figural Language in Rousseau, Nietzsche, Rilke, and Proust* (New Haven, 1979).

37 In *Genesis of Secrecy* (Cambridge, Mass., 1979), Frank Kermode comments on Kafka's parable of The Law in *The Trial*, admitting that his general application of that parable to interpretation is to "make an allegory, once more, of Kafka's parable; but some such position is the starting point of all modern hermeneutics except those which are consciously reactionary" (p. 123). Modernity has even circled around to a point behind the "reactionary" by proceeding in accord with what Kermode describes as the old Hebrew interpretive principle of *midrash*, "a way of finding in an existing narrative the potential of more narrative" (p. xi).

38 Commentators on narrative theory work very hard to distinguish between those works that announce themselves as allegory by design and those that would resist allegory if they could. Robert Scholes and Robert Kellogg, *The Nature of Narrative* (Oxford, 1966), for example, make the useful distinction between illustrative figuration, say, Spenser's *Faerie Queene*, where things are decidedly other than what they are, and representational figuration, say, Proust's *Remembrance of Things Past*, where a good deal of narrative activity contributes to making the "thing" a lot more of what it already is (p. 107). But figuration in narrative operates within a pattern of action that carries meaning; therefore, it is available for allegorization in some degree whether it chooses allegory or has allegory thrust upon it.

39 The Greek further extends the meaning of Odysseus's name to a pun on the word *trouble*. See George Dimock, "The Name of Odysseus," in *Essays on the Odyssey*, ed. Charles Taylor, Jr. (Bloomington, Ind., 1963).

40 In his long third chapter, "The Novel as Beginning Intention," in *Beginnings: Intention and Method* (New York, 1975), Edward Said writes of the contradictory

impulses in narrative wherein the same forces that strive to make a work believable also tend to violate its integrity as illusion. Narrative accounts are "molested" with an abundance of the very materials of life purportedly imitated.

41 *Molloy*, in *Molloy, Malone Dies, The Unnamable*, trans. Patrick Bowles (New York, 1955), p. 86.

42 Ibid.

Chapter One

1 *Ulysses* (New York, 1961), p. 109. All references are to this edition, emended, when necessary, in accord with the new Garland Edition (New York, 1984).

2 *The Life and Strange Surprizing Adventures of Robinson Crusoe*, ed. J. Donald Crowley (London, 1972), p. 142. All references are to this edition.

3 In his essay, "The Displaced Self in the Novels of Daniel Defoe," *ELH* 38 (1971):562–90, Homer O. Brown makes a similar point about temporal doubling in Crusoe's journal: "The journal is an attempt to define a situation by ordering the present as it becomes the past" (p. 585). The present "becomes" the past in the sense that it will both revert to the past in time and reflect the past's essence.

4 David Blewett discusses the action of *Robinson Crusoe* in terms of what he sees as the paradox at its center: "The island expresses the central paradox of the novel. There Crusoe is both imprisoned and set free, and in ways more complex than he at first grasps" (*Defoe's Art of Fiction: Robinson Crusoe, Moll Flanders, Colonel Jack, and Roxana* [Toronto, 1979], p. 31).

5 *Serious Reflections during the Life and Surprizing Adventures of Robinson Crusoe*, in *The Works of Daniel Defoe*, ed. G. H. Maynadier, 16 vols. (New York, 1903), 3:xi. All references are to this edition, as are references to *The Farther Adventures of Robinson Crusoe*.

6 In "*Robinson Crusoe*: 'Allusive Allegorick History,'" *PMLA* 82 (1967):399–407, Robert W. Ayers neatly defines the process as "a story whose literal meaning is augmented by a second meaning which is the construct of allusions in the literal narrative" (p. 400).

7 In his recent *Factual Fictions, the Origins of the English Novel* (Columbia, 1983), Lennard Davis argues that Defoe's position is hopelessly confused on the issue of truth telling. At the heart of Davis's presentation is a rather innocently framed question of why "one man's life should be the allegory of another's" (p. 160), as if Defoe were limited in what he could do with narrative invention because he takes on Crusoe's voice to defend Crusoe's story. But Defoe was playing on the notion that truth "sells"; his defense, after all, was part of the advertising paraphernalia for the Crusoe saga. John Richetti senses as much in *Defoe's Narratives: Situations and Structures* (Oxford, 1975) when he recognizes the art of advertising in the

various commentaries on the story: "It is, obviously, being sold as an extravaganza to people who like all of us value the exotic and the various as a pleasurable relief from the humdrum and uniform quality of daily life" (p. 24). Richetti's use of the word "extravaganza" is calculated; the remote wandering beyond bounds makes this feigned truth stranger than romance fiction.

8 Defoe, *A Collection of Miscellany Letters out of Mists's Weekly Journal* (London, 1722–27), 4:210. See Maximillian E. Novak, "Defoe's Theory of Fiction," *Studies in Philology* 61 (1964):650–68. This seminal essay goes far in addressing the entire matter of fiction, romance, and lying in Defoe's conceptual sense of narrative. Novak maintains, among other things, that Defoe took a traditionally Aristotelian position in privileging probability over verified actuality. What is probable in terms of what might be called the fictional contract is what is useful in extracting the meaning from any fable. Of course Novak knows, as all Defoe's readers ought, that in representing what looks to be probable in fiction Defoe also opens veins of complex narrative psychology that sustain an interest in his work beyond the theory of usefulness Defoe none too modestly advances for it.

9 In a panoramic sense, Robinson Crusoe's allusive allegoric history fulfills a traditional narrative pattern of sustained risk, trauma, and return, a pattern allegorically analogous to biblical history, various national histories, and spiritual and personal lives. See J. Paul Hunter, *The Reluctant Pilgrim: Defoe's Emblematic Method and Quest for Form in Robinson Crusoe* (Baltimore, 1966); George Starr, *Defoe and Spiritual Autobiography* (Princeton, 1965); and, most recently, Leopold Damrosch, Jr., *God's Plot and Man's Stories: Studies in the Fictional Imagination from Milton to Fielding* (Chicago, 1985).

10 *Moby Dick,* chap. 12, "Biographical" (New York, 1964), p. 88. Of course, an opposite argument has been made with a considerable array of facts to back it up. Defoe's biographer, John Robert Moore, in *Daniel Defoe: Citizen of the Modern World* (Chicago, 1958), claims that Defoe set the island specifically near the region of the Orinoco river basin in order to stimulate a scheme he favored for negotiating with Spain for trade rights in that area. Maximillian Novak takes up the thread of that argument in his chapter "Imaginary Island and Real Beasts: The Imaginative Genesis of *Robinson Crusoe,"* in *Realism, Myth, and History in Defoe's Fiction* (Lincoln, Neb., 1983), pp. 23–46. Novak points to a scheme that appeared in Defoe's *Weekly Journal,* 7 February 1719, for the South Sea Company to colonize territory at the mouth of the Orinoco in order to build ships and initiate massive trading operations. Defoe's imagination was, in a way, directed toward the region.

11 When W. Bliss Carnochan describes Crusoe's propensity to read into his island, he addresses one of the central ironies of the novel's allegorical dispensation: "By figuring his island allegorically in his journal he tries to distill its meaning. But the meaning he assigns it jars with the narrative rendering of his experience"

(*Confinement and Flight: An Essay on English Literature of the Eighteenth Century* [Berkeley, 1977], p. 30). One of the points to make about allegorical interpretation, whether it takes place as part of the action within a text or part of the experience of reading it, is that it tends to be overdetermined. In its need to make sense of something "other," allegory almost by design surpasses the range of the material about which it tries to make sense.

12 Defoe's notion of disobedience has a political cast to it that runs counter to the familial disobedience of Crusoe's presumed original sin. Like Locke, he does not confuse patriarchy and patriarchal politics. In fact, the abused doctrine of passive obedience on the patriarchal model stands at the center of Defoe's antagonism toward the Stuarts. In *Jure Divino* (1706), he points out that his long poetic satire against tyranny "had never been Publish'd, tho' some of it has been a long time in being, had not the World seem'd to be going mad a second Time with the Error of Passive Obedience and Non-Resistance" (p. i). The first time was in the latter days of an increasingly desperate James II, and an argument could be mounted that the Jacobite turn of mind existed right through the first several decades of the eighteenth century. For a different development of this notion centering on an economic reading of the fable, see Maximillian Novak's chapter, "Robinson Crusoe's Original Sin," in *Economics and the Fiction of Daniel Defoe* (Berkeley, 1962), pp. 32–48.

13 Crusoe's very name implies a species of wanderer. Robert W. Ayers ("'Allusive Allegorick History'") ponders the original name of the Crusoe family, Kreutznaer. He suggests various possibilities: *Kreutz* = cross, "to cross, to cruise" (a religious version would be a *Kreutzzug* or "crusade"); *naer* or naher = comparative of near; *nahren* = "to journey," "to approach." Crusoe's name, as befits the double exilic pattern, seems to mean both "to wander" and "to come home."

14 If one simply follows Defoe's major heroes and heroines around the globe (discounting sundry pirates and one lunar philosopher, who ascends 250,000 miles up but neglects to come down), one would travel the equivalent of ten times the circumference of the earth. Captain Singleton, the ocean's very waif, is the sweepstakes winner, logging over 100,000 miles. Crusoe places second with over 85,000 miles. Colonel Jack charts in at half that, over 40,000 miles. And Moll Flanders, with a bit of the original gypsy still in her soul, travels close to 20,000 miles.

15 In many attempts to trace the allegorical import of Crusoe's history, commentators have made scant mention of the historical or national coincidence in its timing. J. Paul Hunter is one of the few to notice the temporal parallel of the island exile: "Crusoe's twenty-eight years of isolation and suffering, for example, parallel the Puritan alienation between the Restoration and the accession of William and Mary; the allusion intensifies the sense of Crusoe's alienation from society and suggests the thematic implications of the Puritan emblematic reading

of events" (*The Reluctant Pilgrim*, p. 204). Douglas Brooks acknowledges Hunter and makes the same point briefly in his *Number and Pattern in the Eighteenth-Century Novel* (London, 1972), p. 25. I have developed the notion in an earlier version of this chapter, "Crusoe in Exile," *PMLA* 96 (1981):363–74; and, most recently, Maximillian Novak suggests that the allegory of a nation in exile touches on Defoe's pronounced sympathy for the Scottish covenanters under the reign of the original and restored Stuarts ("Imaginary Islands and Real Beasts," pp. 39 ff.). Of course, the idea of resettling in the New World to sustain values threatened in the old is at the heart of the Dissenters' exodus to New England.

16 In his one sustained autobiographical pamphlet, *An Appeal to Honour and Justice* (London, 1715), Defoe writes in the third person of his reaction to the Stuart cause past and present: "No Man in this Nation ever had a more riveted Aversion to the *Pretender,* and to all the Family he pretended to come of, *than he*" (p. 28). He goes on to write that he came to maturity opposing the Stuart kings, first Charles II and then James II as "A Man that had been in Arms under the Duke of *Monmouth,* against the Cruelty and Arbitrary Government of his pretended Father; That for twenty Years had, to my utmost, opposed him (King *James*), and his Party after his Abdication; That had serv'd King *William* to his Satisfaction, and the Friends of the Revolution after his Death, at all Hazards, and upon all Occasions; That had suffer'd and been ruin'd under the Administration of *High-flyers* and *Jacobites*" (p. 28).

17 In *Daniel Defoe and Middle-Class Gentility* (Cambridge, Mass., 1968), Michael Shinagel remarks on the antagonism Defoe, as Dissenter, felt toward the Stuarts: "The persecutions suffered by the Dissenters during the 1660s served to unite rather than disperse them. They found comfort and succor in their shared afflictions. They felt themselves being tested for their religious beliefs, if not also on trial for their souls" (p. 37).

18 In his *Life and Adventures of Mr. D——— Def——* (1719), Charles Gildon was the first to pick up the possible allegorical identification of Crusoe's exile with Defoe's life: "You are the true Allegorick Image of thy tender Father D———l" (p. x). And Gildon also sensed that there was a political message in the narrative for which Defoe required the protection of fiction: "But honest D- - - -l, I am afraid with all your Sagaciousness, you do not sufficiently distinguish between the Fear of God, and the Fear of Danger to your own dear Carcass" (p. 18). A detailed account of the personal and public events possibly allegorized in *Robinson Crusoe* is offered by George Parker, "The Allegory of *Robinson Crusoe,*" *History* 10 (1925):11–25. Parker concentrates on Defoe's entrepreneurial and political career, citing as the basis for his own speculation Defoe's comment in his *Appeal to Honour and Justice:* "I have gone through a life of wonders, and am the subject of a vast variety of Providences."

19 John Richetti, with little mention of the specific political events of the seven-

teenth and eighteenth centuries, understands as well as any of Defoe's commentators what he calls the "official ideology" of the narrative, one running absolutely counter to the absolutist position: "Indeed, the deep fantasy that Crusoe and his story serve is the dream of freedom perfectly reconciled with necessity, the self using necessity to promote its freedom" (*Defoe's Narratives: Situations and Structures*, pp. 54–55). In *Moby Dick*, Melville makes a similar ideological argument based on extremes of self-sovereignty and cooperative capacity in regard to islanders who make up most of the crew of the *Pequod*. His remarks have allegorical potential for the constitutional structure of American government just as Defoe's might for English rule: "They were nearly all Islanders in the Pequod, *Isolatoes* too, I call such, not acknowledging the common continent of men, but each *Isolato* living on a separate continent of his own. Yet now, federated along one keel, what a set these Isolatoes were!" (chap., 27, "Knights and Squires," p. 166).

20 *Essay upon Projects* (London, 1697), p. 8.
21 *The Compleat English Tradesman* (London, 1726), 2:198–99.
22 Crusoe is on the seas when Oliver Cromwell defeats the remaining royalist forces at Worcester and the future Charles II flees to France. Defoe held no brief for Cromwell the militarist. Crusoe's gradual eclipse from England seems to coincide, at least in terms of Defoe's politics, with worsening stages of English rule. Crusoe is in a Moorish prison and on a plantation in Brazil for the Protectorate and in island exile for the Restoration.
23 In September of 1659 Lambert dismissed the ineffective Rump Parliament as a ruling body, thus leading to the series of events that ushered in the Restoration of Charles II.
24 If the difficult part of Crusoe's working through toward toleration involves the cannibals, the spirited part involves his own political commentary on his reign once he has accommodated himself to its mechanisms: "My Man *Friday* was a Protestant, his Father was a *Pagan* and a *Cannibal,* and the *Spaniard* was a Papist: However, I allow'd Liberty of Conscience throughout my Dominions: But this is by the Way" (p. 241). One of Defoe's severest complaints against the Stuarts in his assessment of state politics in *The Consolidator* is that they used and misused toleration as a hypocritical tool to ease into a Catholic succession in England.
25 In the classic first chapter, "Odysseus' Scar," of *Mimesis* (Princeton, 1953), Erich Auerbach considers the polarities of narrative in terms of surface and background (or depth) sequences, arguing that a sense of immediacy is associated with the Homeric epic, an immanent mode of narration where all things are brought to the fore as stark presence. Background narration is associated with the teleological perspective of the Old Testament where sequences of action recede into a much wider panorama of allegorical history and historical promise. Implicit in Auerbach's summary of narrative potential is the notion that the Western tradition of

prose fiction has, in various ways, worked toward bringing foreground and background closer together. Defoe certainly centers his own discussion of *Robinson Crusoe* and allegory on just such a notion in his *Serious Reflections.*

26 John Richetti, recognizing both the irony and the scope of the footprint episode, writes: "And it is precisely at this point in the narrative, when the island has been totally possessed by Crusoe, when it is fully an extension of himself, that he discovers the footprint on the beach" (*Defoe's Narratives,* p. 50). David Blewett sees the print as the bifurcating point in a bifurcated novel: "It shatters Crusoe's tranquil existence and opens the movement of the second half of the novel" (*Defoe's Art of Fiction,* p. 39).

27 Because of his fear of the print and its unknown maker, Crusoe later says he lived "like one of the ancient Giants, which are said to live in Caves, and Holes, in the Rocks, where none could come at them" (p. 179). If he were like a Cyclopean giant, the print he sees ought to be smaller, not larger, than his own. As Rousseau argues in his *Essay on the Origin of Languages,* size and its perception are often a metaphoric adjustment to fear.

28 Maximillian Novak ("Imaginary Islands: Real Beasts") suggests that readers interested in some of Defoe's seemingly offhand remarks in *Crusoe* refer to his journalistic efforts while at work on the novel. In a *Weekly Journal* for 19 April 1718, Defoe presents a scheme to make all kings emperors and all men with political control of an area kings. Either this occurred to him as a result of his work on *Crusoe* or in conjunction with it.

29 Crusoe claims he leaves the island on 19 December 1686 after twenty-eight years, two months, and nineteen days. These calculations would bring the date of arrival back to 30 September 1658, which is a year earlier than he says when he lands. But we ought to credit the 1659 date because, even admitting the fictional status of the whole saga, that is the year he gives us while in the middle of it. To get to 1658 we have to count backward. Defoe makes a number of hopeless chronological mistakes toward the end of the narrative, and to get himself off the hook he has Crusoe say "nor had I kept even the Number of Years so punctually, as to be sure that I was right, tho' as it prov'd, when I afterwards examin'd my Account, I found I had kept a true Reckoning of Years" (p. 249).

30 *Account of the Growth of Popery and Arbitrary Government in England* (1678), in *Works,* ed. Alexander B. Grosart (London, 1875), 4:303–04. A modern authority on the Restoration writes of 1674 as the year in which "an opposition now national in character" appeared in English life (David Ogg, *England in the Reign of Charles II,* 2d ed. [London, 1956], 2:544).

31 For the full context of Crusoe's experience and the principles of natural law, see Maximillian E. Novak, *Defoe and the Nature of Man* (Oxford, 1963). Cannibalism, of course, is one of the supreme challenges to natural law. And, as Everett Zimmerman points out, it is a charged subject and symbol for Defoe: "The

ubiquitous references to being devoured point to a generalized fear: of being dematerialized—the reversal of the desire to accumulate. It is a fear shared by author and character" (*Defoe and the Novel* [Berkeley, 1975], p. 32). Conrad's oblique parody of the Crusoe legend in the figure of "Cannibal" Robinson in *Lord Jim* is discussed in my second chapter.

32 What Crusoe works out in his response to the persecution of the cannibals touches on the natural propensity toward tyrannical violence that exists in mankind without the check of law and contractual restraint. Defoe observes in *Jure Divino* (1706): "Nature has left *this Tincture in the Blood* / That all *Men would be Tyrants if they cou'd.* / If they forbear their Neighbors to devour, / 'Tis not for want of *Will*, but want of Power" ("Introductory Verses," p. 1). Melville again makes a comparable point with more savage wit in *Moby Dick:* "Go to the meatmarket of a Saturday night and see the crowds of live bipeds staring up at the long rows of dead quadrupeds. Does not that sight take a tooth out of the cannibal's jaw? Cannibals? who is not a cannibal?" (chap. 65, "The Whale As a Dish," p. 393).

33 This conclusion is obviously important for Defoe; he repeats it virtually word for word from an earlier passage in *Crusoe:* "I ought to leave them to the Justice of God, who is the Governour of Nations, and knows how by National Punishments to make a just Retribution for National Offences; and to bring publick Judgments upon those who offend in a publick Manner, by such Ways as best please him" (p. 173).

34 In the same sense that Crusoe thinks, incorrectly it turns out, that there may have been a Dutchman with the English crew (and a Dutchman, indeed, helped the English cause in 1688), all the illegitimate shenanigans at the end of the narrative may reflect, in part, on the desperate last days of James II and his Cabal fighting to hold on to a realm that was more and more ready to expel them.

35 We have an idea from an earlier passage what Crusoe must have looked like and how he might affect an Englishman: "My Beard I had once suffer'd to grow till it was about a Quarter of a yard long; but as I had both Scissars and Razors sufficient, I had cut it pretty short, except what grew on my upper Lip, which I had trimm'd into a large Pair of *Mahometan* Whiskers, such as I had seen worn by some *Turks,* who I saw at *Sallee;* for the *Moors* did not wear such, tho' the *Turks* did; of these Muschatoes or Whiskers, I will not say they were long enough to hang my Hat upon them; but they were of a Length and Shape monstrous enough, and such as in *England* would have pass'd for frightful" (p. 150).

36 Again, it seems to me that John Richetti expresses the implicit ideology of the exilic allegory with precision: "The elaborate games that Crusoe plays as he ends his story are not only strategies for managing the mutineers; they represent an awareness in the narrative of the nature of freedom. They repeat on that trickiest and most difficult level of reality—the social and political—the games that

Crusoe has had to master all through his story in order to 'survive,' that is, to achieve a special kind of autonomy" (*Defoe's Narratives*, p. 61).

37 Not only is this date of historical importance to Defoe as the second anniversary of Monmouth's Rebellion against James II, in which he may have taken some small part, but it was precisely at this time that leading national figures in England invited the Protestant Prince of Orange to mount an invasion and wrest the British Crown from James II.

Chapter Two

1 *Lord Jim*, in *The Works of Joseph Conrad*, Dent Collected Edition (London, 1946; reprint of Dent Uniform Edition, 1923), p. 272. All references to Conrad's works are to this edition unless otherwise noted.

2 Isolation is a crucial element in Albert Guerard's psychoanalytic interpretation of *Heart of Darkness;* he identifies the journey as an interiorization of unconscious urges similar to those represented in *The Secret Sharer* where "morally isolated men . . . meet and commit themselves to men even more isolated" (*Conrad the Novelist* [Cambridge, Mass., 1958], p. 48). Guerard's reading assumes isolation is a metaphor for atavistic indulgence, and the "psychic geography" (p. 41) his reading produces is comparable to that interior space where the bourgeois Ego meets the desiring Unconscious in Freud's *Interpretation of Dreams*.

3 In his *Conrad in the Nineteenth Century* (London, 1980), Ian Watt makes the point about one of the real outcasts upon whom Jim was partially based, a man named Jim Lingard living in isolation with a native wife on the Berau River in the wilds of Borneo, that the reason for the exilic choice of life bears directly on the impulse to impose barriers between it and a more common "reality": "It is a puzzle which occurs whenever one comes across a man living in isolation from all his kind, and the solution that first proposes itself is usually unflattering—the man must be in hiding and for good reason" (p. 267).

4 The best of Conrad's critics are fascinated with the constitutive properties of his narrative voice. See Albert Guerard's "The Conradian Voice," in *Joseph Conrad: A Commemoration*, ed. Norman Sherry (London, 1976), pp. 1–16; also in that same volume, Edward Said's essay on "Conrad and Nietzsche," pp. 65–76, the essence of which is not so much about shared philosophies as shared assumptions on the power, positioning, and failings of language in representing human actions.

5 Guerard, *Conrad the Novelist*, p. 141.

6 In his *Personal Record,* Conrad writes: "The comic, when it is human, soon takes upon itself a face of pain" (p. xvi).

7 J. Hillis Miller's chapter on *Lord Jim* in *Fiction and Repetition in Seven English Novels*

(Cambridge, Mass., 1982) focuses on this key sentence in analyzing the motives and structures of the novel (see especially pp. 27 ff.).

8 From the "1897 Preface" to *Nigger of the "Narcissus,"* Norton Critical Edition, ed. Robert Kimbrough (New York, 1979), p. 147. The "1897 Preface" is not included in the Dent Collected Edition. When I cite the later, 1914, preface elsewhere in this chapter, the reference is to the Dent Edition.

9 Guerard, *Conrad the Novelist,* p. 161.

10 See Miller, *Fiction and Repetition,* where the notion of repetition constitutes the basis of a sustained, detailed reading of the action in *Lord Jim.*

11 See G. W. Kennedy, "Conrad and *Robinson Crusoe,*" *Conradiana* 10 (1978):113–22, and Jeffrey Meyers, "Savagery and Civilization in *The Tempest, Robinson Crusoe* and *Heart of Darkness,*" *Conradiana* 2 (1969–70):171–79. Kennedy understands that the comparisons between Defoe and Conrad are not merely incidental but ideological. In regard to the status of the rehabilitated exile, Kennedy writes that for "Conrad, this notion of the solitary man triumphant in isolation from his native culture is a potentially subversive influence" (p. 114). He seems to reflect the very dementia of ego and power that sustains the worst part of the imperial idea.

12 At the time of *Robinson Crusoe,* Defoe supported a scheme to exploit the Orinoco basin. See note 10 to chapter one.

13 It is interesting that Defoe has an African tale to tell in the imperial vein that adumbrates Conrad's. His Captain Singleton journeys to equatorial Africa and ends up raiding for ivory. Though Conrad named one of his mariners Singleton in *Nigger of the "Naricissus,"* he may not have known of Defoe's novel, *Captain Singleton.* But had he, he would have been intrigued. Defoe's hero makes a long arduous journey through the African continent, passing by the inland Congo region with his expedition. Near the end of his equatorial venture, he comes upon an ivory-factoring English renegade who had cornered the region's market in what he calls elephants' teeth. This powerful white ivory trader thrives under the protection of armed native tribesmen. Singleton wishes he could give him a pair of shoes, a gesture that is of coincidental relevance to the famous exchange between Marlow and the river in *Heart of Darkness.* See my note, "Defoe in Conrad's Africa," *Conradiana* 17 (1985):145–46.

14 For a fascinating look at actual cases of shipwreck and cannibalism, see A. W. Brian Simpson, *Cannibalism and the Common Law: The Story of the Tragic Last Voyage of the Mignonette and the Strange Legal Proceedings to Which It Gave Rise* (Chicago, 1984).

15 See Tony Tanner, "'Gnawed Bones' and 'Artless Tales'—Eating and Narrative in Conrad," in *Commemoration,* pp. 17–36. Tanner focuses on Conrad's story "Falk," but his essential argument reaches as far as the famous and grotesque image of Stevie's remains served up in *The Secret Agent* as if at some cannibal feast.

Tanner might have gone on to mention that Conrad compounds the irony and the violation when he recalls that Winnie Verloc gave up her chance to marry a hardworking butcher only to ally herself with Verloc, supposedly for the sake of her brother's security.

16 Conrad has a character in *Under Western Eyes* remark of the English imperial empire, established in a significant way after the 1688 Revolution: "so much liberty for so much hard cash" (p. 134). In a letter to the *New York Times,* 24 August 1901, Conrad defended himself and Ford Madox Ford, in reference to their volume, *The Inheritors,* against accusations of attacking the British Empire by insisting that they intended only to attack "the materialistic exaggeration of individualism, whose unscrupulous efficiency it is the temper of the time to worship." Conrad's close friend, Edward Garnett, pulled no punches at all. In a review of *Heart of Darkness* for *Academy and Literature* 63 (6 December 1902), he wrote: " 'Heart of Darkness,' to present its theme bluntly, is an impression, taken from life, of the conquest by the European whites of a certain portion of Africa, an impression in particular of the civilising methods of a certain great European Trading Company face to face with the 'nigger.' " For a general study of these matters, with a chapter on Conrad, see Martin Green, *Dreams of Adventure, Deeds of Empire* (New York, 1979).

17 *Conrad in the Nineteenth Century,* p. 144. Watt claims that it is always a Western fear that in the imperial drive to civilize the native the easy street between greed and hypocrisy could run the wrong way and the civilizer turn "primitive."

18 The extent to which *Heart of Darkness* is a parable of underworld descent has caused somewhat of a stir among Conradians. Watt is foremost among the ranks of those who dismiss the notion, though he describes Marlow's role in the narrative as "a man who stumbled into the underworld many years ago, and lived to tell its secrets, although not until much later" (*Conrad in the Nineteenth Century,* p. 253). It seems as though Watt wants what others notice to be considered "heterophoric" and what he says "homophoric," as if he talks only about issues and others talk only about structures.

19 Lawrence Graver, *Conrad's Shorter Fiction* (Berkeley, 1969), has Kurtz in mind when he describes a central condition in Conrad's fiction: "the irreconcilable antagonism between egoism, the moving force of the world, and altruism, its essential morality" (p. 45).

20 James Guetti makes this point in his essay "The Failure of Imagination," in *Conrad: Heart of Darkness, Nostromo, and Under Western Eyes, A Casebook,* ed. C. B. Cox (London, 1981), pp. 65–77: "Language has meaning in *Heart of Darkness* in terms of the exteriors of experience—the coast of a wilderness, the surface of a river, a man's appearance and his voice—and this meaning can exist as a reality so long as one remains ignorant, deliberately or otherwise, of all that lies beyond these exteriors, of what language cannot penetrate" (p. 75).

21 Conrad excised the passage as it appeared in the Rosenbach typescript. Watt discusses the excision in *Conrad in the Nineteenth Century* (pp. 316–17). The passage would have come directly before that beginning "By Jove!" (p. 158) in the Dent Edition of *Lord Jim*.

Chapter Three

1 *A Portrait of the Artist as a Young Man* (New York, 1964), p. 247. All subsequent references are to this edition.

2 Two days after Joyce's death, Louis Gillet wrote a remarkable eulogy, "Farewell to Joyce," trying to recreate from his own memory of the Dublin neighborhood where his friend was born the beginning of Joyce's nomadic life. Gillet misstates some facts but captures the Joycean uprootedness, imagining one of the family's many moves within Ireland as the onset of a life-long Exodus.

> This wandering household, the flight in Egypt with a mother in despair and a bragging father screening his retreat with fanfares, seems to me an image, a symbol of the whole life of the artist who has just died—there he is already in all his entirety. Thus was announced to him the adventure of existence. Thirty-five years of wilful exile, of nomadic sojourns at Venice, Rome, Trieste, Zurich, and finally at Paris where he settled almost twenty years ago: settled is not the word, for he continued wandering between Passy and the Gros-Caillou, Montparnasse and Grenelle, not counting the escapades, the eclipses, the letters which without warning showed him to be in London, Folkestone, Basel, Copenhagen. His page in my address-book is filled with numerous erasures. I never saw him in the same lodging for more than six months. I have known him to have three apartments on his hands simultaneously, one of which was a very expensive flat in Kensington Gardens where he never set foot, while his furniture, in the superfluity of choice, remained in a furniture warehouse. He was something of a meteor, a will-o'-the wisp. He burdened the ground with no more than his shadow which he could fold up as an Arab folds up his carpets and his tent from bivouac to bivouac.

See *Portraits of the Artist in Exile: Recollections of James Joyce by Europeans,* ed. Willard Potts (Seattle and London, 1979), pp. 166–67.

3 *Finnegans Wake* (New York, 1939), p. 171. All references are to this edition.

4 *Exiles* (New York, 1951), p. 114. All references are to this edition.

5 *Ulysses* (New York, 1961), p. 199. All references are to this edition, emended, when necessary, in accord with the new Garland Edition (New York, 1984).

6 Malcolm Cowley was among many who held against Joyce what Robert held against Richard. He writes of Joyce in *Exile's Return: A Literary Odyssey of the 1920's* (New York, 1951): "As he wandered through Italy, Austria, Switzerland and France, he continued to write about the Dublin of his youth and remembered

the sound of Irish voices, but he half forgot that Irish race whose conscience was being forged in the smithy of revolution" (p. 117).

7 *Stephen Hero* (New York, 1963), p. 186. All references are to this edition.

8 *The Letters of James Joyce,* ed. Stuart Gilbert (New York, 1957), 1:146–47.

9 Joyce reserved his own views on the language issue for the Gaelic-growling cur in the "Cyclops" chapter of *Ulysses* where insistence on native Irish merged with the violence and paranoia of nationalist politics: "Our greatest living phonetic expert (wild horses shall not drag it from us!) has left no stone unturned in his efforts to delucidate and compare the verse recited and has found it bears a *striking* resemblance (the italics are ours) to the ranns of ancient Celtic bards" (p. 312). When Joyce was confronted by a mean-spirited Garryown-like Irish mastiff once in Holland, he quipped: "A descendant perhaps who had read that page of *Ulysses* and recognized me." (See Jacques Mercanton, "The Hours of James Joyce," in *Portraits of the Artist in Exile,* p. 233).

10 J. G. Keogh, "*Ulysses'* 'Parable of the Plums' as Parable and Periplum," *JJQ* 7 (1970):337–78.

11 Jacques Mercanton, in "The Hours of James Joyce," remembers a conversation in which Joyce said of Bloom: "Bloom Jewish? Yes, because only a foreigner would do. The Jews were foreigners at that time in Dublin. There was no hostility toward them, but contempt, yes, the contempt people always show for the unknown" (p. 208).

12 Reuben J. Dodd was not a Jew, as his descendants were eager to point out in a law suit directed against the BBC Radio after a reading of *Ulysses* on the air, but referring to him as such by the local Dublin citizenry, at least the citizenry of *Ulysses,* was intended as an insult.

13 Alexandre Dumas, *The Count of Monte Cristo,* 2 vols., Everyman's Library Translation (London, 1955, first printed 1909), 1:412. All references are to this edition. Eighteen English translations of Dumas's romance were printed in London between 1847 and the publication of Joyce's *Portrait of the Artist,* and several others were printed in the United States. It is doubtful whether Joyce's memory of the text was a detailed one, so it is a fool's errand to try to guess which translation the young Dedalus or the young Joyce read. In those instances when passages in *Monte Cristo* (rendered similarly in most translations) touch, coincidentally, on some of Joyce's own phrasings, I checked them against the original French. Again, except for the muscatel grape scene, claims for direct allusion ought to be limited.

14 Stephen's comment in *Ulysses* in reference to Mulligan—"Now I eat his salt bread" (p. 20)—is an allusion to the famous exile canto of Dante's *Divine Comedy, Paradiso, xvii,* 58–59, "Tu proverai sì come sa di sale / lo pane altrui, e come è duro calle." I doubt Joyce had the *Monte Cristo* scene from *Portrait* in mind, though it makes a nice comparison.

15 The rival vocations of priest and artist is a well-warmed topic in Joyce studies. It

is enough to cite Daedalus in *Stephen Hero:* "Was it anything but vanity which urged him to seek out the thorny crown of the heretic while the entire theory, in accordance with which his entire artistic life was shaped, arose most conveniently for his purpose out of the mass of Catholic theology?" (p. 205).

16 Joyce wrote in answer to a question on the proofs of Herbert Gorman's biography of him that Europe was his "spiritual father." The Europeanization of the Irish artist is a constant theme in Joyce's work, but, like every other Joycean theme, it is subject to parody. In *Exiles*, for example, the slightly questionable Robert says to the returned exile Richard, slightly questionable in his own right: "If Ireland is to become a new Ireland she must first become European. And that is what you are here for, Richard. Some day we shall have to choose between England and Europe. I am a descendant of the dark foreigners: that is why I like to be here. I may be childish. But where else in Dublin can I get a bandit cigar like this or a cup of black coffee? The man who drinks black coffee is going to conquer Ireland" (p. 43). Of course Robert's own exile at the end of the play is ironically to England, not Europe, and to the home of a cousin in Surrey with the bullish name Jack Justice.

17 "Silent and sure" seems to have been the cliché picked up by several of the translations of Dumas's novel as an equivalent for the French cliché, *basse et haute*. Again, the connection to Joyce's exilic program is more paradigmatic than direct.

18 See Georges Borach, "Conversations with James Joyce," in *Portraits of the Artist in Exile*, p. 70.

19 This notion seems to have interested Joyce right through the various "progresses" of *Finnegans Wake*, including one of the Wake's heroes, Odin, whose name means "movement." In the first lecture of *Heroes and Hero Worship*, Carlyle mentions the etymology of *"Wuotan*, which is the original form of Odin, a word spread, as name of this chief Divinity, over all the Teutonic Nations everywhere; this word, which connects itself, according to Grimm, with the Latin *vadere*, with the English *wade* and suchlike;—means primarily *movement"* (*Works* [New York, 1969], 5:24).

20 When a young critic, Carola Giedion-Welcker, approached an older Joyce on the significance of his brief note on *Exile*'s characters, he responded with a question that seemed to make an automystic of the automobile: " 'Tell me, what sort of an idea do you think the word 'automobile' would have aroused in the Middle Ages?' 'Certainly only that of a divine being,' he added without waiting my answer, 'a self-mover, thus a god.' " (See "Meetings with Joyce," in *Portraits of the Artist in Exile*, p. 257). In describing the automobile, Joyce seems to have forgotten, or not cared, that the particular character on whom he originally bestowed the tag was the rather dismal Robert.

21 *Third Census of Finnegans Wake* (Berkeley, 1977), p. ix.

22 Joyce had also touched on Judas as rival in *Exiles*. Richard says to Robert: "There is a faith still stranger than the faith of the disciple in his master." Robert: "And that is?" Richard: "The faith of a master in the disciple who will betray him" (p. 44). In a sense here, mastery is the total knowledge that includes, or perhaps causes, the act of betrayal.

23 Many have plotted the means by which Joyce transforms his life into a national archive, but none has done so more forcefully than John Paul Riquelme in his recent book, *Teller and Tale in Joyce's Fiction: Oscillating Perspectives* (Baltimore, 1983).

24 When Joyce saw a picture in the *Irish Times* of a low-life tramp leaning against the Dublin statue of Daniel O'Connell and mimicking the nationalist's pose, he remarked, with a nod to Marx's *18th Brumaire*: "Altogether the meaning of 'Work in Progress': history repeats itself comically." See Jacques Mercanton, "The Hours of James Joyce," p. 234.

25 See Lindsey Tucker, *Stephen and Bloom at Life's Feast: Alimentary Symbolism and the Creative Process in James Joyce's "Ulysses"* (Columbus, 1984).

26 It was clear to Joyce that violence could turn on its own cause. As a just matriculated college student, he wrote an essay on the futility of "Force" and always defended the more moderate members of Arthur Griffith's Sinn Fein party against the radical remnants of the old Fenian movement like the Citizen in "Cyclops": "Anyone who studies the history of the Irish revolution during the nineteenth century finds himself faced with a double struggle—the struggle of the Irish nation against the English government, and the struggle, perhaps no less bitter, between the moderate patriots and the so-called party of physical force." See the newspaper article "Fenianism" Joyce wrote for the Triestine *Piccolo della Sera*, in *James Joyce: The Critical Writings* (New York, 1959), p. 188.

27 Bloom's nature is rarely violent, and he would rather ignore slights than confront antagonists, as is the case with the Ajax figure in "Hades," the lawyer Menton: "Be sorry after perhaps when it dawns on him. Get the pull over him that way" (p. 115). In "Conversations with James Joyce," Georges Borach records the following: "The Talmud says at one point, 'We Jews are like the olive: we give our best when we are being crushed, when we are collapsing under the burden of our foliage.' Material victory is the death of spiritual predominance" (p. 71).

28 Though the subject obviously irritates him, August Sutter records in "Some Reminiscences of James Joyce" that in "Zurich Joyce had introduced his wife to Greeks and Jews, models for Bloom, and apparently he would have liked, with a touch of curiosity, to see his wife discomposed. Mrs. Joyce realized that he was playing with her virtue, and refrained from thus serving as a model for her husband's books. She had more character and constancy than coquettishness" (in *Portraits of the Artist in Exile*, p. 64). William Empson makes much of these biographical and marital intrigues, though he seems to forget that others have

mentioned the matters before him. See his essay, "The Ultimate Novel," in *Using Biography* (Cambridge, Mass., 1984), pp. 217–59. Joyce himself conceived of the subject of cuckoldry as part of the history of novelistic realism. He writes in his notes for *Exiles:* "Since the publication of the lost pages of *Madame Bovary* the centre of sympathy appears to have been esthetically shifted from the lover or fancyman to the husband or cuckold. This displacement is also rendered more stable by the gradual growth of a collective practical realism due to changed economic conditions in the mass of the people who are called to hear and feel a work of art relating to their lives" (p. 115).

29 *James Joyce and the Making of Ulysses* (Bloomington, 1960), pp. 314–15.

Chapter Four

1 Sterne may have planned to bring Yorick back, but he died shortly after the publication of the first two volumes of *A Sentimental Journey.*

2 *A Sentimental Journey Through France and Italy by Mr. Yorick,* ed., Gardner Stout, Jr. (Berkeley, 1967), p. 65. All references are to this edition.

3 *A Treatise of Human Nature,* ed. P. H. Nidditch (Oxford, 1978), p. 393 (Book 2, Pt. 2, Sec. 10).

4 *The Works of Laurence Sterne,* 12 vols., introduction by Wilbur Cross (Cambridge, Mass., 1904), 9:330. Stout thinks this sermon crucial enough for *A Sentimental Journey* that he reprints several pages of it in Appendix E to his edition, pp. 327–30.

5 *Works,* 9:330.

6 Sterne writes to Garrick from France in April of 1762: "Here every thing is hyperbolized" (*Letters of Laurence Sterne,* ed. Lewis Curtis [Oxford, 1935], p. 161).

7 See James W. Garvey's "Translation, Equivocation, and Reconstitution in Sterne's *Sentimental Journey,*" *Southern Humanities Review* 12 (1978):339–49. Garvey defines translation as "immersing oneself in an alien experience until it is no longer alien" (p. 342). Martin Battestin has a wonderful essay, though he gets a bit dewy-eyed on the subject of grace, that treats of translation as part of linguistic and metaphysical systems of syntax in the novel. See *"A Sentimental Journey* and the Syntax of Things," in *Augustan Worlds,* ed. J. C. Hilson et al. (Leicester, 1978), pp. 223–39.

8 In the "Prodigal Son" sermon, Sterne had this to say about speaking in a foreign tongue: "Conversation is traffic; and if you enter into it, without some stock of knowledge, to ballance the account perpetually betwixt you,—the trade drops at once" (*Works,* 9:333).

9 In his *Portraits of Places* (London, 1883), Henry James writes of crossing the border into France that "the 'administration' is the first thing that touches you;

in a little while you get used to it, but you feel somehow that, in the process, you have lost the flower of your self-respect" (p. 84).

10 *Critical Review* 25 (1768):181.

11 In *Confinement and Flight: An Essay on English Literature of the Eighteenth Century* (Berkeley, 1977), W. B. Carnochan has much to say on these matters generally and much to say on Sterne in relation to them specifically.

12 In an impressive essay on *A Sentimental Journey*, "Language and Hartleian Associationism in *A Sentimental Journey*," *Eighteenth-Century Studies* 13 (1980):285–312, Jonathan Lamb makes the point, among dozens of others, that the appearance of hands is so prominent in the novel that one can almost "construe sentimental travel as manual dexterity" (p. 293). Battestin also notes: "In *A Sentimental Journey*, indeed, hands are often the means of syntactical connection" ("Syntax of Things," p. 230).

13 Raymond Williams, *Keywords, a Vocabulary of Culture and Society* (Oxford, 1976), pp. 143–44.

14 See R. S. Crane's classic essay, "Suggestions toward a Genealogy of the 'Man of Feeling,'" *ELH* 1 (1934):205–30. Arthur Hill Cash's full-length study of Sterne's novel, *Sterne's Comedy of Moral Sentiments: The Ethical Dimension of the Journey* (Pittsburgh, 1966) provides ample information on the subject of the sentimental code, but Cash's bias against Sterne's exploitation of sexuality makes reading his book a bit grim. For a short, supple essay on the sentimental novel in general, see Leo Braudy's "The Form of the Sentimental Novel," *Novel* 7 (1973):5–13.

15 See, for example, Hume's explanation of the principle of natural virtue called *sympathy*, which is the philosopher's major salvo against Hobbes's premise of natural vice:

> As in strings equally wound up, the motion of one communicates itself to the rest; so all affections readily pass from one person to another, and beget correspondent movements in every human creature. When I see the *effects* of passion in the voice and gesture of any person, my mind immediately passes from these effects to their causes, and forms such a lively idea of the passion, as is presently converted into the passion itself. In like manner, when I perceive the *causes* of any emotion, my mind is convey'd to the effects, and is actuated with a like emotion" (*Treatise of Human Nature*, p. 576 [Book 3, Pt. 3, Sec. 1]).

16 Lamb points out: "Carelessness with cash is firmly associated with sentimental profit" ("Hartleian Associationism," p. 296).

17 The issue of Sterne's seriousness as a sentimentalist has been hacked over for years, but surely Alan McKillop had it right in the 1950s when he wrote that Yorick was a "comic figure representing at the same time sentimentalism and the ultimate refinement or attenuation of the comedy of humors" (*The Early Masters of English Fiction* [Lawrence, Kans., 1956], p. 216). Gardner Stout reinforces McKillop's argument in "Yorick's *Sentimental Journey:* A Comic 'Pilgrim's Pro-

gress' for the Man of Feeling," *ELH* 30 (1963):395–412; and Joseph Chadwick reinforces Stout's in "Infinite Jest: Interpretation in Sterne's *A Sentimental Journey*," *Eighteenth-Century Studies* 12 (1978–79):190–205.

18 *Old Curiosity Shop* (Harmondsworth, Eng., 1972), chap. 14, p. 163.

19 For an essay that touches on this notion, see Eve Kosofsky Sedgwick, "Sexualism and the Citizen of the World: Wycherley, Sterne, and Male Homosocial Desire," *Critical Inquiry* 11 (1984):226–45.

20 *Treatise*, p. 402 (Book 2, Pt. 3, Sec. 1).

21 In a letter (probably to John Wodehouse) Sterne admits that he, too, makes love in the French manner, by sentiments, though he complains of French attitudes toward love that "they make such a pother about the word, they have no precise ideas annex'd to it" (*Letters*, p. 256).

22 *Fable of the Bees*, ed. F. B. Kaye, "Remark 'M'" (Oxford, 1924), 1:129.

23 Since I intend to treat Henry James's *The Ambassadors* as a kind of sentimental journey in my next chapter, I will mention, for comparative purposes, a scene in that novel where Lambert Strether has occasion to comment on the purchase of a pair of gloves: "Mere discriminations about a pair of gloves could thus at any rate represent—always for such sensitive ears as were in question—possibilities of something that Strether could make a mark against only at the peril of apparent wantonness" (in *The Novels and Tales of Henry James*, New York Edition [New York, 1961], 1:41).

Chapter Five

1 "Project" for *The Ambassadors*, in *The Notebooks of Henry James*, ed. F. O. Matthiessen and Kenneth B. Murdock (New York, 1947), p. 415. All references are to this edition.

2 *The Ambassadors*, 2 vols., in *The Novels and Tales of Henry James*, New York Edition (New York, 1961), 2:282. All references to James's novels are to the New York Edition.

3 *The Middle Years* (New York, 1917), p. 11. All references are to this edition.

4 *The American Scene*, ed. Leon Edel (Bloomington, Ind., 1968), p. 366. All references are to this edition.

5 *The Notebooks of Henry James*, p. 26.

6 James, *The Art of the Novel*, ed. R. P. Blackmur (New York, 1934), p. 195.

7 *A Small Boy and Others* (London, 1913), p. 292.

8 This observation comes in a letter to Edith Wharton. See *The Letters of Henry James*, ed. Percy Lubbock, 2 vols. (New York, 1920), 2:57.

9 My colleague Jeffrey Perl and I discussed the Iliadic contours of *The Ambassadors* when we were both working on the nature of epic form in modern narrative. Perl

treats the subject in his *The Tradition of Return: The Implicit History of Modern Literature* (Princeton, 1984), especially pp. 163 ff.

10 In *The American Scene,* James makes a distinction that is implicit in *The Ambassadors,* that between the old and new France, France of the First Empire and the Restoration and the modern France of the Third Republic. Social and material conditions "tend to alter everywhere, partly by the very force of the American example, and it may be said that in France, for instance, they have done nothing but alter for a hundred years" (p. 160).

11 James labors under no delusions about the virtue of the South's cause in the Civil War. In speaking of the region's present "infelicity," he writes that it is "something more than the melancholy of a lost cause. The whole infelicity speaks of a cause that could never have been gained" (*American Scene,* p. 394).

12 *Literary Essays of Ezra Pound,* ed. T. S. Eliot (London, 1954), p. 298.

13 In *Antony and Cleopatra,* a citizen central to the well-being of an expanding western order, the Roman Empire, is lured to a much older, refined, eastern place by an attraction difficult to ignore—Cleopatra's name in the play is literally interchangeable with "Egypt." See U. C. Knoepflmacher, " 'O rare for Strether!': *Antony and Cleopatra* and *The Ambassadors,*" *Nineteenth Century Fiction* 19 (1964–65):333–44.

14 Richard Blackmur, "The Loose and Baggy Monsters of Henry James: Notes on the Underlying Classic Form in the Novel," in *The Lion and the Honeycomb, Essays in Solicitude and Critique,* rev. ed. (New York, 1955), p. 288. This generative essay on James's absorption of classical impulses into his fiction speaks of the "deep-breathing economy" (p. 272) in *The Ambassadors* and of its compelling formal structures that still allow for life's essential background rhythms. Blackmur touches on some of the same issues taken up in the earlier work of the Hegelian Georg Lukács in *The Theory of the Novel,* though each would take radically different solace from similar conclusions. Whereas Blackmur advances a case for the refinement of novelistic consciousness as the classical saving remnant of individualism in the West, Lukács writes of the havoc wreaked upon epic immanence either by the bourgeois conventionalism of novelistic realism or by the irony directed *against* bourgeois conventionalism.

15 *Letters,* 2:245.

16 See Ronald Wallace, "Comic Form in *The Ambassadors,*" *Genre* 5 (1972):31–50. Wallace speaks mostly of the thematics of comic action, comparing the Parisian experience to festive comedy's dip into the transformative green world.

17 T. S. Eliot, "In Memory of Henry James," *Egoist* 1 (January 1918):1–2.

18 The night-raid is, of course, one of the conventions of epic action, usually an attempt to accomplish a tactical maneuver without engaging in the niceties of epic honor. The language of *The Ambassadors* is generally charged with tactical and martial talk, as is James's earlier *The Spoils of Poynton.* Tony Tanner discusses

the martial aspect of *The Ambassadors* in "The Watcher from the Balcony: Henry James's *The Ambassadors*," *Critical Quarterly* 8 (1966):35–52. Strether readies to "gird" himself (1:154) for battle, and at one point he jokes that Chad put out excitement as "he put out his washing," Strether feeling a "personal analogy with the laundress bringing home the triumphs of the mangle" (2:232). (I do not know if anyone has suggested the iron mangle as the unnamed vulgar item of Woollett manufacture.)

19 In an oft-cited notebook reference to *The American*, James writes of his choice to situate his novels on a continent other than his own: "No European writer is called upon to assume that terrible burden, and it seems hard that I should be. The burden is necessarily greater for an American—for he must deal, more or less, even if only by implication with Europe; whereas no European is obliged to deal in the least with America" (*Notebooks*, p. 24).

20 Frederick Crews, in *The Tragedy of Manners: Moral Drama in the Later Novels of Henry James* (New Haven, 1957), makes the point that the struggle with Europe for an American is to gain a sense of added range, sophistication, and tradition without abandoning his or her native being. But he also makes the point that James's characters, including Strether, are really after something that is often more inhibited than facilitated by any single cultural perspective. He says of the conflicting systems of national expression in *The Ambassadors:* "But the central judgment of the novel is that both systems are inadequate. Neither Woollett's abstemious Puritanism nor Paris' amoral secularism can account for the sense of Life that Strether has [through] the expansion of his social and moral awareness" (p. 55).

21 Tony Tanner spends a good deal of time excoriating the bourgeois *arriviste* Americans in the novel. He centers on Waymarsh and Sarah Pocock, arguing that when they do not pander to their own sense of spectacle in Europe they merely spend money: "They are enthusiastic purchasers (to buy something is to show your power over the seller; thus to reduce Europe to a shop is to treat it like a contemptuous patron)" ("The Watcher from the Balcony," p. 45).

22 Laurence Holland, in *The Expense of Vision, Essays on the Craft of Henry James* (Princeton, 1964), points out that the word *appreciate* implies both appraisal and enlargement (p. 238). Strether can in all regards count appreciation as part of his experience.

23 Quentin Anderson's tough-minded reading of the novel argues that for all Strether's desire to intensify experience, his imagination works on the double principle of willed expansion and willed exclusion. He wills not to see what he wishes not to contemplate, and sexuality is among the items on the exclusionary side. See *The American Henry James* (New Brunswick, 1957).

24 For an extremely informative and subtle essay that traces the range or, it might be better to say, the arena of this phrase, see Charles Feidelson, "James and the 'Man

of Imagination,'" in *Literary Theory and Structure*, ed. Frank Brady, John Palmer, and Martin Price (New Haven, 1973), pp. 331–52.

25 Ian Watt makes this point in his analysis of the novel's opening paragraph, where a phrase such as Strether's reference to Waymarsh—"he both wanted extremely to see him and enjoyed extremely the duration of the delay" (1:5)—forecasts in its syntax the temporal "need" that plays itself out in the design of the novel. See "The First Paragraph of *The Ambassadors:* An Explication," *Essays in Criticism* 10 (1960):250–74.

Chapter Six

1 *Pale Fire* (New York, 1962), p. 56. All references are to this edition. In the note to this line of Shade's poem in *Pale Fire,* the Nabokovian commentator, Charles Kinbote, lists seventeen pairs of apposite languages. Among the listings, English and Russian appear four separate times without any hint, except as a symptom of Kinbote's mad anguish, why this should be so. We can infer that conjurings in these tongues meant something special to Kinbote and to Nabokov. The last pair on the list is not even linguistic but territorial; Kinbote locates the axis of his exile as "American and European" (p. 235).

2 *Speak, Memory, An Autobiography Revisited* (New York, 1966), p. 250. All references, hereafter cited in text as *SM,* are to this edition.

3 In "An Interview with Vladimir Nabokov conducted by Alfred Appel, Jr.," Nabokov rejects national classification and says point blank: "The writer's art is his real passport." See *Wisconsin Studies in Contemporary Literature* 8 (1967):127.

4 *The Gift* (New York, 1963), p. 100. All references are to this edition.

5 The word *interest* was prelude and perspective for Sterne in *A Sentimental Journey* as well. See my discussion on pp. 118–19.

6 "On a Book Entitled *Lolita,*" in *Lolita* (New York, 1955), pp. 318–19.

7 Nabokov wrote this essay for the Berlin Russian-language periodical, the *Rudder.* Andrew Field excerpts and translates from the essay in *Nabokov: His Life and Art* (Boston, 1967), p. 183.

8 *Ada or Ardor: A Family Chronicle* (New York, 1969), p. 538. All references are to this edition. In *Lolita,* Humbert Humbert notes that he has published an essay called "Mimir and Memory" in which he argues "a theory of perceptual time based on the circulation of the blood and conceptually depending (to fill up this nutshell) on the mind's being conscious not only of matter but also of its own self, thus creating a continuous spanning of two points (the storable future and the stored past)" (p. 262). Mimir, by the way, is a Norse god who keeps company with the triplet phases: past, present, and future.

9 In the Appel interview, Nabokov makes the link between memory and the imagination explicit: "I would say that imagination is a form of memory. Down,

Plato, down, good dog. An image depends on the power of association, and association is supplied and prompted by memory. When we speak of a vivid individual recollection we are paying a compliment not to our capacity of retention but to Mnemosyne's mysterious foresight in having stored up this or that element which creative imagination may use when combining it with later recollections and inventions. In this sense, both memory and imagination are a negation of time" ("An Interview with Vladimir Nabokov," p. 140). For a detailed, thorough treatment of these matters in Nabokov's fiction, see William Anderson, "Time and Memory in Nabokov's *Lolita*," *Centennial Review* 24 (1980):360–83, and Jeffrey Leonard, "In Place of Lost Time: *Ada*," in *Nabokov: Criticism, Reminiscences, Translations, and Tributes,* ed. Alfred Appel, Jr., and Charles Newman (Evanston, Ill., 1970), pp. 136–46.

10 "On a Book Entitled *Lolita,*" p. 314.

11 *Lolita* (New York, 1955), p. 144. All references are to this edition.

12 George Steiner writes of Nabokov: "Whereas so many other language exiles clung desperately to the artifice of their native tongue or fell silent, Nabokov moved into successive languages like a traveling potentate. Banished from Fialta, he has built for himself a house of words. To be specific: the multi-lingual, cross-linguistic situation is both the matter and form of Nabokov's work" (see *Extraterritorial: Papers on Literature and the Language Revolution* [New York, 1971], p. 7).

13 For a sustained look at Van Veen in relation to the generic proportions of Nabokov's narrative, see Paul H. Fry, "Moving Van: The Neverland Veens of Nabokov's *Ada,*" *Contemporary Literature* 26 (1985):123–39.

14 *Despair* (New York, 1966), p. 127.

15 For an excellent essay on this and other subjects, see Robert Alter, "*Ada,* or the Perils of Paradise," in *Vladimir Nabokov, His Life, His Work, His World: A Tribute,* ed. Peter Quennell (London, 1979), pp. 103–18.

16 "An Interview with Vladimir Nabokov," p. 151.

17 "Wordsmithy" is Cherdyntsev's phrase in Nabokov's *The Gift* for the poet endowed with an overplus of vision.

18 Other Avernian (Cumaean) places for the imagination are picked up in earlier titles of Shade's collections preceding "Pale Fire": *Dim Gulf* and *Night Rote.* For the land of eternal youth, Shade offers *Hebe's Cup* (p. 68).

19 It is important in *Pale Fire* that the poet Shade knows that the phrase for his title seeps in through allusion: "Help me, Will! *Pale Fire*" (p. 68), whereas Kinbote does not, even though the phrase comes from the one play of Shakespeare's, *Timon of Athens,* perpetually at Kinbote's disposal, the only play for which he possesses a Zemblan translation. "Pale fire" in *Timon* refers to the reflection or theft of the sun's light by that arrant thief, the moon: "pale fire she snatches from the sun." Perhaps the Zemblan translator, Conmal, whose name means "badly known," botched the line; more likely, the phrase suggests the quality of reflection that

defines the secondary status of Kinbote in his New Wye exile. The best Kinbote can do is ghost the phrase "pale fire" in his own voice: "My commentary to this poem, now in the hands of my readers, represents an attempt to sort out those echoes and wavelets of fire, and pale phosphorescent hints, and all the many subliminal debts to me" (p. 297).

20 In the Appel interview, Nabokov parodies postintentionality by assuring us that Kinbote killed himself "after putting the last touches to his edition of the poem" (p. 137).

21 Paul H. Fry, *The Poet's Calling in the English Ode* (New Haven, 1980), p. 145.

22 *Solus Rex* was the title of one of Nabokov's unfinished narratives about a mythical northern king and kingdom.

23 *Pnin* (New York, 1957), pp. 38–39.

24 In a recent, somewhat troubled essay on Nabokov's *Pale Fire*, Alvin Kernan ponders a number of issues that not only disturb the very notion of imaginative projection in the novel but spill over to affect the contemporary literary enterprise as a whole, especially in America: the insularity of narrative vision, the jetsam and flotsam of post-Romantic aesthetics, the heartlessness of academic literary appropriation. But he concludes his piece with a powerful, albeit not entirely assured, conviction that something in the design or texture of imaginative projection suffices for the damage inflicted by the bleak circumstances of *Pale Fire*'s subjects and actions. Shade and Kinbote are commonly inspired even if they are not commonly displayed. See Kernan's "Reading Zemblan: The Audience Disappears in Nabokov's *Pale Fire*," in *Imaginary Library: An Essay on Literature and Society* (Princeton, 1982), pp. 89–129.

Epilogue

1 *The Ambassadors*, in *The Novels and Tales of Henry James*, New York Edition (New York, 1961), 1:xvi.

2 Ibid., p. xvii.

3 Gide, *The Counterfeiters*, trans. Dorothy Bussy (New York, 1973), p. 186.

4 *Remembrance of Things Past*, vol. I, trans. C. K. Scott Moncrieff and Terence Kilmartin (New York, 1981), p. 423.

5 Alain Robbe-Grillet, "Time and Description in Fiction Today," in *For a New Novel* (New York, 1965), p. 65.

Index

Allegory: and exile, 8, 10, 13–14; and
    narrative, xiii, 3, 4, 14–16, 21–27,
    29, 31, 35, 37, 64, 75, 87, 89,
    107, 115, 117, 160, 173, 197,
    205n, 206n, 209n. *See* Exile: and
    narrative duplication
Alter, Robert, 226n
Anderson, Quentin, 224n
Anderson, William, 226n
Appel, Alfred, Jr., 225n, 226n, 227n
Arendt, Hannah, 203n
Auden, W. H., 3, 203n
Auerbach, Erich, 210n
Ayers, Robert W., 206n, 208n

Balogh, E., 203n
Battestin, Martin, 220n, 221n
Baudelaire, Charles-Pierre, 185
Beckett, Samuel: his *Molloy*, 15–16,
    37, 206n
Benjamin, Walter, 5, 203n
Bergin, Thomas Goddard, 202n
Bernheimer, Charles, 6, 203n
Bishop, Elizabeth: her "Crusoe in En-
    gland," 20, 22, 26
Blackmur, Richard, 139, 222n, 223n
Blake, William, xi, 165
Blewett, David, 206n, 211n
Borach, Georges, 218n, 219n
Boswell, James, 183
Bowles, Patrick, 206n

Brady, Frank, 225n
Braudy, Leo, 221n
Brecht, Bertolt, x
Brooks, Douglas, 209n
Brown, Homer O., 206n
Brownley, Maxine, 204n
Budgen, Frank, 101, 220n
Bunin, Ivan Alekseyevich, 168
Bunyan, John: his *Pilgrim's Progress,* 24
Burgess, Anthony, 3
Burry, J. B., 204n
Bussy, Dorothy, 227n
Bryon, George Gordon Lord, 84, 122,
    123

Carlyle, Thomas, 218n
Carnochan, W. Bliss, 207n, 221n
Cash, Arthur Hill, 221n
Caroll, Lewis (Charles Dodgson): his
    Adventures of Alice, 6
Cervantes, Miguel de: his *Don Quixote,*
    94, 159
Chadwick, Joseph, 222n
Conrad, Joseph: mentioned, xiii, 3; his
    "Geography and Some Explorers,"
    55, 59, 202n; his *Heart of Darkness,*
    44–70 passim, 213–16n *passim;* his
    Lord Jim, xi, 1, 44–70 *passim,*
    202n, 212n, 213–16n *passim;* his
    Nigger of the "Narcissus," 52, 214n;
    his *Nostromo,* 48, 58; his *Personal*

Index

Index

Index

Index

Lévi-Strauss, Claude, 57
Levin, Harry, 201n
Lewes, George, 204n
Locke, John, 38, 208n
Lubbuck, Percy, 222n
Lukács, Georg: his *Theory of the Novel,*
  201n, 223n

Mabbot, Thomas Olive, 205n
Mann, Thomas, x, 11
Mandeville, Bernard, 127, 222n
Marvell, Andrew, 38, 211n
Marx, Karl, xii, 219n
Matthiessen, F. O., 222n
Maynadier, G. H., 206n
McKillop, Alan, 221n
Melville, Herman: mentioned, 164;
  his *Moby Dick,* 26, 207n, 210n,
  212n
Mendelson, Edward, 203n
Mercanton, Jacques, 217n, 219n
Meredith, George, 72, 123
Meyers, Jeffrey, 214n
Miller, Frank Justus, 202n
Miller, J. Hillis, 203n, 213–14n
Milton, John, 6, 91, 174
Mitchell, W. J. T., 203n
Molière (Jean-Baptiste Poquelin), 127
Moncrieff, C. K. Scott, 227n
Moore, John Robert, 207n
Moses, 2, 12, 73
Muir, Edwin, 203n
Muir, Wila, 203n
Murdock, Kenneth, B., 222n

Nabokov, Véra, 177, 183
Nabokov, Vladimir: his *Ada,* xiii, 3,
  164–80 *passim,* 202n, 203n, 225–
  27n *passim;* his *Despair,* 4, 177,
  203n; his *Gift,* x, 2, 165, 167–68,
  181, 192, 201n, 225n, 226n; his
  Lolita, 166, 170–71, 174–76, 179,
181, 225n, 226n; his *Pale Fire,* x,
  xi, xiii, 164–196 *passim,* 198,
  201n, 225–27n *passim;* his *Pnin,*
  190, 227n; his *Speak, Memory,* x, 5,
  164, 168, 177, 181, 201n, 203n,
  225n
Narrative: and "interest," 118–19,
  122, 149, 165, 221n. *See also* Allegory; Exile
Newman, Charles, 226n
Nidditch, P. H., 220n
Nietzsche, Friedrich, 14, 62, 205n
Nohrnberg, James, 14, 205n
Nostos. See Exile: and homecoming
Novak, Maximillian A., 207n, 208n,
  209n, 211n

Ogg, David, 211n
Oldmixion, John, 38
Ovid, x, 2, 9–10, 202n, 203n

Palmer, John, 225n
Parker, George, 209n
Parnell, Charles Stewart, 100
Passports, 112, 114, 117, 164–65,
  225n. *See* Exile: and narrative
  authority
Pater, Walter, 203n
Perl, Jeffrey, 222n
Perry, Ruth, 204n
Plato, 3, 190, 226n
Poe, Edgar Allan, 13, 205n
Politics. *See* Exile: and politics
Pope, Alexander, 184, 188
Potts, Willard, 216n
Pound, Ezra, 138, 223n
Price, Martin, 225n
Proust, Marcel: mentioned, xi, 164,
  193, 203n; his *Remembrance of Things
  Past,* 5, 198, 205n

Quennell, Peter, 226n